GREECE
Splendours of an Ancient Civilization

D1464672

Thames & Hudson

SPLENDOURS OF ANCIENT GREECE

CONTENTS

Text: *Furio Durando*
Editorial co-ordination: *Fabio Bourbon / Valeria Manferto De Fabianis*
Graphic design: *Patrizia Balocco Lovisetti / Anna Galliani / Clara Zanotti*
Translation: *Ann Ghiringhelli (text) / Studio Traduzione / Vecchia Milano (captions)*
Drawings: *Monica Falcone / Roberta Vigone*

First published in the United Kingdom in 1997 by
Thames & Hudson Ltd, 181A High Holborn, London WC1V 7QX

© 1997 White Star S.r.l. Vercelli, Italy

British Library Cataloguing-in-Publication Data
A catalogue record for this book is available from the British Library

ISBN 0-500-28337-0

Printed and bound in Italy

(Note: caption numbers refer to the pages on which the illustrations appear.)

1 Her draperies flying, the Nike of Samothrace appears to alight on a staircase in the Louvre. She is a masterpiece by a sculptor from Rhodes.

2–3 The Parthenon of Athens (447–432 BC) is the symbol of the high achievements of Greek architects.

4–5 All the beauty of the island sacred to Apollo is encapsulated in this view of the Hellenistic 'Theatre Quarter' on Delos.

6–7 Segesta, the powerful Elymian city in Sicily, had a splendid Greek-style theatre and a large Doric temple.

8 Two beautiful silver rhyta of Greek manufacture from the Thracian necropolis of Borovo (Bulgaria, 4th century BC).

8–9 The vivid realism of 5th-century BC Greek sculpture is evident in this marble horse's head from the east pediment of the Parthenon.

10–11 Teeming with life and energy, this view of a port of the 16th century BC is a detail from a miniature fresco found in a house in Akrotiri, on the island of Santorini (Thera).

12–13 The intimate atmosphere of a symposium of Greek aristocrats is reproduced in the painted wall panels of the 'Tomb of the Diver', Paestum (480 BC), with music, toasts and tender gestures between the participants.

FOREWORD

The influence of Ancient Greece, the cradle of western civilization, is still felt today in all spheres of modern life, from philosophy and politics to literature and art. Through the centuries, the power of Greek history and culture to fascinate each new generation has shown no sign of waning. Tourists still flock to visit the splendid remains of Greek antiquity; exhibitions on the ancient Greeks continue to draw huge crowds. Every year, general and specialist studies, excavations and research reveal whole new areas of knowledge and intellectual and aesthetic delights.

And yet no book intended for the general reader and no textbook for students has yet succeeded in approaching this fascinating and complex subject in a way that combines the wealth of topics, with concise coverage of each, matching informative text with dazzling illustrations.

Our objective is therefore to take readers on an amazing journey in search of ancient Greece and its civilization and to offer them new insights into the Classical world through outstanding pictures, many of them never previously published. All the illustrations have been selected to reflect the narrative sequence and also to help place each topic addressed in its historic and cultural context. It is hoped, too, that this work will stimulate the interest of anyone intending to study ancient Greece and its civilization in greater depth.

An overview of the history and culture of the Greek and Hellenistic worlds is followed by an outline of developments in art, from its Aegean origins to the Roman conquest. Here

14 Oedipus and the Sphinx, from the central tondo of an Attic red-figure kylix of the late 6th to the early 5th century BC. This well-known mythical story symbolizes man's quest for truth and knowledge in the face of the unknown.

14–15 Signed by Exekias as potter and also attributed to him as painter, this beautiful black-figure amphora is dated to between 540 and 530 BC. The scene depicted, with such graphic realism, shows Achilles slaying the Amazon queen Penthesilea.

15 Attic vase painting often drew on the repertory of epic literature, as seen in this black-figure amphora, signed by Exekias, of about 540 BC. Here the Greek heroes Achilles and Ajax are intent on a game of knucklebones.

descriptions are brought to life by splendid and detailed illustrations, together with reconstructions of the most significant monuments and entire cities, specially commissioned for this book.

Completing the volume is a spectacular itinerary which takes in the most beautiful cities and colonies of ancient Greece – the mainland, the islands, Asia Minor and *Magna Graecia*.

Finally, a brief glossary of technical terms and a selection of titles for further reading should assist the reader to a fuller understanding of ancient Greece – one of the most formative and influential periods of human history.

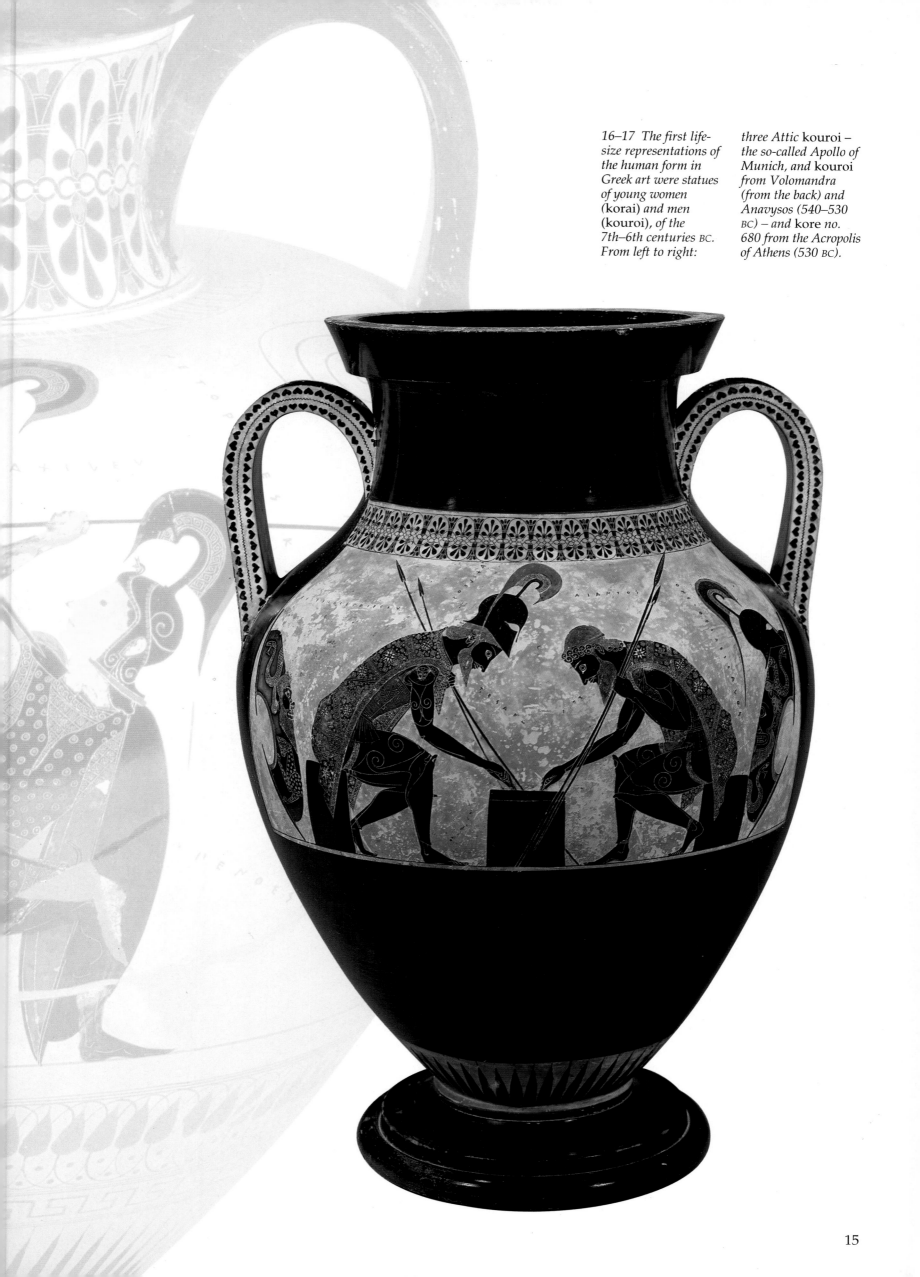

16–17 The first life-size representations of the human form in Greek art were statues of young women (korai) and men (kouroi), of the 7th–6th centuries BC. From left to right: three Attic kouroi – the so-called Apollo of Munich, and kouroi from Volomandra (from the back) and Anavysos (540–530 BC) – and kore no. 680 from the Acropolis of Athens (530 BC).

Greek history from Minos to Augustus

18-19 A scene from the late Archaic Ionic frieze of 525 BC on the Siphnian Treasury at Delphi shows a dramatic moment in the battle between the Gods and the Giants (the Gigantomachy). The skill of the Greek artists in portraying dynamism and depth of space is already evident.

GREECE BEFORE THE GREEKS: PREHISTORY

20 A combination of materials and skills was used by the Neolithic artist of this painted clay figurine from Sesklo of a woman nursing an infant – known as a kourotrophos (3500–3000 BC). It has been argued that such figurines represent a primitive Mother Goddess, and are perhaps a reflection of the fact that Neolithic societies were matriarchal.

The earliest evidence of the presence of human populations in Greece can be dated to the Middle and Upper Palaeolithic (45,000–13,000 BC) with finds from Epirus, Thessaly and Argolis. At this period there is nothing to distinguish these groups from peoples scattered elsewhere in the Balkans and Danube region. The focal importance of the Greek peninsula, even before its inhabitants can be called Greeks, only becomes apparent around 6800 BC, with the development of agricultural communities in Crete, the Cyclades, the Peloponnese and Thessaly. Evidence for the first sea voyages across the Mediterranean - probably hopping across the Aegean from one of its countless islands to another – is found in the distribution of obsidian, a black volcanic glass from Melos. Presumably other goods, such as flint to be made into tools, and perhaps surplus food, were carried along the same routes. Such trade may have taken the form of gifts exchanged by high-ranking individuals in distant villages, an early form of 'diplomatic' relations.

By the middle and late Neolithic the largest villages had already reached high levels of sophistication. As early as the 5th millennium BC, Sesklo and Dhimini in Thessaly were surrounded by strong walls. And it was not long before metal-using cultures appeared and the spread of metallurgy, by a process still not entirely understood, got under way. By the middle of the 5th millennium metal artifacts had already appeared in the 'proto-urban' community of Sesklo, with its flourishing agricultural and pastoral economy. A fundamental source of wealth and prestige, metal eventually became the source of conflicts over access to, and control of, sites where the precious raw materials were found.

THE SECOND MILLENNIUM BC: CRETE, THE CYCLADES AND MYCENAE

A Andros   E Syros   I Siphnos
B Tinos   F Seriphos   J Melos
C Mykonos   G Paros   K Thera
D Delos   H Naxos

21 (below) The elegant simplicity of this head of a Cycladic figurine from Antiparos resembles the work of Modigliani. It also reveals the delicacy of execution of Aegean artists in the second half of the 3rd millennium BC.

21 (right, above) A typical violin- or fiddle-shaped marble Cycladic figurine from Paros. These extreme simplifications of the human figure date from the earliest phase of Aegean art, around 3000–2500 BC.

The geographical position of the Cyclades, like stepping stones across the Aegean Sea between Greece and Anatolia, made these islands one of the pre-eminent areas of civilization in the ancient Mediterranean. Between the end of the 3rd and the early 2nd millennium BC trade in valuable raw materials, such as obsidian from Melos, marble from Paros, Tinos and Syros, and copper from Siphnos, increased in scope and importance. In exchange, the communities of the Cyclades perhaps received foodstuffs to supplement the archipelago's variable agricultural production.

The most flourishing period in the Cycladic islands, both south (especially Melos and Thera) and north (Tinos, Paros, Naxos, Syros, as well as the 'minor Cyclades' like Keros and Despotiko, Amorgos, Siphnos, Kythnos, Kea), would appear to have been between 2200 and 1700 BC. From then on the islands gradually came increasingly within the orbit of Crete and its emerging civilization.

In the 'golden age' of Cycladic civilization its trade covered the whole Aegean sea and extended throughout the eastern Mediterranean. Important settlements grew up and their inhabitants enjoyed great prosperity, as shown by the varied and cosmopolitan origins of objects found in burials.

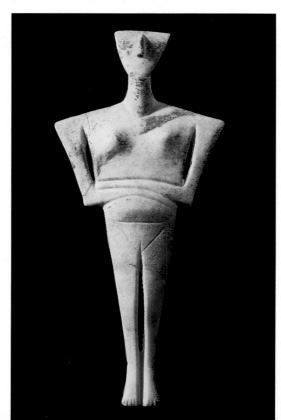

21 (right) This female figurine from Syros, with an indication of sexual characteristics, dates to a later stage of Aegean art (2200–2000 BC).

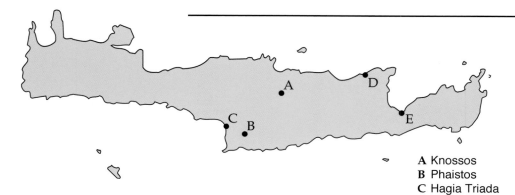

A Knossos
B Phaistos
C Hagia Triada
D Mallia
E Gournia

The first palaces, which lacked any features designed for defence, were comprised of hundreds of rooms grouped around a central court. In these complex architectural structures the symbols of religious authority – horns of consecration and double axes – were placed alongside brightly coloured frescoes which embellished rooms and corridors.

Trade thrived, with steady flows of foodstuffs and exquisite objects made by skilled potters, woodworkers, goldsmiths and metalworkers, apparently employed in the royal workshops of the palaces. Writing, using a form of script still not deciphered, known as Linear A, may have been used for both accounting procedures of the state and also for religious purposes. It is certainly testimony to the complex organization and amazing efficiency of the palace-settlements of Crete.

Around 1700 BC the first palaces were destroyed. The cause of the destruction is uncertain, though perhaps it was a disastrous

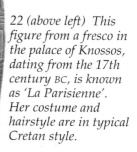

22 (above left) This figure from a fresco in the palace of Knossos, dating from the 17th century BC, is known as 'La Parisienne'. Her costume and hairstyle are in typical Cretan style.

22 (left) The 'Peak Sanctuary' rhyton from the palace of Zakros is a masterpiece of the Cretan stonecarver's art, carved from serpentine. The scene depicted is of a shrine in a natural landscape setting, with Cretan wild goats heraldically placed on top.

Towards the end of the 3rd millennium BC, Crete – the largest island in the Aegean – began its own progress to becoming the first European civilization. Around 1900 BC the first palaces at Knossos and Phaistos formed the core of imposing settlements. Arthur Evans, who rediscovered the Cretan civilization, named it Minoan, after Minos, the legendary king of Crete, and sometimes its rulers are referred to therefore as 'minos'. There is no evidence, however, for a single ruler of the whole island, rather it seems that there were several important centres, with Knossos perhaps dominant in the Second Palace Period. Trade was an important factor in the growth of Crete, and Cretan supremacy over Aegean trade routes and its links with Egypt and the Near East led to what has been described as the Minoan thalassocracy – control of the sea. Other territories of the Aegean came increasingly under the influence of Cretan civilization, which developed in ever more grandiose forms.

considerations clearly took priority over purely functional ones, such as the road's destination – possibly a temple or rural settlement.

Minoan cultural influence in the southern Cyclades was especially strong in Thera, modern Santorini. Here the excavation of the site of Akrotiri has brought to light spectacular remains of an impressive town with buildings up to four storeys high. Ornately frescoed rooms are only one sign of the riches and prosperity wiped out forever by a cataclysmic event.

Around the year 1450 BC (the date is still much disputed by archaeologists) the volcano from which the island had originated many thousands of years earlier erupted and turned Thera into history's first Pompeii, burying the settlement under a great depth of ash. It seems its inhabitants had time to escape as no bodies have been found in excavations.

23 (left) A faience figurine representing a Snake Goddess or her human attendant, from the Temple Repositories in the palace of Knossos, 17th century BC. The Minoans may have worshipped a nature goddess, with chthonic aspects, as shown by the snakes. She may also have been a goddess of fertility and Mistress of Animals, an antecedent of the Potnia theron *of the Linear B tablets.*

earthquake. However, they were rapidly rebuilt on an even larger scale than before. The earlier palaces were agglomerations of living quarters and areas used for administration, production and storage, comprising large halls, throne rooms and shrines, artisans' workshops and magazines for produce. The later palaces usually included a western court, overlooked by rows of steps, probably a theatral area, where collective rites were celebrated or ceremonies performed, including perhaps the bull sports.

In the so-called Second Palace Period (1700–1450 BC) not only were palaces at Knossos, Phaistos, Zakros and Mallia built, but also houses we could label 'country residences', such as Tylissos and Hagia Triada, a large villa not far from Phaistos. Paved roads are also found in this period. The splendid 'Royal Road' at Knossos, for example, offers evidence of the attention paid by architects to the urban setting of the palace and to its surrounding landscape. Such

23 (right) A beautiful rhyton *carved in the shape of a bull's head – a masterpiece of neopalatial Cretan sculpture. Great care was taken in producing this ritual vase, with its gilded horns, rock crystal eyes with jasper surrounds and mother-of-pearl muzzle. It was possibly used to hold and pour out a liquid for a sacred libation – whether bull's blood or something else is not known.*

24 (below) Minoan fresco painting was the first ancient art to express true naturalism, moving away from the stereotyped images of ancient Egyptian art. The graceful lines, the rich range of bright colours and the appreciation of nature are all evident in the famous fragment of a fresco from the second palace of Knossos. A brightly coloured garden is populated by birds – partridges and a hoopoe – a prototype of similar designs found much later, in the Hellenistic and Roman periods.

24 (right) Skilled Cretan craftsmen produced many beautiful objects, specializing in luxury items made in workshops in the palaces. Actual workshops have been identified at Knossos and Zakros, where imported raw materials have been found, for instance copper and elephants' tusks, as well as beautiful finished products such as this rhyton. It is carved from a single piece of rock crystal, with a handle of bronze wire threaded with beads of rock crystal.

Some archaeologists believe that the side effects of this catastrophe were among the factors that triggered the decline of Cretan civilization. According to this theory, the entire southern Aegean was affected by disastrous earthquakes, tidal waves and clouds of ash that darkened the skies and rained down on the earth, with ensuing climatic changes. A debilitated Crete was then left to face the expansionist ambitions of the Mycenaeans.

Minoan Crete can be called the first European civilization, as amply demonstrated by architecture, art and religion. In religion, a powerful goddess of fertility occupied an important place. She was associated with the bull – an animal frequently represented in art. The youth of the island performed initiation rites in her honour, taking the form of a kind of bloodless corrida in which young men and women showed great acrobatic skill in leaping and somersaulting over the back of a charging bull.

In their art, the Cretans express the imagination and originality of an essentially peaceful people. Although highly organized and productive, they appreciated life's pleasures rather than displays of power or the glorification of weapons. Evidence of the Cretan love of luxury and finery is found in the beautiful apparel worn by figures in frescoes and by the exquisite objects made by skilled craftsmen which can be seen today in the Archaeological Museum in Iraklion. It is also shown by the sophisticated facilities for washing and drainage found in the palaces.

25 *The Cretans' intimate relationship with the sea is apparent in countless works of art, especially frescoes. This fresco of the 16th century BC comes from a house in the town of Akrotiri on Thera which was destroyed by the eruption of its volcano. It is a portrait of a lithe young fisherman, captured by the artist carrying the fruits of an abundant haul. The detail is so fine and vivid that it is possible to identify the fish — they are either large mackerel or perhaps small tuna.*

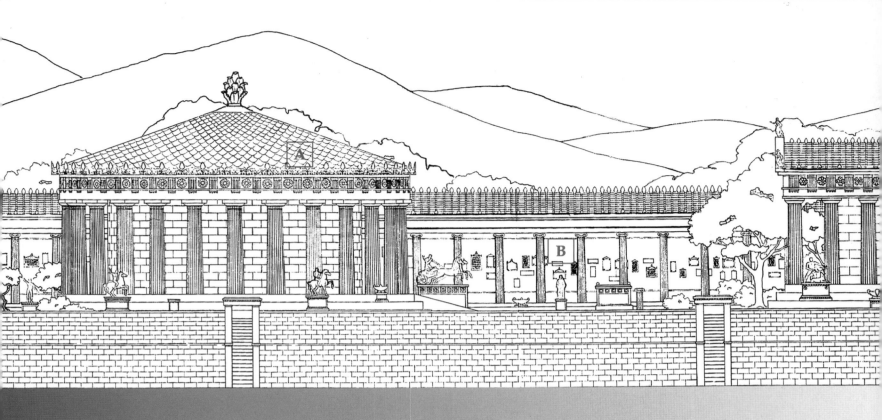

THE SANCTUARY OF EPIDAURUS

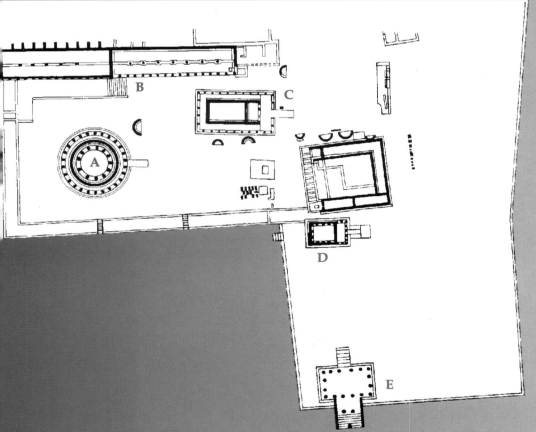

A Tholos
B Incubation Stoa
C Temple of Asclepius
D Temple of Artemis
E Propylaea

From the artist's reconstruction on the following pages we can gain some impression of the former splendour of the sanctuary of Epidaurus – one of the most renowned in ancient Greece. Visible, from left to right, are the Tholos, or rotunda, of Asclepius; the portico used for the incubation ritual, where patients slept hoping for cures in their dreams; the Temple of Asclepius and the Temple of Artemis, partly hidden from view by the north Propylaea (foreground). Pausanias' description adds lost details: 'Over from the temple is where the ritual supplicants of the god go to sleep. A round construction of white stone called round house which is worth a visit has been built near by. Inside is a picture by Pausias in which Eros has discarded his bow and arrows and carries a lyre instead. "Drunkenness" is also there, painted by Pausias drinking from a wine glass; you can see a wine glass in the painting and a woman's face through it.'

GREECE THROUGH THE AGES

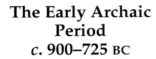

Prehistory *c.* 45,000--2800 BC	Bronze and Iron Ages *c.* 2800–1220 BC	The Dark Ages *c.* 1220–900 BC	The Early Archaic Period *c.* 900–725 BC	The Middle Archaic Period *c.* 725–610 BC

Prehistory
c. 45,000--2800 BC

Evidence exists of sporadic human presence in the region (nomads, hunter-gatherers; cultural affinities with the Balkans) in the Middle and Upper Palaeolithic and Mesolithic periods. Around 7000 BC Europe's first groups of farmers/herders appear in Macedonia, Thessaly, the Peloponnese, the Cyclades and Crete, possibly involving migrations from the east. A thriving exchange network is established, with land and sea routes extending across the region, for obsidian, amber, salt in particular. Around 6000–4000 BC large settlements develop, several (Sesklo, Dhimini) with a 'proto-urban' structure and large stone walls. Around 4500 BC the working of native copper begins; widespread use of the metal contributes to agricultural development and population growth, with more organized social structures.

Upper Palaeolithic and Mesolithic periods
(*c.* 45,000–6800 BC)

Neolithic period and earliest use of copper
(*c.* 6800–3500 BC)

The Copper Age
(*c.* 3500–2800 BC)

Bronze and Iron Ages
c. 2800–1220 BC

With the Bronze Age come the first waves of Indo-European migration; cultural affinities emerge between mainland Greece, the Aegean islands and the Anatolian seaboard. The Cyclades are the first to become a flourishing centre of trading activities. In around 1900 BC the first palaces are built in Crete and become centres of political power and production. After the destruction and rebuilding (1700 BC) of the palaces, the Minoan thalassocracy dominates the Aegean. The eruption of Thera (possibly around 1450 BC) has serious consequences for Crete, preparing the way for the takeover by the Mycenaeans. The splendid Mycenaean culture, with its fortified palace-settlements, dominates the Aegean. In the 14th and 13th centuries BC, trade-oriented expansionism results in 'pre-colonial' trading posts in the western Mediterranean. Around 1250–1120 BC, the site of 'Homeric' Troy is destroyed.

'Golden age' of Cycladic culture
Development of Minoan culture
(*c.* 2800–2000 BC)

First Minoan palaces
(*c.* 1900–1700 BC)

Destruction and rebuilding of Minoan palaces
The 'golden age' of Mycenaean culture
(*c.* 1700–1450 BC)

Collapse of Minoan culture
(*c.* 1450 BC)

Hegemony of Mycenaean traders in the Mediterranean
(*c.* 1450–1250 BC)

Destruction of Homeric Troy
(*c.* 1250–1220 BC)

The Dark Ages
c. 1220–900 BC

The 'Sea Peoples' bring devastation to the eastern Mediterranean, and trade comes to a halt. At the same time the Dorians, another Indo-European race, invades Greece from the Balkans, triggering the demise of the Mycenaean kingdoms in the 12th century BC. There follows a long period known as the 'Helladic Dark Ages', characterized by the breakdown of settled conditions, with many sites abandoned, cultural impoverishment and the disappearance of Mycenaean political and socio-economic structures. Dorians, Ionians and Aeolians determine the development of Greek 'dialects' in areas they occupy after over a century of migrations. With the aid of weapons or wealth, aristocracies based on families or clans emerge: they adopt the 'heroic' funeral practice of cremation. Use of iron starts to spread. In the 10th century BC general economic recovery leads to the foundation of new urban settlements, trade activities and 'colonial' expansion along the coasts of Anatolia.

Raids of the 'Sea Peoples'
(*c.* 1220–1180 BC)

Movements of Indo-European peoples and end of Mycenaean culture
(*c.* 1220–1120 BC)

Foundation of the first urban centres and early developments of the colonizing movement
(1100–900 BC)

The Early Archaic Period
c. 900–725 BC

Demographic and economic growth slowly strengthens the newly established poleis. Athens, Argos, Thebes, Sparta, Corinth, Chalcis, Eretria, Miletus, Smyrna, Phocaea and others burst on to the Mediterranean trade scene and begin founding colonies and trading posts in both east and west, competing peacefully with Phoenicians and Etruscans. Constitutional structures take root, with aristocracies firmly in control. Monarchies are transformed into oligarchies (with Sparta's system of joint rule by two kings the sole exception). The development of writing, adapted from the Phoenician alphabet, provides the means to preserve the poems of Homer – the Iliad and the Odyssey – for posterity. Production of fine pottery and metal artifacts and exports of oil and wine put Athens, Corinth, Argos and the Euboean cities in prominent positions.

First Olympic Games
(776 BC)

Foundation of the first western colony, at Pithekoussai
(*c.* 770 BC)

First 'constitutions' in Athens and Sparta
(*c.* 754–753 BC)

First Messenian War
(743–724 BC)

Colonies founded in southern Italy
(740–708 BC)

The Middle Archaic Period
c. 725–610 BC

Trade between Egypt and the east and the Greek poleis (particularly Corinth) and their colonies thrives, as does business/competition throughout the Mediterranean, with the Phoenicians and Etruscans (who control important metal sources in the west). As a result, Greece experiences strong growth, not only economically: cultural activities also flourish in the fields of literature, philosophy and art. Greek artists and craftsmen are much influenced by Oriental models, imported in great quantities to satisfy the taste for luxury of the dominant aristocracies. In Corinth, Argos and Sicyon social tension between nobles and the people (demos) brings tyrants to power, while colonization continues in both east and west. The religious and political importance of the Panhellenic sanctuaries of Delphi and Olympia is strengthened.

Further colonies founded in southern Italy
(688–648 BC)

Second Messenian War
(684–668 BC)

Tyranny at Corinth under the Cypselids
(657–583 BC)

Tyranny at Argos under Pheidon
(650–630 BC)

Foundation of Cyrene
(631 BC)

Law-code introduced by Draco in Athens
(624–620 BC)

The Late Archaic Period
c. 610–510 BC

While Sparta extends its hegemony over the entire Peloponnese (only Argos retains its autonomy), socio-economic conflicts between the oligarchies and the productive classes of the demos, who demand a greater say in politics, leads to attempted reforms of the kind instituted by Solon at Athens. The failure of these initiatives results in an increasing number of tyrannies which sweep away the dominant aristocracies in cities like Athens, Megara, Samos, Naxos and Miletus. Further afield in the Greek world, old-established colonies become increasingly autonomous, found colonies of their own and fight for regional hegemony. Athens becomes the leading economic centre under the tyranny of the Pisistratids, who are eventually banished. In the mid-6th century BC the Persians start to extend their empire, thus posing a threat to the poleis of Ionia.

Law-code of Solon in Athens
(c. 594–591 BC)

Three phases of tyranny under Pisistratus in Athens
(561–527 BC)

Fire at the sanctuary of Apollo at Delphi
(548 BC)

Polycrates tyrant of Samos
(546–522 BC)

Persian conquest of Near and Middle East
(559–513 BC)

Expulsion of the Pisistratids from Athens
(514–510 BC)

The Persian Wars
510–449 BC

Cleisthenes establishes a democracy in Athens. Darius I, the Persian king, threatens the cities of Ionia, which react by revolting against the recently installed satraps (governors). After resisting valiantly, Miletus and the others fall, and are harshly punished. In 490 BC the first Persian War ends with the victory of the Athenians led by Miltiades at Marathon. Xerxes I declares war again in 480 BC; after several successes and the sack of Athens, the Persians are defeated at Salamis. With Ionian support hostilities continue under the leadership of Athens, which founds the Delian League. The western Greeks defeat Carthagians and Etruscans. Under Themistocles and Cimon, Athens begins a period of military and economic imperialism, in conflict with the other poleis. Callias signs a peace treaty with Persia (449 BC).

Ionian revolt against the Persians
(499–494 BC)

First Persian War
(490 BC)

Second Persian War Battle of Himera between Greeks and Carthaginians
(480 BC)

Second Ionian revolt against the Persians
(479 BC)

Delian League
(478 BC)

Naval battle of Cumae between Greeks and Etruscans
(474 BC)

Third Messenian War Wars of Athens against Aegina and Corinth
(464–455 BC)

Peace treaty between Greeks and Persians
(449 BC)

The Classical Age
449–338 BC

Under Pericles Athens reaches the apex of economic success and cultural splendour. Its expansionist foreign policy triggers revolts and hostilities against the Athenian empire throughout the Hellenic world. Rivalry with Sparta, Corinth, Thebes and Syracuse leads to the Peloponnesian War. After alternating fortunes, Athens eventually capitulates and spends the last decade of the 5th century BC under short-lived oligarchic governments. The new century opens with the restoration of democracy in Athens, Spartan attacks on Persia and Carthaginian expansion in Sicily, while other wars are waged in Greece. Sparta dominates the Greek scene for several decades before being deprived of its hegemony by Athens and Thebes, the emerging power. In 356 BC Philip II of Macedon begins his conquest of Greece, completed in 338 BC at Chaeronea. With the Corinthian League peace is imposed on the Greek states under the aegis of Macedon.

Hegemony of Pericles at Athens
(449–429 BC)

Peloponnesian War
(431–404 BC)

Oligarchic revolution at Athens
(411 BC)

Wars between Greeks and Carthaginians in Sicily
(409–392 BC)

Surrender of Athens and fall of the Thirty Tyrants Restoration of democracy
(403 BC)

Hegemony of Sparta
(404–379 BC)

Hegemony of Thebes
(379–362 BC)

Philip II of Macedon overlord of Greece
(356–338 BC)

Macedonian Rule
338–323 BC

Macedonian hegemony over the Greek poleis takes the form of an alliance which survives the assassination of Philip II at Aegae, the capital. His heir, Alexander III – called 'the Great' on account of his amazing conquests – takes up his father's plan to invade the Persian empire, involving all the Greeks in the liberation of cities dominated by the satraps of the King of Kings. His expeditions become a triumphant march of conquest, battle after battle, across the Persian empire. Alexander reaches the banks of the Indus and present-day Afghanistan, establishing cities which bear his name. He founds the first universal empire of history, promoting the cultural Hellenization of the countries conquered. His death in Babylon, at only 33 years of age, triggers fierce struggles among contending successors and several poleis make futile attempts to gain control.

Corinthian League between Greeks and Macedonians
(338 BC)

Assassination of Philip II
(336 BC)

Reign of Alexander III, the Great
(336–323 BC)

Alexander the Great conquers the Persian Empire
(334–329 BC)

Alexander the Great's campaigns in India and Bactria
(328–327 BC)

Alexander the Great dies in Babylon
(323 BC)

The Hellenistic Period
323–146 BC

Antipater suppresses a revolt by the Greeks but for forty years Alexander's Macedonian generals struggle to gain the upper hand, eventually dividing the great empire into Hellenized kingdoms, founding long-lasting dynasties. Powerful states come into being, their political, economic and cultural activities centred on splendid capitals. The Greek poleis found leagues, such as the Aetolian League which routs the invading Celts in 280 BC and the Achaean League which puts an end to Sparta's independence. But the hegemony over all Greece of the Antigonid dynasty remains intact. Likewise, the Seleucids in Asia Minor, Syria and Mesopotamia, the Ptolemies in Egypt and the Attalids in Pergamum continue to reign until Rome completes its conquest.

Greek revolt against Macedonia
(323–322 BC)

Foundation of the Hellenistic kingdoms
(322–281 BC)

Absolute Macedonian monarchy over Greece
(276–239 BC)

Foundation of the Kingdom of Pergamum
(240 BC)

'Democratic' revolution in Sparta. End of Spartan independence
(227–222 BC)

Rome frees the Greeks from Macedonian dominion
(200–196 BC)

Rome defeats Macedonia
(171–168 BC)

Rome makes Macedonia and Greece provinces Siege and destruction of Corinth
(147–146 BC)

34 (right) Colour was an important feature of many monumental buildings in ancient Greece; sadly, most of it has now almost completely faded. This reconstruction gives some impression of the vibrant colours that once set off the reliefs decorating the Tholos at Epidaurus. Above the narrow peristyle, with its 26 close-set Doric columns, was a frieze of triglyphs and metopes decorated, unusually, with rosettes in relief. Along the projecting moulding – or cyma – gargoyles in the form of splendid and realistic lions' heads alternated with elegant palmettes on a background of ornate foliage. Patterns created from different shades of finest-quality marble completed the overall dynamic effect.

A Mycenae
B Nauplion
C Tiryns
D Vapheio
E Pylos

During the period when Cretan civilization flourished, between 2000 and 1600 BC, Indo-European peoples moved into and occupied mainland Greece and the Peloponnese. Sometimes referred to as Achaeans, they may perhaps be the Ahhiyawa mentioned in the records of the Hittite Empire.

The new groups settled in Thessaly, Boeotia, Attica, Argolis and Messenia, rapidly changing their semi-nomadic lifestyle. The region they settled in naturally looked towards the Mediterranean and was rich in resources in terms of cultivable land and animal life, which were soon put to good use. It was not long before the princes of Iolkos, Argos, Mycenae, Tiryns and Pylos – men at the top of the rigid social pyramid – learned to take advantage of the trade routes of the region. Precious artifacts, made of gold, silver and bronze, textiles and fine pottery were traded by enterprising merchants throughout the whole Aegean and eastern Mediterranean.

Since the late 19th century, when the importance of Mycenae was revealed by the excavations of Heinrich Schliemann (whose approach may now be considered amateurish but whose work undeniably produced results), the peoples who occupied this whole region have generally been known as the Mycenaeans.

36 (above) Romantically called the 'Cup of Nestor' by Schliemann, who found it in the rich Grave IV of Grave-Circle A at Mycenae (16th century BC), this kantharos of sheet gold weighs nearly 300 grams. Two birds sit on top of the spool-shaped handles.

36 (right) The Mycenaeans used a script now called Linear B, incising the syllabic signs – an early form of Greek – into wet clay tablets. Many such tablets, including the one illustrated here, were found at the Mycenaean palace of Pylos, in Messenia, accidentally baked in the fire that destroyed the site in the 12th century BC.

37 *An excellent example of the skills of Mycenaean metalworkers, this beautiful lion's-head* rhyton, *from Shaft Grave IV of Grave-Circle A at Mycenae, dates to the 16th century* BC. *Its form is clearly derived from Cretan models, but the result is less naturalistic and has the formality and greater rigidity typical of Mycenaean art.* Rhyta, *both in Crete and in the Mycenaean world, were vases intended for ritual ceremonies, with one hole for liquids to be poured into the vessel and another for them to flow out of. It is thought that they were used in religious and funerary libations.*

Mycenaean society hinged on centralized power and an economy based on large landed estates and on trading activities which relied on the work of skilled craftsmen and a network of experienced mariners. At the centre of each Mycenaean city-state was a fortified palace and 'town' surrounded by massive defence walls. At the top of its social hierarchy was the *wanax*, the supreme ruler who represented the warrior and land-owning aristocracies – the *lawos* and the *damos* - who, thanks to their estates, were very wealthy. At the right hand of the *wanax* was a military commander, the *lawagetas*. Consultants and officials assisted the ruler in the political and administrative functions of government. The village authorities were the *basilewes*, who controlled collective ownership of farmland not directly owned and used by the *wanax*. Little is known about the structure of the lower classes, apparently comprised of artisans and agricultural workers, though it seems there was a caste of slaves.

Much of our information about Mycenaean civilization has come from the clay tablets found in excavations at the palaces of Pylos, in Messenia, Knossos, under Mycenaean control from the 15th century BC, and – to a lesser extent – Mycenae, Tiryns and Thebes. The tablets are written in an early form of Greek, using a syllabic 'alphabet' derived from ideograms. This script – deciphered by Michael Ventris and John Chadwick – is known as Linear B. As well as indicating the number and functions of personnel in the palace, the tablets contain lists of tributes, inventories, administrative procedures and records of property ownership. The Mycenaean economy was based on agriculture and livestock breeding. Production of oil, flax and wool also allowed the manufacture of cosmetics and textiles to flourish. Overseas commerce expanded: the palace of Knossos alone exported no less than 30 tons of wool a year.

From as early as the 16th century BC, Mycenaean craftsmen excelled in work

38 (right) This gold signet-ring from Mycenae was made by a Mycenaean artist, though the scene of a religious rite, with the symbol of the double axe, probably derives from a Minoan model.

in gold and bronze. Their activities were controlled by the palace, which supplied the workshops with copper from Cyprus and tin from central and western Europe. Precious metals, amber and glass-like materials were used in abundance, testifying to wide-ranging Mycenaean trade routes which, until the 13th century BC, extended from Egypt to Syria, from Rhodes to Cyprus, from Cilicia to Ionia. When the Mycenaean empire was at its peak (14–13th centuries BC), its traders pushed further and further afield throughout the Mediterranean, but above all in the west. Some scholars even talk of Mycenaean 'pre-colonization' along the same routes taken by the Greeks in the 8th to 6th centuries BC. Settlements sprang up along the coasts of Italy and southern

Spain, for example at Vivara on the Gulf of Naples, in the southern part of Puglia, on the eastern side of Sicily and in the Aeolian islands. Mycenaean merchandise also reached the Upper Adriatic and Po Delta, as shown by finds from Frattesina, near Rovigo. Testimony of the level of prosperity and power attained during this period is seen in the enlargement of the walls of centres like Mycenae and Tiryns. This is also a reflection perhaps of the most significant characteristic of Mycenaean civilization – its martial nature. An echo of this has persisted through the ages in the tradition of a war fought by peoples from all over Greece against Troy. The Phrygians of Troy had established a powerful kingdom and controlled the Dardanelles Strait, a strategic passage between the Aegean and the Black Sea fringed by areas rich in ore deposits and vast cultivated plains. And into

38–39 (below) Created by a Cretan artist, but discovered in Shaft grave IV of Grave-Circle A at Mycenae, this bronze dagger inlaid with scenes in niello, gold and silver, on both sides, features the aristocratic theme of lion hunting.

39 (left) Another gold signet-ring from one of the most ancient royal tombs of Mycenae (16th century BC) vividly illustrates a lively scene of stag hunting.

39 (above) The subject of war appears on this gold ring, similar in style to the previous one and, perhaps surprisingly, also from a woman's tomb.

the Black Sea flowed the Danube, a river of enormous importance. As related by Homer in his celebrated epic poem, the *Iliad*, an exceptional coalition of the most powerful Achaean cities, from Thessaly, Boeotia, Argolis, Messenia, Laconia, came together and defeated Troy. In fact one of the levels at the site of Troy was destroyed around 1250 BC. The 'Trojan War' can be seen as a symbol of the last moment of glory of a civilization destined to collapse and disappear within the space of decades. One explanation is that lands around the Mediterranean were disrupted by the so-called Sea Peoples. Trade – the mainstay of the Mycenaean economy – came to a halt. There is evidence of depopulation, cultural and material impoverishment, and destruction and abandonment of settlements – events which marked the beginning of the period now known as the Helladic 'Dark Ages'.

39 (below) Mycenaean goldsmiths produced objects that show a clear Minoan influence as well as ones which decoratively were more oriented to the 'schematic naturalism' typical of mainland art. Sometimes simple and elegant shapes of drinking vessels were preferred, renouncing any decoration, such as this kantharos.

THE HELLADIC 'DARK AGES'

The precise origins of the Sea Peoples whose raids contributed to the destruction and chaos around the Aegean and eastern Mediterranean have not been identified with certainty. Prominent among them, in the 12th and 11th centuries BC, were Phoenicians and Philistines. However, they were not the only cause of the upheavals. Further incursions by Indo-European peoples brought the real founders of Greek civilization. First and foremost were the Dorians, who came from the impenetrable valleys of the Balkans and settled mainly in Epirus, Acarnania-Aetolia, the Peloponnese and the southern Aegean islands, even reaching the southwest coasts of Anatolia. Other groups of 'Greeks', the Ionians and Aeolians, correspond to the division of the region into areas identifiable through their use of three different dialects of a single language: Greek. The demise of urban centres and the absence of a state and its structures encouraged the development of a social model based on the *genos*, a kind of aristocratic clan which gained power and prestige through bravery, the forceful appropriation of lands and riches and the possession of material goods and weapons. In funeral rites burial was replaced by cremation, with its 'heroic' attributes. In the political sphere the Mycenaean *wanax* was replaced by the *basileus*, a 'king' who was simply the leader of the community, a member of the aristocratic élite supported by other heads of households. The first embryonic city-state – the *polis* – developed as early as the 11th–10th centuries BC among Ionian and Aeolian immigrants settled on the coast of Anatolia.

On the Greek mainland the decline in population, material and cultural impoverishment and the absence of commerce had reached their lowest point. Signs of recovery begin in the 10th century BC as seen at Karphi and Dreros, in Crete. Around the same time cities rebuilt on the remains of ancient Mycenaean centres or permanent clusters of village communities in areas previously unoccupied presaged the emergence of the *polis*: Athens, Argos, Corinth and Sparta are prominent examples.

The epic past of the Mycenaeans became the cultural heritage of the aristocrats. Poetry formerly transmitted orally was transformed into literature by the adaptation of the Phoenician alphabet to the dialects of Greece (irrespective of whether Homer actually existed as a historic figure). And the old Mycenaean settlements became cult centres which were the precursors of sanctuaries at Olympia, Delphi, Dodona, Isthmia and Nemea.

40 (left) A bronze of the 8th century BC, discovered in Crete, preserves for us the image of a bard of the epic poems. He is a typical figure of Achaean and Archaic Greek culture, symbolized by the most famous bard of all – Homer. In the Geometric style, the singer of ballads bends over his lyre, his hands on the strings, searching for suitable notes for 'winged words'.

40 (right) Clear evidence of the economic recovery of Greece and an increase in population in the Geometric period comes from finds from cemeteries. The wealth and high artistic value of funerary assemblages document the prestige of the wealthier families. This amphora from a tomb in the Dipylon cemetery in Athens (around 750–740 BC) provides a fine example.

THE ARCHAIC PERIOD

Areas in orange represent Greek territories between the 11th and 10th centuries BC

The Greek *polis* (plural *poleis*) emerged around 1000–900 BC as a community of individuals from different socio-economic classes who concentrated their activities in a place suitable for habitation, easy to defend, and with available resources and trade prospects. Rural settlements of earlier periods – with an economy based on self-sufficiency and limited trading activities – lost importance and became subordinate to the new centres, forming their *chora*.

In the *poleis*, artisans, merchants and entrepreneurs grew in number and prosperity, and their wealth became a challenge to the power of the aristocratic families. The importance of cultivable land, horses and herds diminished as attention was increasingly focused on the value of goods produced, successful craft activities and services which were no longer offered solely to a ruler, but rather to an expanding and thriving community.

With the growth in population and more widespread prosperity, political institutions had to be brought into line with new social structures. Members of the old aristocracy were, however, reluctant to share their power. Unable to maintain the existing social order, they instead founded colonies in the western Mediterranean. This practice, initially begun in the 8th century BC, and more widespread in the 7th century, reduced internal strife and avoided pointless conflict.

41 (left) The famous 'Goddess of Auxerre', an important early example of Greek statuary, represents either a goddess or perhaps the dedicator of the statue in a devotional attitude. It was probably made in Crete around the mid-7th century BC and is almost a paradigm of the so-called Archaic style of Greek sculpture.

41 (above) A typical Corinthian amphora of the 7th century BC typifies the commercial success of Corinth between the 7th and 6th centuries BC. From its advantageous position on the isthmus, Corinth exported these products of high-quality artistic craftsmanship throughout the whole Mediterranean area.

42 (below) This beautiful terracotta statue of an enthroned deity, perhaps Demeter, goddess of fertility, comes from Grammichele, in Sicily and is late Archaic in style. The sculptor has clearly been influenced by Greek sculpture.

42 (right) This painted terracotta plaque either decorated the façade or was a metope of a temple in Syracuse (575 BC). It portrays the terrifying Gorgon Medusa, from whose blood the winged horse, Pegasus, was born.

In the western Mediterranean, Greek colonies were mainly bridgeheads set up to strengthen the economic role of the old *emporia*, which they gradually replaced. The oldest of these existing trade settlements – such as the first, Pithekoussai on Ischia (770 BC) – continued to operate as 'open' ports where merchants of varying ethnic origin gathered to trade. But many new colonies were established for agricultural reasons. In South Italy and Sicily 'Greekness' took on a new dimension in the form of *Megale Hellas* or *Magna Graecia*, 'Great' Greece: an offshoot of Greece proper, closely linked to the motherland by a shared culture, shared aims and shared needs.

In the space of a few decades after founding Pithekoussai the Greeks established colonies in Cuma (740 BC), Naxos (733 BC), Syracuse (732 BC) and nine other sites around the shores of Sicily, Calabria, Puglia and Lucania. By the 7th century BC Greece had consolidated its political, economic and cultural position in the Mediterranean. It had secured colonies in the Levant, increasingly under threat from the Assyrians, and in the west, where it competed with the expansionist goals of the Phoenicians, and it also traded intensively with the Orient. It was not only merchandise that travelled along routes linking far-distant cities. 'Culture' in the broadest sense was also disseminated by the dominant aristocracies. They continued to indulge their taste for luxury and were increasingly fascinated by the forms and styles of Oriental civilizations.

Colonies had also been established in the east, from the Bosphorus to the Black Sea, with its mineral sources,

43 Times of unrest
and conflict between
rival poleis *or*
between tyrants and
aristocrats must have
resulted in numerous
casualties, as testified
by the many tomb
monuments found, in
Attica in particular.
On the famous stele of

Aristion, a work by
Aristokles and datable
to around 510 BC, the
dead man is shown
wearing his hoplite
armour (cuirass,
helmet, shin guards,
lance), portrayed with
the typical technical
precision of the
Archaic style.

from the coastal regions of Anatolia to Macedonia and Thrace. These centres became outposts of both trade and ideology, offering an arena for political and scientific experimentation, inspired by philosophers, scientists, artists and writers, and influenced by the cultural and material effects of trade.

In the 8th to mid-6th centuries BC trade and cultural exchanges between east and west increased. Tolerance and even peaceful co-operation seem to have prevailed, a supposition endorsed by archaeology. For instance, a huge number of amphoras probably from the Etruscan city of Caere (Cerveteri) were found in the earliest levels of Carthage, and vast quantities of Phoenician products have been discovered along the colonial Greek seaboards of Italy and in the non-Greek hinterland of Campania, Etruria and Lazio. A trade axis clearly existed between Pithekoussai and the Phoenician colonies of Sardinia, probably only one arm of a vast trading network from Gibraltar to the eastern Mediterranean.

We also have evidence of the presence of Levantine 'trade offices' in Greek urban settlements, and of a similar series of Greek trading posts along the coast of modern Tunisia. The existence of a kind of 'common market' is demonstrated by a system of accounting tables for converting the units of weight and measurement used by the various peoples of these regions – two centuries before Pythagoras codified precision mathematics.

In politics, conflicts within the aristocratic oligarchies brought the tyrants to power (the word *tyrannos*, of Anatolian origin, simply means 'lord'). Although often of aristocratic origin, the tyrants gained control by finding

favour with the new, productive members of society. The authority inherent in tyranny put an end to social and political tensions. Some tyrants ruled with a rod of iron, others by gaining popular support through demonstrations of good government. These might take the form of economic incentives, or public works on a grand scale – such as religious buildings of the kind erected in Samos by Polycrates (540–520 BC) or in Corinth.

In the 7th century BC Corinth was the trade capital of Greece and produced very popular pottery in the so-called Orientalizing style, with which Athens, the Cyclades and the Ionian islands tried to compete in vain. In 657 BC the Cypselid tyranny overthrew the Bacchiad dynasty. It assisted trade by developing the ports of Kenchreai and Lechaion, founded agricultural and trading colonies, and built the *diolkos*, a stone causeway which allowed ships to be hauled across the isthmus from the Aegean to the Gulf of Corinth.

Elsewhere, social conflict was addressed by lawmakers. In Athens, for instance, first Draco and later Solon introduced constitutional and fiscal reforms. To a great extent, however, both met with failure and tyranny was the eventual outcome. Sparta, with a constitution combining communism and nationalism based on ethnic origin and caste, was one of the few cities to remain united. In the period when the other *poleis* were in the throes of serious crises, it conquered Messenia and the Peloponnese, meeting with insurmountable resistance only in Argos. The 7th and 6th centuries BC also saw the panhellenic sanctuaries at Delphi and Olympia established as centres of cult, sporting events and

44 *A small bronze statue representing a hoplite, armed from head to foot, as he launches an attack on an imaginary enemy. This figure is at the same time a quotation of the 'heroic' past of Greece, as reflected in Homer's epic, and a document of the ceaseless opposition of the small Hellenic city-states to the expanding power of the Persians. Just as the Mycenaeans defeated the Trojans, the Greeks strove to defend their political independence against the imperialism of the Persian King of Kings. Memories of the past thus became the propaganda of the present. The age of the heroes was back.*

literary and theatrical contests, which attracted competitors from all over the Greek world. These sanctuaries provided a venue for the diplomatic resolution of tensions and conflicts. City-states vied with one another to gain influence over the priesthood, resorting to ostentatious worship and lavish offerings. On a practical level this meant expropriating huge sums for erecting splendid buildings, dedicating works of art to the gods and devoting one-tenth of war booty

to creating monuments with a lasting impact on the whole of Greece.

In 561 BC Athens had its first taste of tyranny. Control of the city was seized by Pisistratus. He promoted the cause of small landowners and businesses, built a fleet, pursued an expansionist foreign policy and re-established harmony among quarrelling social groups, with the exception of his personal enemies, the powerful house of the Alcmaeonidae. The period of tyranny ended in 510 BC after a decade of resistance against Pisistratus' sons, Hippias and Hipparchus. In 514 BC Hipparchus was killed in a plot by the nobles Harmodius and Aristogeiton; four years later Hippias chose exile. The Alcmaeonidae returned in triumph and, under Cleisthenes, Athens had its first experience of democracy. But a new threat was moving towards Greece. Under Cyrus and then Cambyses the Persian empire began to expand, taking over the kingdoms of the Near East and gaining control of the western regions of Anatolia. The flourishing city-states of Ionia – Miletus, Ephesus, Phocaea, Smyrna, Samos – risked conquest, primarily because of the pro-Persian attitude of some tyrants, who had collected tribute for the Perisan king Darius. The outcome was the tragic series of Persian Wars.

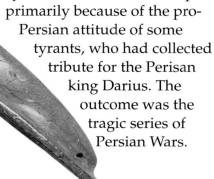

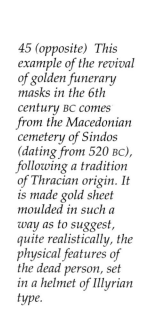

45 (opposite) This example of the revival of golden funerary masks in the 6th century BC comes from the Macedonian cemetery of Sindos (dating from 520 BC), following a tradition of Thracian origin. It is made gold sheet moulded in such a way as to suggest, quite realistically, the physical features of the dead person, set in a helmet of Illyrian type.

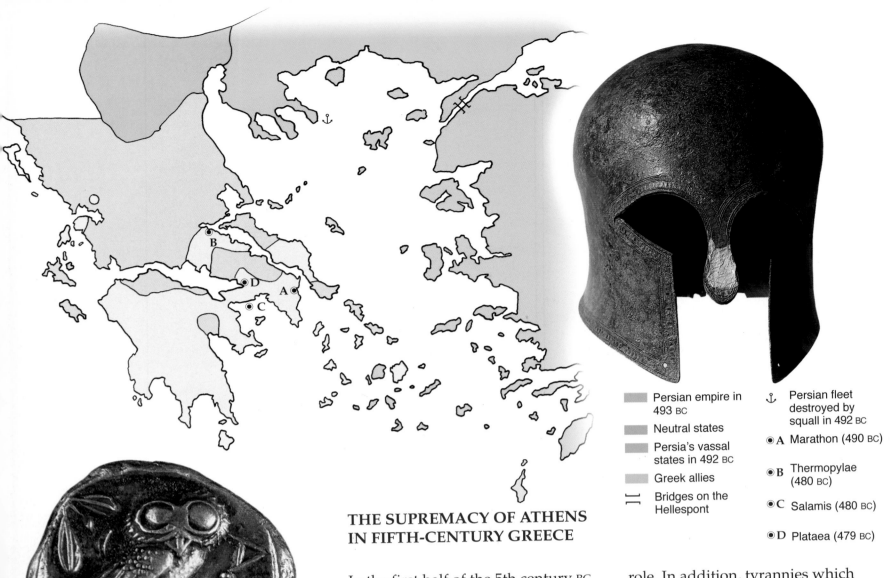

Legend

▨ Persian empire in 493 BC	⚓ Persian fleet destroyed by squall in 492 BC
▬ Neutral states	◉ A Marathon (490 BC)
▬ Persia's vassal states in 492 BC	◉ B Thermopylae (480 BC)
▬ Greek allies	◉ C Salamis (480 BC)
⊨ Bridges on the Hellespont	◉ D Plataea (479 BC)

THE SUPREMACY OF ATHENS IN FIFTH-CENTURY GREECE

In the first half of the 5th century BC the Greek world faced critical moments in the defence of its territory, identity and autonomy. In earlier periods a number of factors had contributed to a fragile equilibrium. These same factors now became weak links, particularly in the face of Persian expansion westwards, forcefully relaunched by Darius I. One such factor was the limited influence of Athens outside Attica, barely threatening the hegemony of Sparta, Corinth and Argos. In the Aegean, political fragmentation meant that many of its thriving islands could focus their attention on trade. Many inland areas, with economies still dependent on agriculture and pastoral activities, instead played a secondary role. In addition, tyrannies which enjoyed notable popular support had gradually brought the Ionian cities of Asia Minor into the orbit of Persian imperialism and had encouraged the overseas colonies to achieve greater autonomy from their mother-cities.

At the beginning of the 5th century BC mainland Greece experienced an event that was to have unimaginable reverberations: an innovative political model was introduced which would revolutionize the Greek world, and even the history of the human race.

A democracy was established in Athens – the equation 'state = citizens' was established for the first time – and government of the *polis* was entrusted to the assembly of the *demos* ('people') and its elected representatives. With

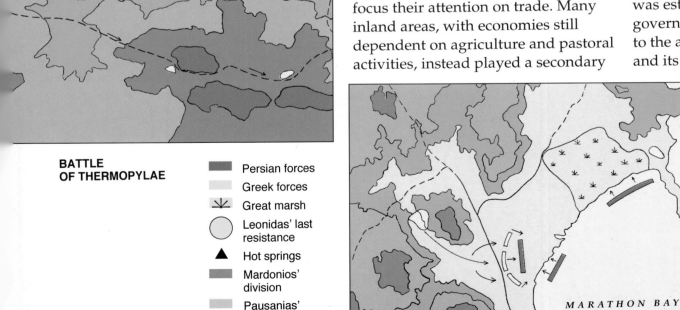

BATTLE OF THERMOPYLAE

▬	Persian forces
▬	Greek forces
↯	Great marsh
◯	Leonidas' last resistance
▲	Hot springs
▬	Mardonios' division
▬	Pausanias' division
– –	Path

MALLIA GULF

TRACHIS

MARATHON BAY

BATTLE OF MARATHON

the various social and productive classes now directly involved in political decisions, in the space of half a century Athens and Attica became the leading economic, trading and cultural centre of the Mediterranean.

The new political model was exported from Piraeus, the city's busy port, along with merchandise and the products of Athenian culture and art. The aristocratic oligarchs and tyrants who held control elsewhere in Greece saw it as a very real threat. Divisions and conflict increased, with violent struggles for power between pro-Persian 'parties' and 'enlightened' aristocrats, won over – though to what extent it is impossible to say – by the doctrine of equal rights and free trade implicit in democracy. An immediate repercussion was the Ionian revolt against the Persians in 499–494 BC. Though crushed by Darius I, it triggered an attack on Greece itself, whose heterogeneous city-states were considered too untrustworthy to be left independent. Many prosperous *poleis* of Asian Ionia were overcome. Thousands of spectators were later moved by the tale of the conquest of Miletus, dramatized by the tragedian Phrynicus and presented in the Theatre of Dionysus in Athens. In 490 BC the army of Darius I, under the command of Artaphernes and Datis, attacked Eretria and Athens. The extraordinary victory at Marathon, when 10,000 men led by the Athenian Miltiades routed the Persians, brought Persian expansion to an end. But not for long. Ten years later, Xerxes I, son of Darius, attacked again at the head of a huge army and fleet. Once more the Persians met with strong resistance and a forceful counter-attack from Athens and its less-powerful allies. Initially the allied city-states suffered huge setbacks: the Spartans under Leonidas were defeated at Thermopylae, a mountain pass that opened the way to the plains of Boeotia and Attica; the Greek fleet lost at Cape Artemisium; Athens was itself sacked and the sanctuary of Athena on the Acropolis defiled. And yet at the naval battle of Salamis the Athenians won the day. Led by Themistocles, the Greek ships even dared to chase the Persians as they

fled in disarray. And throughout 479 BC they were a threat to Persian supremacy in Ionia, restoring independence in several cities.

Another eastern power had set its eyes on the flourishing colonies of *Magna Graecia*. From around 550 BC, Carthaginian trade ambitions were transformed into an imperialism that was bound to come into conflict with Greek interests. Tyrrhenian Italy was in effect divided between Carthage and the Etruscan cities of Caere, Tarquinia, Vulci and Populonia, and harsh treaties had been imposed by the old colony of Tyre on the young republic of Rome. An attempt to make Sicily a Carthaginian island met with failure at Himera in 480 BC, at the hands of a coalition led by Gelon, tyrant of Syracuse. In 474 BC a new coalition of Western Greeks led by Syracuse ended Etruscan hegemony over Tyrrhenian Italy with a naval victory at Cumae, the old Chalcidian colony which became the most active trading centre of the Western Greeks for over half a century.

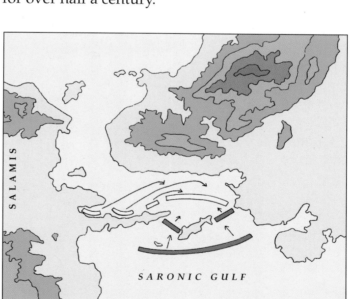

SALAMIS

SARONIC GULF

BATTLE OF SALAMIS

47 (Above) This portrait bust of Themistocles, the Athenian strategist and victor at Salamis, shows him in idealized style, according to the contemporary Greek sculptural tradition. The bust is a Roman copy of a Greek original and is now in the National Archaeological Museum, Naples.

46 (opposite, centre) An Athenian silver tetradrachm, minted at the time of the Persian Wars, features the owl sacred to the goddess Athena and the first three letters of the name of Athens, the city that twice valiantly resisted the Persians.

46 (opposite, above) The Corinthian helmet, with nose and cheek guards, was used particularly in the Persian Wars. Countless examples, from the north to the south of Greece, attest to its wide diffusion.

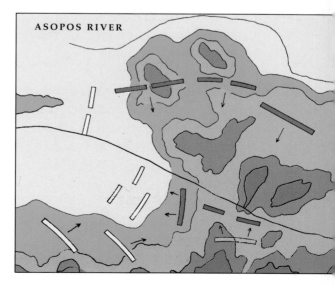

ASOPOS RIVER

BATTLE OF PLATAEA

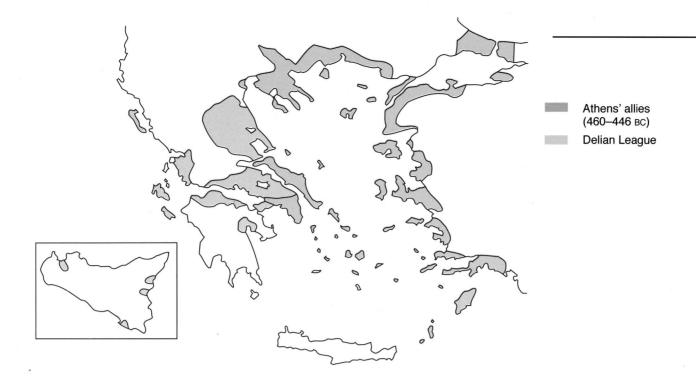

Athens' allies
(460–446 BC)

Delian League

In Athens, democracy now enjoyed an exceptional, and unique, level of popular support and participation. It developed along two main lines, of decisive importance for Greek history in the second half of the 5th century BC. On one hand, strong figures occupied an increasingly prominent role in government, while in both trade and military affairs the city's foreign policy took on an aggressive slant that smacked of imperialism; on the other, Athens gradually became the established capital of Greek culture, in philosophy and literature, art and science. These phenomena became particularly evident from the middle of the century, when Pericles – successor of the 'conservative' Cimon – took over the reins of the democratic party. He initiated a vast political programme which raised Athens to the greatest heights ever seen in the ancient world in terms of standards of living, trade supremacy and culture.

Athens was also the founder of the Delian League to which numerous cities and Aegean islands belonged. The League's objective was to continue the war against the Persians until the eastern cities had been liberated, and to provide for communal defence in the event of aggression. Its base and treasury, initially situated on the tiny Cycladic island of Delos, with its sanctuary of Apollo, was moved to Athens in 454 BC. This Athenian initiative, motivated by a need for greater security and made possible by Athens' leading role in the alliance, met with protests from other League members.

48 (left) Our image of the great Athenian statesman Pericles comes from this portrait bust by Cresilas, commissioned by some citizens to commemorate him posthumously on the Acropolis (Athenian laws prohibited the portrait of a living person or public tribute to politicians, even deserving ones). This head, a Roman copy, lacks the individualized features of a true portrait, according to Greek artistic conventions. Only the strategist's helmet, slightly raised on the head, allows us to see the 'egghead', mocked by the playwrights of his time.

49 (opposite) The so-called 'Blond Boy', a masterpiece by an unknown Attic artist in the Severe style (c. 485 BC) still retains traces of the colour that once gilded the hair of the youth – perhaps an athlete or a warrior fallen in battle. It shows how the stiff conventions of Archaic art were being broken.

After the 449 BC peace treaty with the Persians, the League continued under the increasing supremacy of Athens, which used it to reinforce growing hostility towards its own traditional economic and political rivals. After victory over Aegina in 456 BC, Athens still had to teach a lesson to Corinth, Megara and, above all, Sparta, which dominated the Peloponnese and did nothing to disguise its strong anti-Athenian feelings (more than matched by the Athenians' hostile attitude towards the Spartans). For Athens and – to a lesser degree – its allies, the Delian League brought many economic advantages. Its members formed a kind of 'common market' and played a central role in trade in the Mediterranean.

In the space of a few decades Athens became enormously wealthy. Its unrivalled economic strength was due to the discovery of silver, mined with slave labour, at Laurion (Sounion), and privileged access to ore deposits in the northern Aegean. Legislation further fostered the entrepreneurial dynamism of its producers and merchants. Before long the city dominated the Mediterranean, and its growing expansionist tendencies and agression were founded on popular consensus. Athens had by now established its own 'empire' in the midst of the Mediterranean. Initially its power was strictly economic, as shown, for example, by its pre-eminence as an exporter of finest-quality Attic oil or by the enormous demand for its pictorial pottery (by now commonly found in all aristocratic and 'middle-class' households of the ancient world)

50 Inspired by the remarkable development of philosophy in 5th-century Greece, art historians named this beautiful bronze head, discovered in a shipwreck near Villa San Giovanni (Reggio Calabria), the 'Philosopher of Porticello'. It is in fact regarded by some as the earliest example of a Greek portrait (dating to around 460–440 BC). The skilful artist and bronzesmith studied the reality of the human face and individual features and was capable of reproducing them in telling detail.

and other objects created by Attica's talented artists and craftsmen. Rather than increasing its flourishing commercial activities, however, Athens' later political and military imperialism paved the way for a serious decline. The tragedy of the Peloponnesian War provides a very clear picture of the consequences of empire-building ambitions based on extinguishing the ideals and political identities of others, simply because they are considered weaker.

In the ancient world, however, imperialism was the course inevitably followed by all the most important powers. When a state's original territory, natural resources and trading arena were no longer sufficient to sustain a growing population and people's demand for prosperity – that is, when it was no longer possible to find new resources and increase production, maintain levels of consumption and extend markets – then forceful expansion was the route chosen, irrespective of that state's political model. Wars were fought to colonize or annihilate possible rivals, and empires were created on the basis of political, economic and military supremacy. Other powers that followed this course before Athens were Sparta (although its action was limited to the Peloponnese, in the 7th and 6th centuries BC) and Carthage (certainly from 550 BC on); much later – between the 3rd century BC and the 2nd century AD – the same expansionist line was taken by Rome.

In Athens, a climate of euphoria led the majority of its roughly 40,000 citizens (women, non-Athenians living in the city and slaves were not entitled to vote) to support Pericles' ambitious building programmes. His plans for the transformation of public architecture and the construction of numerous splendid monuments eventually turned Athens into the first real 'capital' of the ancient world. And yet in 431 BC this same politician involved Athens in the catastrophic Peloponnesian War, which lasted for thirty long years.

The city which became Athens' arch-enemy in this war was Sparta. For many, the rivalry between Athens and

51 *The funeral stele of a rich Athenian woman, Hegeso, daughter of Proxenos, is one of the most impressive documents of the frank gaze on mortality of Greek art at the end of the 5th century* BC, *when the tragedy of the Peloponnesian War eroded optimism and human certitude. In the quiet interior of a home, in a melancholy atmosphere, the woman, sitting on an elegant* diphros, *takes a necklace out of the casket offered to her by her handmaid. She is dressed in fabrics that reveal her blooming young body. These are the bride's preparations for her last, eternal, black wedding to the infernal prince, Hades.*

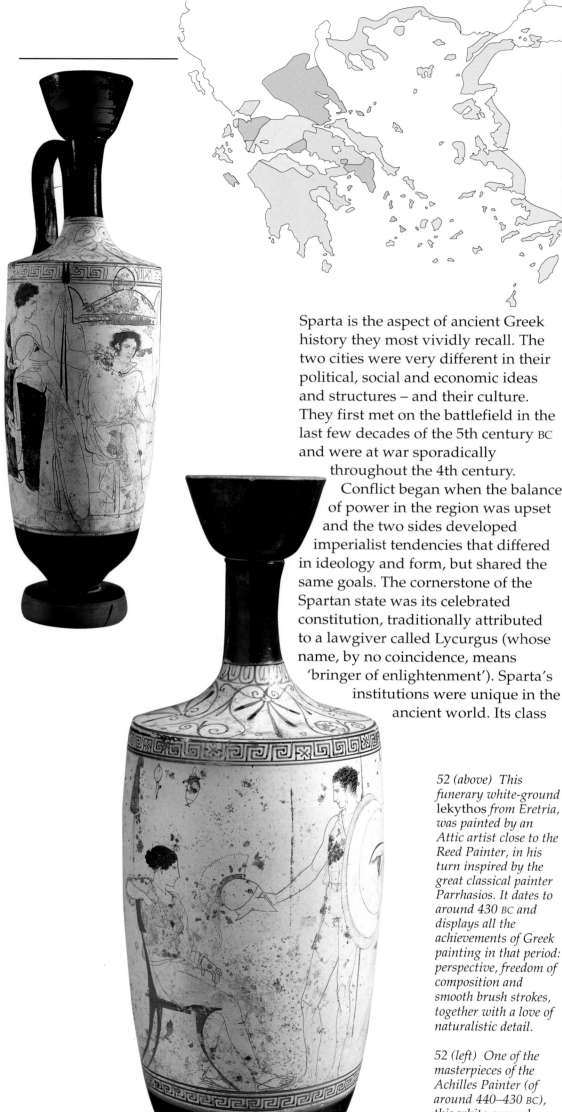

Sparta is the aspect of ancient Greek history they most vividly recall. The two cities were very different in their political, social and economic ideas and structures – and their culture. They first met on the battlefield in the last few decades of the 5th century BC and were at war sporadically throughout the 4th century.

Conflict began when the balance of power in the region was upset and the two sides developed imperialist tendencies that differed in ideology and form, but shared the same goals. The cornerstone of the Spartan state was its celebrated constitution, traditionally attributed to a lawgiver called Lycurgus (whose name, by no coincidence, means 'bringer of enlightenment'). Sparta's institutions were unique in the ancient world. Its class

structure had ethnic and aristocratic origins: only descendants of the founder warriors had full citizenship status. The political structure was simple – it was headed by two kings who were supervised by ephors and who received advice from a council of elders (*gerousia*) and from a public assembly comprised of citizens aged over thirty (*apella*). The economic and administrative structures of the state were based on a kind of communism (total equality, but only within Sparta's rigid ethno-social classes) and on maintenance of a colossal military machine to enforce law and order at home and bolster its aggressive policy beyond the state's borders. From early childhood Spartans were trained for military service and citizenship by a strict disciplinary system that excluded the family from the process of education. Manufacture and trade were handled by semi-free citizens (*peroikoi*) who themselves had few rights, although their work provided considerable wealth for their austere state. Serfs (*helots*) were bound permanently to the soil, tilling the land and herding livestock, from one generation to the next; they were descendants of conquered peoples originally from this same region, and of prisoners of wars fought in nearby areas (most notably Messenia).

It was an Athenian act that sparked off the Peloponnesian War. Pericles issued a decree placing a stranglehold on trade by their neighbouring rival, Megara. Well aware of the enemy's strength, Pericles ordered the entire population of Attica to take refuge inside the city walls of Athens, abandoning their fields and crops. His intention was to use a 'hit and run' technique to put continuous pressure on the Spartans. But Athens' strong financial position, far superior fleet

Athens and her allies

Athenian 'empire'

Sparta and her allies

Neutral states

52 (above) This funerary white-ground lekythos *from Eretria, was painted by an Attic artist close to the Reed Painter, in his turn inspired by the great classical painter Parrhasios. It dates to around 430 BC and displays all the achievements of Greek painting in that period: perspective, freedom of composition and smooth brush strokes, together with a love of naturalistic detail.*

52 (left) One of the masterpieces of the Achilles Painter (of around 440–430 BC), this white-ground lekythos *portrays a warrior taking leave of his wife, a metaphor for the heroic leave-taking of life, and therefore alluding to death.*

and her supremacy over the Aegean assured by allies who, on the whole, stayed loyal, served nothing in the event of a plague which, between 430 and 428 BC, killed one-fifth of the population including Pericles himself (in 429 BC). In the early years of the war the two sides experienced alternating fortunes: repeated invasions of Attica by the Peloponnnesian forces were followed by an upsurge by the Athenians from 425 BC onwards. But by 421 BC both sides were exhausted, demotivated and more than ready to negotiate peace. A new phase in the hostilities opened in 420 BC, linked with the rise to power of dangerous warmongering politicians like Alcibiades and Nicias. In the wake of the battle of Mantineia (418 BC) Sparta regained leadership over the Peloponnese, while Athens was renounced by part of its allies and dismayed its own citizens with the massacre of Melos and the disastrous expedition to Sicily (415–413 BC). With Sparta's aid, Syracuse inflicted a crushing defeat on the Athenian fleet and army, killing thousands of soldiers and condemning countless prisoners to die of starvation.

The third phase coincided with the period when democracy in Athens had been challenged and temporarily overthrown by the oligarchs who sought peace with Sparta. But war was resumed as soon as full democracy was restored. Athens, now isolated, achieved several victories. Before long, however, the Spartans had gained the upper hand, led by their admiral Lysander. He made a triumphant entry into Piraeus and ordered an unconditional surrender. The terms of surrender demanded dismantling of Athenian fortifications and its fleet, and membership of the Peloponnesian League – with an implicit abandonment of democratic government.

Athens was once more ruled by tyrants for a while. When democracy did return, thanks to a bold coup by Thrasybulus, it was not opposed by Sparta, perhaps well aware that Athens would never again be the great power that had held sway in the century then drawing to a close.

53 A poignant testimony to the loss and grief caused by the Peloponnesian War, this beautiful funeral stele portrays two fallen young Athenian warriors, Chairedemos and Lykeas (420–410 BC), setting off to war. The sober language of classical naturalism lends itself to the celebration of the two foot-soldiers, shown in perspective, as if in slow motion, with the idealized features of a 'godlike' man – the true hero – whose beauty is in his deeds and his virtues. This ideal is translated into the harmonious shapes and reflected in the fascination with anatomy which echoes Phidias in the treatment of the heads and Polyclitus in the modelling of other parts of the body.

METAPONTUM

PAESTUM

TARENTUM

SYBARIS

IONIAN SEA

SEGESTA

LOCRI

HIMERA

SELINUS

AGRIGENTO

SYRACUSE

Classical Greece
AND *MAGNA GRAECIA*

AEGEAN SEA

ASSOS

PERGAMUM

DELPHI

MYCENAE

ATHENS

EPHESUS

PRIENE

CORINTH

LYMPIA

DELOS

HALICARNASSUS

SPARTA

EPIDAURUS

KNOSSOS

MEDITERRANEAN SEA

ALEXANDRIA

THE FOURTH CENTURY BC AND THE RISE OF MACEDONIA

With the tragedy of the Peloponnesian War not long over, the 4th century BC saw Greece facing a series of regional conflicts and tensions. These resulted in the alternating and short-lived supremacy of Sparta and Thebes, the intermittent re-emergence of Athens and the rise of leagues of *poleis* (Arcadia and Acarnania-Aetolia, for example) whose policies were moulded by an aspiration to emerge from the peripheral position they seemed condemned to occupy (not just geographically). In the Western Greek world, meanwhile, the old-established colonies had severed all bonds with their ancestral cities. A prominent example was Syracuse which, after its victory over Athens (413 BC), pursued a policy of aggression, from the Tyrrhenian Sea to the Adriatic. The Western Greeks realized they had to rely on their own resources to hold at bay the imperialist aims of the Carthaginians, who had left many flourishing settlements in Sicily in ruins, such as Selinus, Himera, Gela, Camarina.

The Peloponnesian War and the state of permanent conflict in the first half of the century were the cause or effect – according to interpretation – of the erosion of the absolute values which for centuries had been the mainstay of Hellenism. Gone was the unwavering belief in principles like a profound sense of belonging to a community, the city-state; gone was the certainty that came with being part of a society that approached perfection as spiritual and ethical values grew stronger; gone was the perception of self as 'part of a whole' and 'all of one part'; gone was love of knowledge ('philosophy') as a logical process that made the infinite its ultimate goal. Instead there was a short-sighted anthropocentrism as men came to see themselves as the measure of all things, along with rampant individualism and the cult of personality. People were increasingly aware of the precariousness of the human condition; reason became clouded by a turmoil of 'feelings' which no philosophy or religion could reconcile. From a historical viewpoint the supremacy of Sparta had no great impact. Realizing its pro-Persian policy had left Ionia in the hands of a weak and unpopular emperor, Artaxerxes, Sparta opted to support his brother and rival, Cyrus II. Athens, however, felt seriously threatened by the possible success of the people of Lacedaemon in regions traditionally under its influence. It therefore 'courted' the Persian king and helped thwart Spartan schemes, eventually obtaining financial support and control over the Dardanelles, a strategic point of access to the rich colonies of the Black Sea. The peace brokered by Persia (386 BC) was short-lived: Sparta attempted to install a pro-Spartan oligarchy in Thebes, triggering a reaction which, in just a few years, led to Theban hegemony over the whole of Greece, until 362 BC.

Kingdom of Macedonia

Macedonian expansion up to 336 BC

56 A beautiful bronze statue of Athena (430 BC) in the Piraeus Museum is perhaps the most telling image of the goddess of wisdom, clothed in the long peplos, *armed and encircled with the* aegis *decorated with a gorgon's head.*

57 This superb bronze head, perhaps of Satyros – we know he won the prize for boxing in the Olympic Games in about 330 BC, was sculpted by Silanion, a pupil of Lysippus. The athlete's face is battered and bruised, marked by swellings, wrinkles and a bristly, thick beard of great realistic impact.

In an increasingly involved political situation, with cities ideologically at loggerheads, it was perhaps inevitable that the expansionist aims of Macedonia, an emerging monarchic power on the northern periphery of Greece, should pay off so handsomely. A vast mountainous region sloping down from the remote valleys of the southern Balkans to the northwestern shores of the Aegean and as far as Mount Olympus, Macedonia was inhabited by Doric peoples who had been in contact with the Mycenaeans in the second millennium BC. And yet they had long remained on the fringe of Greek history.

The ruling dynasty of the Argeads, in power since the 7th century BC, was based in the old capital city of Aegae; in the 6th and 5th centuries it made several attempts to unify the region and gain control of Thrace. During and after the period of Persian threat (513-480 BC) it made friendly overtures towards southern Greece. Alexander I eventually made an expansionist move towards Pangaeum and its silver mines, east of the river Strymon. In the second half of the 5th century BC Macedonia moved cautiously into the Greek arena, forming alliances alternately with Athens and Sparta and gaining control of the region east of the river Axios. Perdiccas II extended the sphere of Macedonian influence to the Chalcidic peninsula,

an important crossroads for trade in the north Aegean, previously within the orbit of Athens. In the 4th century the Argeads bided their time and prepared to intervene in the struggles for leadership between Athens, Sparta and Thebes. The outstanding military tactics with which Macedonia was to conquer the world – based on a special combat unit, the famous Macedonian *phalanx* – had been perfected and well tried and tested.

Philip II (359–336 BC) was astute in his foreign policy, adapting it to suit the regions and political situations he faced; he brought Macedonia and the northern Aegean together under his rule, establishing a protectorate over neighbouring Thessaly. Meanwhile, the *poleis* of southern Greece were still divided into ephemeral 'leagues' whose policies ranged from short-sighted regionalism to political and economic lobbying. Diplomacy was the key to Philip's initiatives in establishing Macedonian hegemony, operating, for example, through traditional panhellenic associations like the Amphictyony of Delphi. Later, open Macedonian support was offered to political forces and regimes able to further the cause of Philip's leadership within their own regional ambit. After years of warfare, during which the *poleis* entered a phase of terminal decline, the Macedonian victory at Chaeronea (338 BC) settled

58 (top) Philip II is probably represented in this ivory head, just 3 cm (1¹⁄₁₀ in) high, found in his tomb at Vergina. Along with four other heads, it perhaps formed part of a miniature replica of the group executed by Leochares for the Philippeum of Olympia.

58 (centre) Philip II's splendid gold quiver is unusual and has prompted scholars to suggested a Scythian origin. It was decorated with a bloody scene of a plundering.

58 (right) This small but heavy gold casket contained the cremated remains of Philip II. It is a miniature masterpiece in which Macedonian goldsmiths gave free rein to their decorative imagination, combining elegance and delicacy with the sumptuousness of material and the solemn function of the object. On the lid is the symbol of the Macedonian kingdom, the 16-pointed star; the sides are decorated with rosettes and friezes in gold and glass paste.

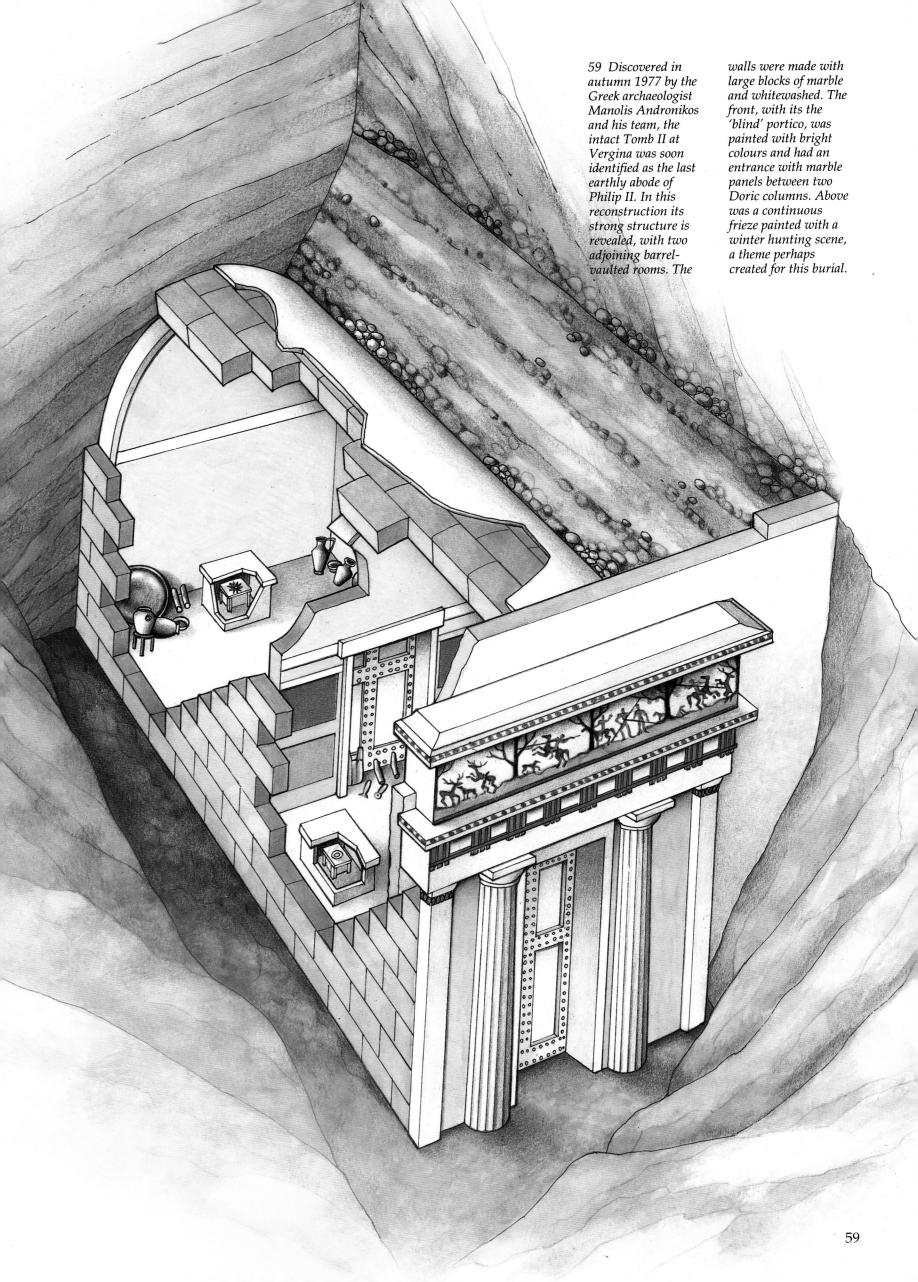

59 Discovered in autumn 1977 by the Greek archaeologist Manolis Andronikos and his team, the intact Tomb II at Vergina was soon identified as the last earthly abode of Philip II. In this reconstruction its strong structure is revealed, with two adjoining barrel-vaulted rooms. The walls were made with large blocks of marble and whitewashed. The front, with its the 'blind' portico, was painted with bright colours and had an entrance with marble panels between two Doric columns. Above was a continuous frieze painted with a winter hunting scene, a theme perhaps created for this burial.

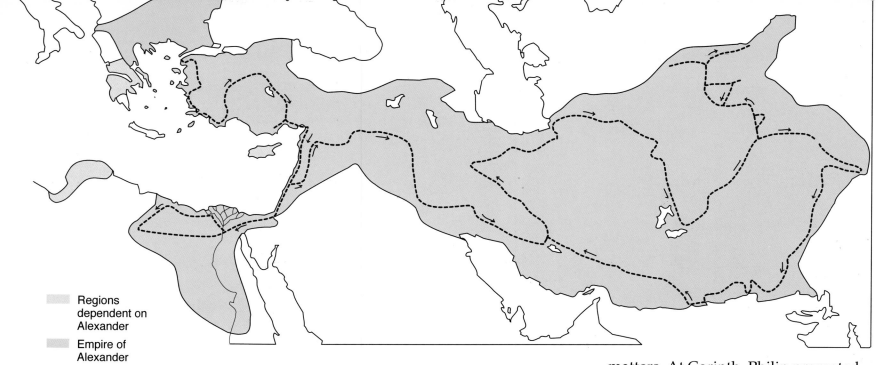

Regions
dependent on
Alexander

Empire of
Alexander

Alexander's route

matters. At Corinth, Philip promoted
the formation of a panhellenic league
which allowed the cities to retain their
autonomy and institutions. He
imposed peace on all the Hellenes and
laid plans for resuming war against
the Persians, to free all the Greek cities
of Asia from the dominion of the
imperial satraps. On the eve of the
expedition against the Persians, Philip
II was assassinated in the theatre at
Aegae. His place on the throne was
taken by his young son, Alexander III,
whose amazing exploits earned him
the name of *Megas* ('the Great'). One
of the greatest figures of antiquity,
Alexander honoured his father's
political legacy: the plan to free the
Asian Greeks became a huge military
adventure, with the outcome that,
between 334 and 329 BC, the Persian
empire, with its vast provinces, was
brought to its knees. In 328–327 BC the
conqueror marched on, advancing as
far as remote regions of the Caspian
Sea and the shores of the Indus. But at
this point his army refused to go on.

Testifying to his successes were tens
of cities named Alexandria in the east,
Egypt and Anatolia. Alexander next
initiated a policy of ethnic mixing, to
join Greeks and Macedonians with the

*60 Alexander the
Great was the first
western person to be
the subject of a
personality cult while
still alive. The myth
that grew around his
feats generated
various images, but
only Lysippus and
perhaps Leochares
were allowed to
portray the king*
*officially. This
beautiful image of a
youthful Alexander is
attributed to the
latter. It is
characterized by the
typical* anastolè *of the
hair – a lock of hair
with an off-centre
parting – and by the
deep, penetrating
gaze, turned to distant
and glorious horizons.*

races they had conquered. An entirely new political ideal – reaching far beyond the *poleis* of the previous era – made its mark on Greek history. It was the idea of universal Hellenism, 'Greece wherever Greeks have set foot', far larger than *Magna Graecia*. Greece would be the home of culture and civilization for a world which, with ethnic and regional barriers overcome, would unite thousands of different cultures and give them new life.

Alexander's early death at the age of 33, in Babylon in 323 BC, when his Persian wife Roxane was carrying the heir to the throne, halted this amazing adventure. But Alexander's deeds had, for the first time in history, introduced the idea of a universal, almost divine monarchy, capable of gathering humanity together under a single flag and within a single splendid and varied culture. The end of the journey of Alexander the Great did not mean the end of the Greek world: on the contrary, with 'universal Hellenism' Greek culture became part of the heritage of all races who came into contact with it, far beyond the boundaries of the *poleis*. Hellenism, it can be said, originated with Alexander.

61 (top) The myth of the deeds of Alexander the Great was illustrated in countless works of art produced in the territories he touched in his conquests, as demonstrated by this impetuous image of the young king on a famous sarcophagus found in Sidon (Lebanon).

61 (above) A detail of the famous mosaic of the battle of Issus between Alexander the Great and Darius. It was found in the House of the Faun in Pompeii and is thought to be a copy of a fresco by Philoxenos of Eretria for the Macedonian dynast Cassander (end of the 4th century BC).

THE THIRD CENTURY BC AND 'UNIVERSAL HELLENISM'

- Ptolemy I
- Antigonus I
- Seleucus I
- Paphlagonia
- Armenia
- Atropatene
- Thrace
- Macedonia

Not long after Alexander's death, the *diadochoi* – the Macedonian generals who had participated in his triumphs – were engaged in fierce struggles over the succession. But Hellenism was already making its mark, as new centres of economic and cultural vitality were established outside the traditional Greek world. Athens, Rhodes and Syracuse were joined by the new capitals of the kingdoms into which the empire had been divided: Alexandria, Antioch, Pergamum and – slightly less important – Pella, the new Macedonian capital of the Antigonids.

As the crisis over the succession continued, a revolt by the Greeks was quickly crushed by Antipater, ruler in Aegae (322 BC). Struggles, involving Cassander, Antipater's son, Lysimachus, Antigonus the One-Eyed, Seleucus and Ptolemy, continued for some forty years before the empire was divided into kingdoms, some huge, some smaller. Cassander initially gained control of Macedonia, later taken over by Antigonus Gonatas, conqueror of the Celts who invaded Asia Minor in 277 BC; Seleucus became master of Asia Minor, as far as Mesopotamia and the Iranian plateau; Lysimachus received Thrace (until ousted by Seleucus); Ptolemy acquired Egypt and founded the dynasty that bore his name. In 240 BC the kingdom of Pergamum entered the Hellenic sphere under the Attalids who zealously encouraged trade and patronized the arts. Antigonid Macedonia retained its hegemony in a declining Greece. Athens alone continued to enjoy the cultural prestige worthy of its splendid past. Sparta, after an attempt to impose a

62 The frieze of the Great Altar of Zeus in Pergamum is almost the symbol of Hellenistic art. Here the theme of the battle between gods and giants became an allegory of the Attalids' victorious wars.

63 Hellenistic art also had an intimate aspect, focusing on the representation of feelings – as shown by this beautiful statue of a young boy wrapped in a short cloak, found at Tralles in Asia Minor.

'popular' framework on its institutions, was overcome by the Achaean League with Macedonian support (227–222 BC). Greece's island cities – Kos and Rhodes in particular – enjoyed significant growth, benefiting from their excellent position for trade. They were run by moderate oligarchies capable of exporting local products to distant places (amphoras from Rhodes and Kos, dated 230–220 BC found in the Po Valley are proof that wine was shipped to the Celts).

In Egypt, Alexandria under the Ptolemies was unrivalled as a centre of trade and culture. The city's museum and library were institutions of great cultural importance, while its school of art was one of the most admired of the Hellenistic world, equal to that at Pergamum. Towards the middle of the century, the city was the point of departure for expeditions which conquered Cyrenaica, Lycia, Pamphylia and Cyprus. Egypt's power began to wane in the early years of the 2nd century BC, the result of corruption among its rulers and the stirrings of expansionism from Rome which, having conquered Carthage, had set its sights on dominating the whole Mediterranean.

Antioch became the capital of the vast Seleucid kingdom. The city played a key role in Hellenizing the melting-pot of cultures that had existed for thousands of years in this region, one of the most prosperous of the world. The liberal policies of its rulers remained constant throughout the century but Seleucid dominions were eventually split up into a series of states, large and small, from India, Bactria and Persia to Anatolia, where the kingdoms of Armenia, Cappadocia and Pergamum emerged.

	Macedonia		Cyprus
	Epirus		Bithynia and Pontus
	Achaea		Galatia
	Asia		Cappadocia
	Lycia and Pamphylia		Cilicia

With the 2nd century BC came the decisive clash between the declining power of Macedonia and the rising force of Rome. Not content with punishing Philip V for his support of Hannibal in the war of 215–205 BC, the Romans took further action in 200–196 BC, under the pretext of freeing the old *poleis* from Macedonian dominion. At the head of the Roman armies, Titus Quinctius Flamininus was victorious at the battle of Cynoscephalae and proclaimed the liberty of all Greek cities at the Isthmian Games of 196 BC. This was the first step towards the subjugation of a region whose culture captivated the more sophisticated members of Rome's senatorial élite.

After a series of wars against the dynasties of Syria, Rome gained control of the Seleucid kingdom (in 129 BC 'demoted' to a mere province). The battle of Pydna in 168 BC brought the Third Macedonian War to a close and signalled the end of the Macedonian monarchy; the region was divided into four republics under the protection of Rome. In the first half of the century Rhodes supported the enemies of Rome, a strategy the island paid dearly for: in 166 BC the Romans declared Delos a 'free port' and sealed the doom of Rhodes' economy. The last Macedonian revolt, supported by numerous Greek cities, led by Corinth, ended with another Roman victory: in 146 BC Corinth was razed to the ground (Carthage was destroyed in the same year). Except for some 'open' cities, Greece became the Roman province of Achaea. The myriad states formed from the dismembered kingdoms of the *diadochoi* were taken over by Rome in the 2nd and 1st centuries BC, generally by force but occasionally ceded voluntarily – as with Pergamum, bequeathed to Rome by the last Attalid. Egypt held on to its autonomy until the fateful year 31 BC. On the day after the battle of Actium, with the defeat of Mark Antony by Octavian, Cleopatra VII, last queen of the Ptolemies, committed suicide and the ancient kingdom of the pharaohs fell to the new prince of Rome.

64 Delos became a free-port and experienced a time of great prosperity in the Roman period (2nd–1st century BC), at the expense of Rhodes. The arts flourished, as is evident in this head of a lost bronze statue, depicting an unknown character, who does, however, have realistically individualized features (c. 100 BC).

65 Roman admiration for Greek art was reflected above all in the systematic creation of copies of the most beautiful and famous works, with copyists varying considerably in skill. This detail is taken from a very fine statue of Hermes, a copy of an original by Praxiteles of the first half of the 4th century BC.

Civilization and Culture in Ancient Greece

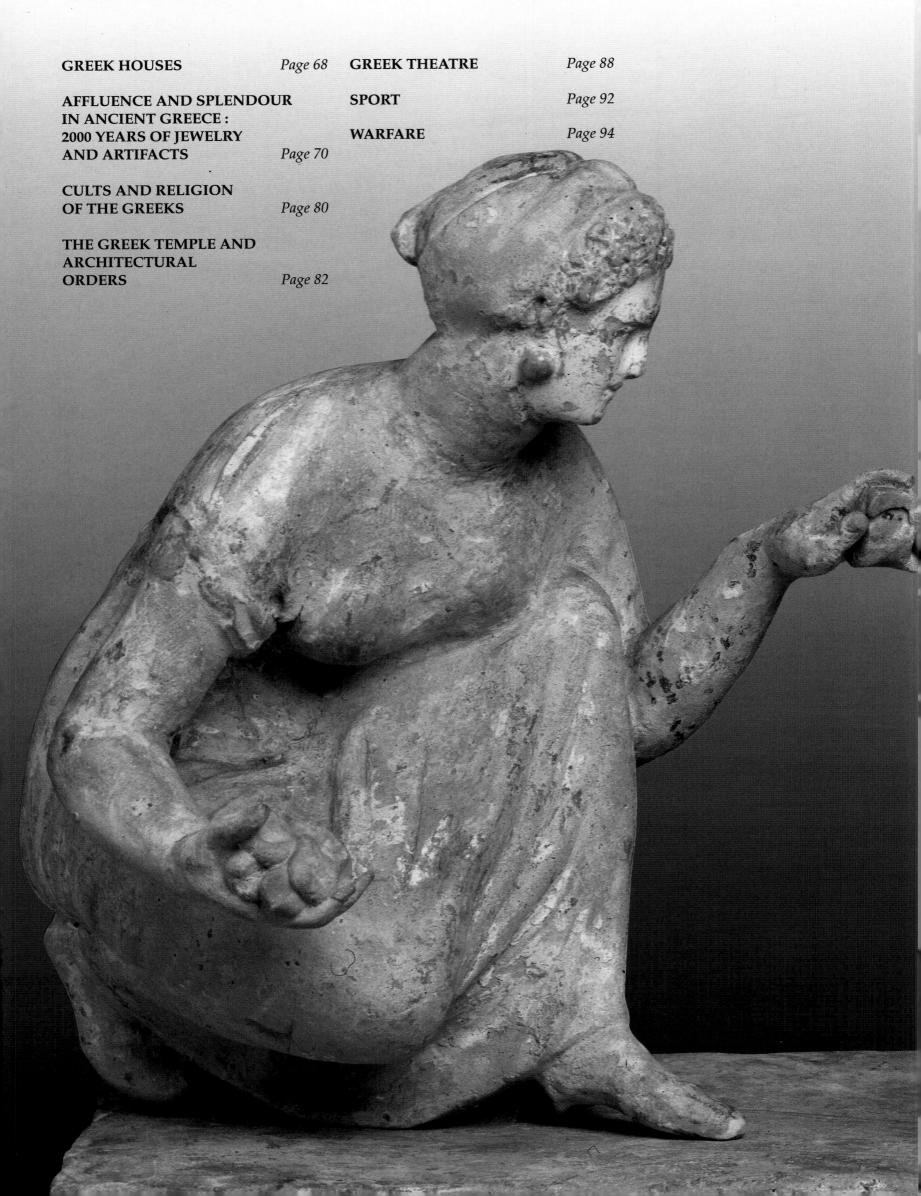

66–67 An intimate daily scene is depicted in this painted pottery group found at Capua and dating to around 300 BC. Two young girls are shown in the midst of a game of knuckle-bones, which was played with dice made from sheep or cattle vertebrae. The individualized features, freedom of composition and variety of gestures presage the Hellenistic style.

GREEK HOUSES

68 *Although perhaps a mythological scene, this painted clay plaque from Locri Epizephyrioi (Calabria) depicts a delightful and detailed image of domestic life. A goddess seated in a room equipped with various pieces of furniture lifts the lid of a wicker basket.*

For many centuries the house had a marginal role in the everyday life of the Greeks. The excellent climate meant that most activities, whether work or leisure, took place outdoors, and most meals were consumed there. Houses mainly provided shelter at night. For Greek women, irrespective of class, the house was a 'prison without bars' where they spent most of their enclosed existence: the sole exceptions were women who chose the morally reprehensible but socio-economically rewarding position of *hetaera*, a cross between a cultured mistress of a salon, secret lover – from genuine passion or economic necessity – and high-class courtesan. In the Archaic period houses quickly evolved from primitive and basic structures, derived from the *megaron*, to a variety of more articulated layouts. Houses were either square or rectangular in shape (sometimes with an apsidal form). Floor plans were organized so that rooms were aligned in a row or faced one another. In some cases they gave on to a private court, in others on to yards shared with other dwellings. Building methods varied, with widespread use of timber framework and pisé as an alternative to plaster-finished unbaked bricks on stone foundations. Roofing was more uniform: only occasionally did single or twin sloping roofs replace the flat, Cycladic-type roof, which served to collect, store and channel rainwater.

With the new, rational urban planning that emerged in the second half of the 5th century BC, styles changed and builders apparently paid more attention to the function and comfort of domestic space. This is perhaps an early sign of the trend to a more individualistic approach to life. This is certainly the impression given by the buildings of Olynthus, a town of the Chalcidic peninsula. Although

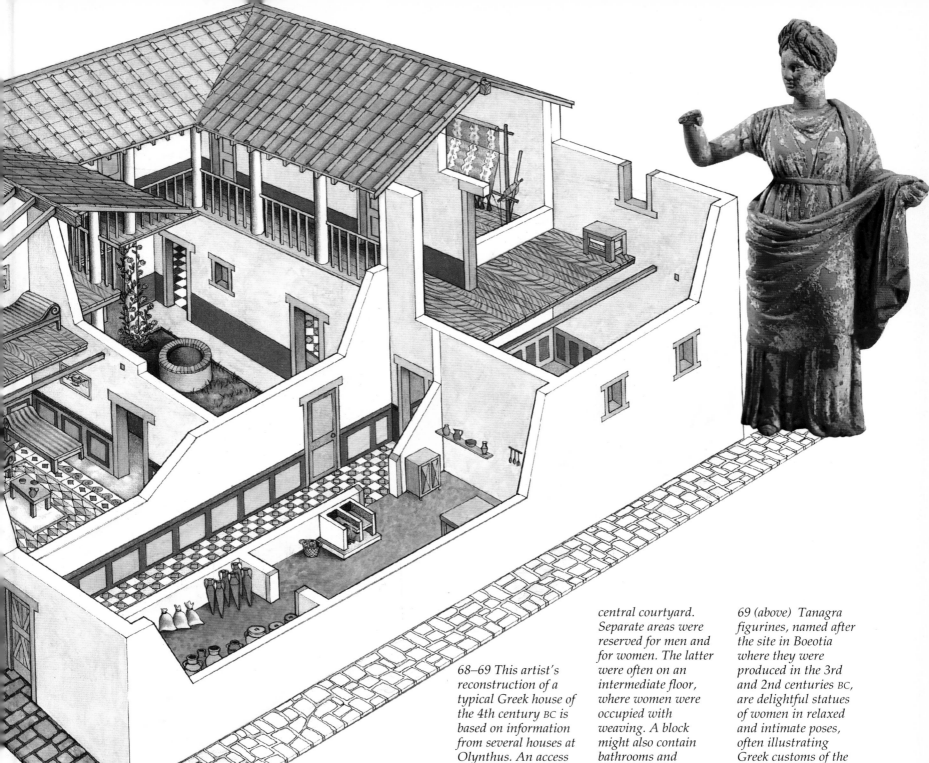

in a peripheral area of Greece, Olynthus attained great prestige and was in many ways comparable with the most powerful cities of the time. It retained this position until 348 BC when it was razed by Philip II of Macedon, preserving precious insights into the urban layout and architectural features of a town of about 20,000 inhabitants. The town plan was based on a grid, with wide north–south arteries intersected by narrower streets. But the character of the terrain and the need to expand led to variants, for example diagonal routes.

When older areas were rebuilt they were brought into line with the new residential quarters in the north of the town. These were organized in long blocks divided along the main axis by an alley, for the circulation of air and people, separating two rows of five standard dwelling units.

Olynthus in fact marked a turning point in the development of the Greek house, with a shift towards more articulated, standardized forms. The most common floor plan consisted of rooms ranged around a courtyard with at least one arcaded side; these generally included a living room, a kitchen and a small bathroom. Evidence has been found in some buildings of an upper floor covering at least part of the dwelling. On the east side of the town numerous detached houses have been unearthed. These often boast an unusually large number of rooms around an arcaded central court and can be seen as precursors of the aristocratic villas of later Hellenistic and Roman periods.

Floor mosaics are another typical feature of these houses: created from river pebbles, they depict mythological figures.

In the Hellenistic age the Greek house reached the apex of its development. Peristyle houses, with many rooms giving on to a porticoed inner court, included more 'mod cons'. There was widespread use of stone or mosaic paving, with decorative detail inspired by textiles, tapestries and carpets or, more probably, wall paintings. The artists attempted to create more varied and scenic effects, often related to the local landscape.

Through the centuries the house evolved from a humble shelter to the small, private 'castle' of law-abiding citizens, satisfied with themselves and with the solid walls of their home – a modest showcase of a lifestyle in which appearances were all that mattered.

AFFLUENCE AND SPLENDOUR IN ANCIENT GREECE: 2000 YEARS OF JEWELRY AND ARTIFACTS

A wide range of precious materials was used by the Minoans, Mycenaeans and Greeks to embellish their homes, for personal adornment and to flaunt luxury as evidence of their wealth, prestige and high social status. These included timbers such as cypress, cedar of Lebanon, Aleppo pine, boxwood and – more rarely – ebony; ivory; semiprecious stones such as chalcedony, carnelian, amethyst, quartz – pink-tinged, green and smoke-grey – rock crystal, lapis lazuli, turquoise, as well as the more humble crystalline calcite, tourmaline, obsidian and garnet; glass paste coloured by skilful Phoenician and Egyptian craftsmen; and, most important of all, precious metals. Greece never yielded much gold: mines existed only in the outlying mountainous regions of Thrace and Macedonia, and on a few Aegean islands. The gold for the artifacts of Minoan Crete and the Mycenaean world came from the east. In the 2nd millennium BC the Hellenic peoples maintained flourishing commercial and diplomatic relations with Egypt, Syro-Palestine, Anatolia and Mesopotamia. By the 7th century BC, once the Greeks had emerged from the long period of impoverishment of the Dark Ages, Oriental jewelry was being imported in large quantities and, before long, was extensively copied by Orientalizing workshops in the homeland and colonies. But it was not until the 6th century BC that an

70 A wonderful boat-shaped earring created using a variety of techniques – moulding, embossing, granulation and filigree – displays the skills of the goldsmiths of Tarentum in the 4th century BC. At the sides, separated by a palmette and two rosettes, are two nikai, or winged victories, with two birds below. Seven amphora-shaped pendants suspended from fine gold chains complete the piece.

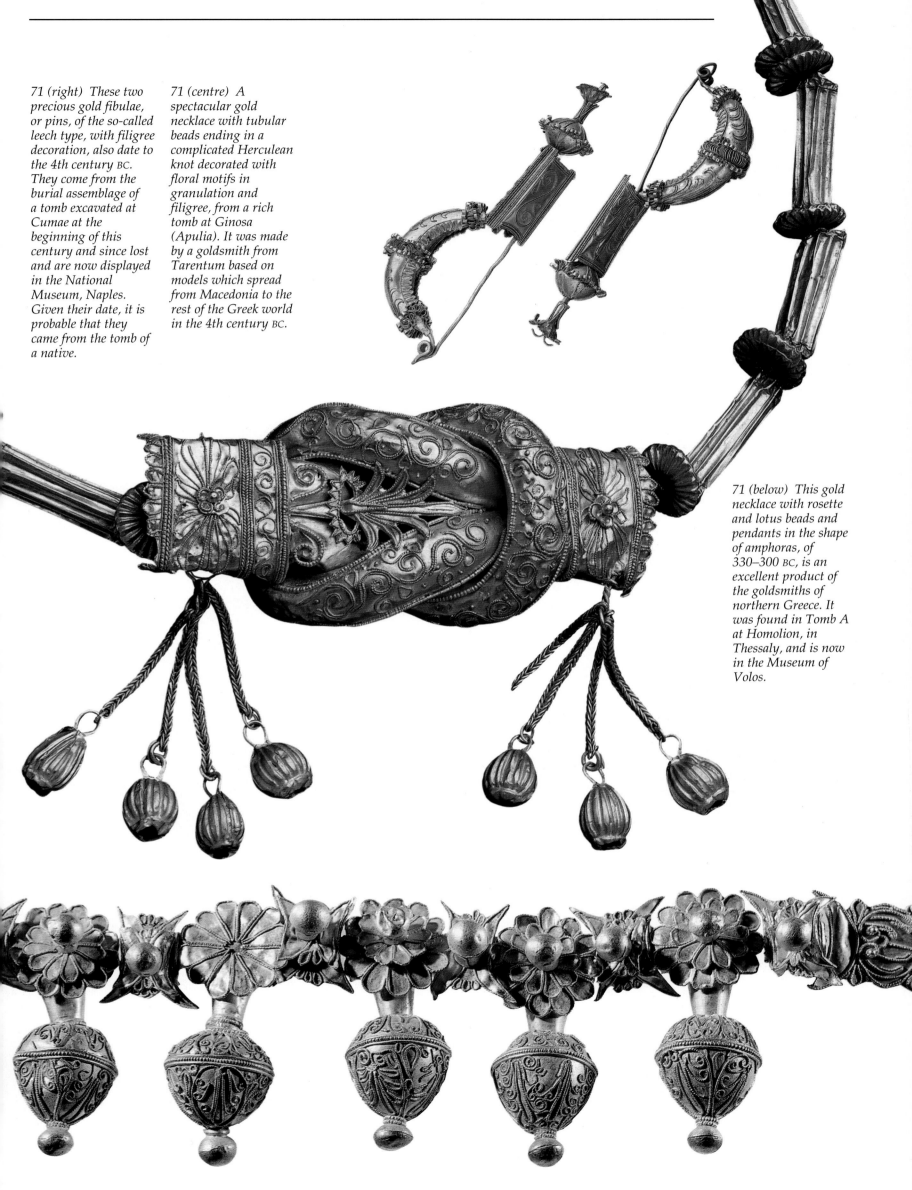

71 (right) These two precious gold fibulae, or pins, of the so-called leech type, with filigree decoration, also date to the 4th century BC. They come from the burial assemblage of a tomb excavated at Cumae at the beginning of this century and since lost and are now displayed in the National Museum, Naples. Given their date, it is probable that they came from the tomb of a native.

71 (centre) A spectacular gold necklace with tubular beads ending in a complicated Herculean knot decorated with floral motifs in granulation and filigree, from a rich tomb at Ginosa (Apulia). It was made by a goldsmith from Tarentum based on models which spread from Macedonia to the rest of the Greek world in the 4th century BC.

71 (below) This gold necklace with rosette and lotus beads and pendants in the shape of amphoras, of 330–300 BC, is an excellent product of the goldsmiths of northern Greece. It was found in Tomb A at Homolion, in Thessaly, and is now in the Museum of Volos.

awareness of gold's value resulted in a coinage-based economy and more widespread use of this metal to make jewelry and artifacts.

Minoan jewelry is stunningly beautiful. Stylistically it reflects the naturalism typical of Cretan art, but technically it has more in common with Egyptian and Oriental models, with an abundant use of repoussé, incision, inlay, gilding and combination with semiprecious stones and terracotta. In the main centres of the Peloponnese, Mycenaean goldsmiths responded to ideas picked up from a vast cultural network, adapting and experimenting with new

techniques and motifs to produce innovative formal and decorative solutions. Numerous examples can be found: a Minoan cup beside a Mycenaean imitation in the *tholos* tomb at Vapheio; Oriental motifs copied – sometimes rather clumsily – on the heads of pins or on signet rings; daggers with inlaid designs using the Anatolian technique of niello; remarkable funerary masks; plant- or marine-style wares; animal-shaped *rhyta* in tombs at Mycenae, Midea-Dendra and Tiryns, where local pieces are found next to imports from Crete and places under Minoan influence.

72 (below left) A magnificent earring with a pendant in the form of the head of a woman, herself adorned with jewels of the Tarentum tradition, from a tomb at Crispiano.

72 (below right) Although these earrings date to the 4th century BC, the iconography of the griffin-head terminals harks back to the 7th century BC and the

Orientalizing period. They therefore demonstrate the continuity of certain decorative themes in Greek art, especially perhaps in its minor expressions.

72–73 A superb gold diadem with flowers of gold and enamel delights the eye. It was probably produced by goldsmiths from Tarentum and placed in a rich tomb at Canosa in the 3rd century BC.

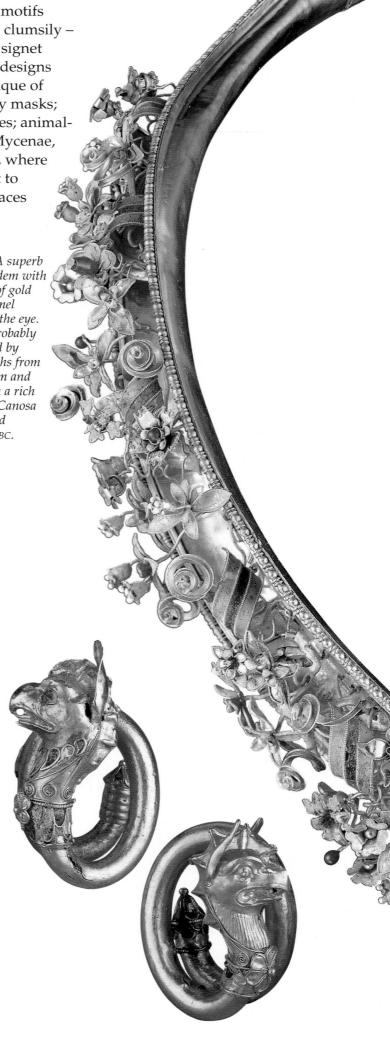

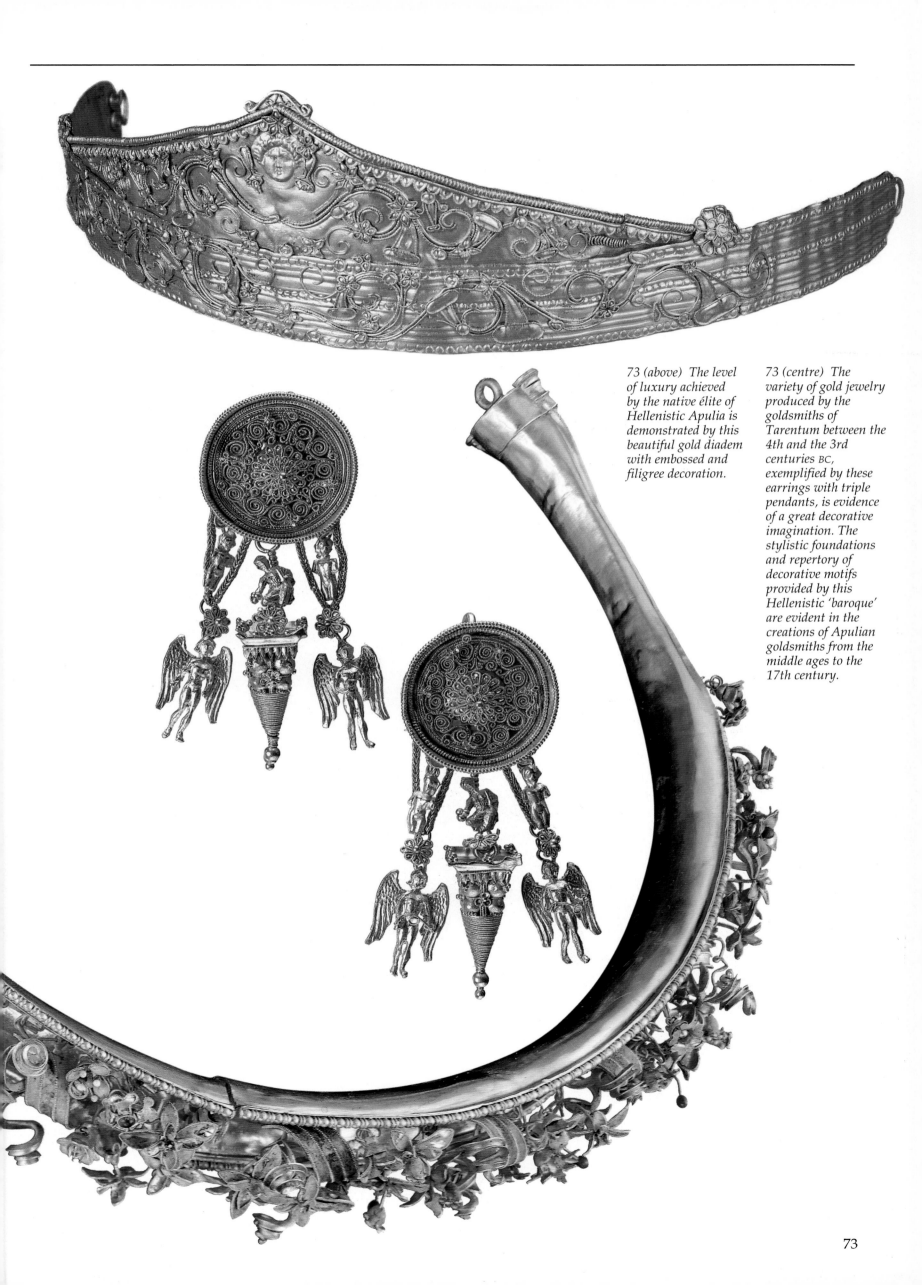

73 (above) The level of luxury achieved by the native élite of Hellenistic Apulia is demonstrated by this beautiful gold diadem with embossed and filigree decoration.

73 (centre) The variety of gold jewelry produced by the goldsmiths of Tarentum between the 4th and the 3rd centuries BC, exemplified by these earrings with triple pendants, is evidence of a great decorative imagination. The stylistic foundations and repertory of decorative motifs provided by this Hellenistic 'baroque' are evident in the creations of Apulian goldsmiths from the middle ages to the 17th century.

74 (above) This golden spray of myrtle flowers originally belonged to a luxurious gold crown of the second half of the 4th century BC, found in central Macedonia.

74 (below) The artistic connection between goldsmiths of Greece and those of Magna Graecia in the 4th and 3rd centuries BC is apparent in this diadem with bronze leaves and insects and berries made of clay and covered with gold leaf. The piece comes from Campania.

74–75 A victor's crown with gold laurel and oak leaves is a testimony to the skill of Thessalian goldsmiths in the Hellenistic age. It was found near Volos and dates between the end of the 4th and the beginning of the 3rd century BC.

75 (centre) A gold diadem, contemporary with the previous one, but from Tarentum, faithfully reproduces a wreath of oak leaves, the tree sacred to Zeus.

75 (below) The charm and inexhaustible creativity of Greek goldsmiths is often encapsulated in a comparatively simple object, such as this small sceptre covered by a thin gold mesh, surmounted by a Corinthian capital, from which oak leaves sprout.

75

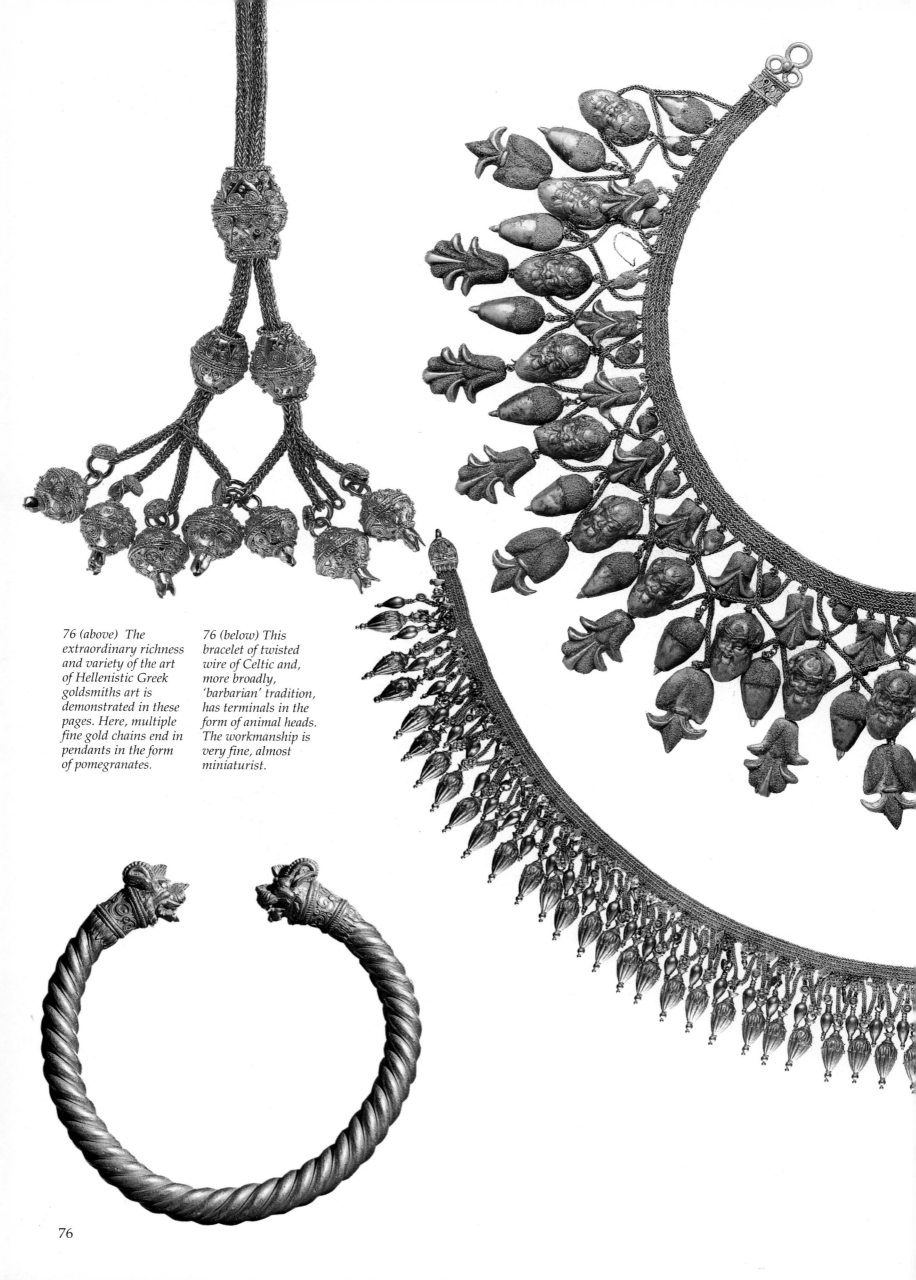

76 (above) The extraordinary richness and variety of the art of Hellenistic Greek goldsmiths art is demonstrated in these pages. Here, multiple fine gold chains end in pendants in the form of pomegranates.

76 (below) This bracelet of twisted wire of Celtic and, more broadly, 'barbarian' tradition, has terminals in the form of animal heads. The workmanship is very fine, almost miniaturist.

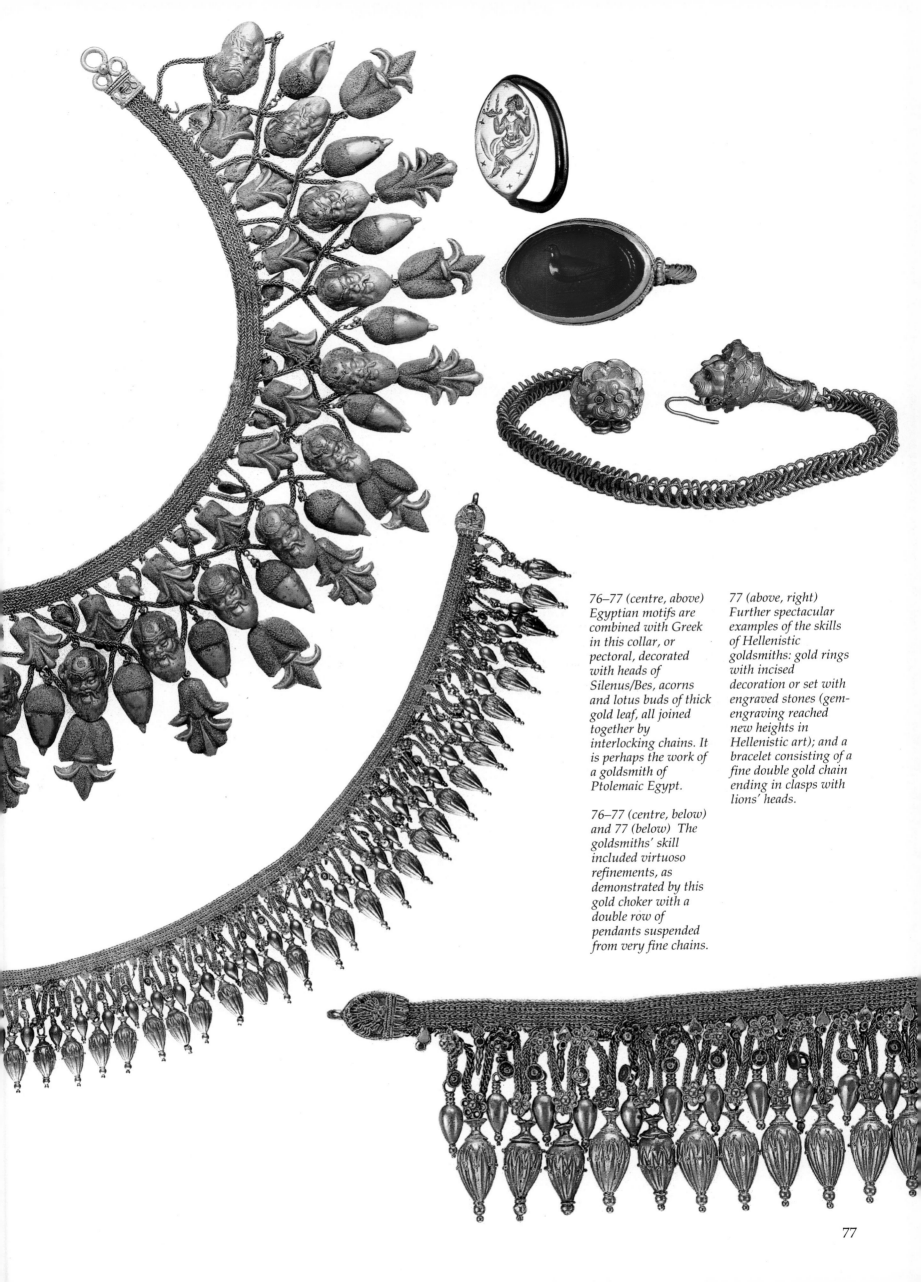

76–77 (centre, above) Egyptian motifs are combined with Greek in this collar, or pectoral, decorated with heads of Silenus/Bes, acorns and lotus buds of thick gold leaf, all joined together by interlocking chains. It is perhaps the work of a goldsmith of Ptolemaic Egypt.

76–77 (centre, below) and 77 (below) The goldsmiths' skill included virtuoso refinements, as demonstrated by this gold choker with a double row of pendants suspended from very fine chains.

77 (above, right) Further spectacular examples of the skills of Hellenistic goldsmiths: gold rings with incised decoration or set with engraved stones (gem-engraving reached new heights in Hellenistic art); and a bracelet consisting of a fine double gold chain ending in clasps with lions' heads.

Relatively small amounts of gold jewelry were produced in the Geometric period. Goldsmiths followed the prevailing trend for abstract designs and non-figurative geometric motifs on earrings, rings and bracelets made for their aristocratic clientele in 8th-century Athens, Eleusis and Eretria. Also datable to this period are the origins of techniques of gold mesh and microgranulation. These were very popular in the following century in the Orientalizing style, with its repertoire of animal and fantastic motifs, its elegant, 'baroque' gems – true masterpieces of jewelry – and the huge variety of decorative appliqués for clothes, household goods and personal accessories. A major role in these developments was played by the easternmost towns of

78 (right) and 79 (left) Two gold plaques with embossed, engraved and filigree decoration from tumulus III at Kralevo (Thrace), dating from the first half of the 3rd century BC. The griffins on them are mythical animals admired by the barbarians and here used to decorate elements of the trappings of a horse that must have belonged to a Thracian prince.

78 (above) The splendour of the age of Alexander the Great and the inventiveness and creativity of the Macedonian artists are exemplified in this famous large krater of gilded bronze, with volute handles and richly decorated in
relief and three-dimensional figures. Found in a tomb at Derveni, near Salonika, and dating from 330 BC, it may have belonged to an aristocrat, Astiounios, son of Anaxagoras of Larisa, according to an inscription on the
rim. On the body is the scene of the wedding of Dionysus and Ariadne, with unrestrained dancing Maenads, carried away in the ecstasy of a sensual dance, and Satyrs excited by the frenzied swaying of the disciples of
Dionysus. Everything in the vase seems to be designed to astonish the fortunate guests at banquets at which the krater must have been used to serve the finest wine – a gift within a gift, a hymn to the fleeting pleasures of this earthly life.

the Greek world, with their close ties to the sources of these influences in the Levant, and perhaps also due to the economic strength of local aristocratic or tyrannical patrons. This is evident in finds from Rhodes, but cemeteries of Crete, Melos and Corinth have also yielded many significant items.

The affluence of the sanctuaries in the Archaic and Classical periods helps explain the quality and quantity of jewelry and artifacts unearthed at Delphi, Olympia, Metapontum and Locri. Greek ascendancy over the trading powers of the Mediterranean led to the production of precious ornamental objects on a large scale, in very different and widely scattered places, sometimes on the fringe of the Greek world, including colonies. Precious metals were used for tablewares and decorative elements for furnishings made of wood or bronze, and these, and the jewelry mirrored tastes in contemporary Greek art. But it is the goldsmiths of the 4th century BC and the Hellenistic period who created the most stunning objects, outstanding for the richness of their design, composition, weight and decoration. Western Greek colonies – Tarentum, Ruvo, Crispiano, Ginosa, Canosa, Roccagloriosa – followed the lead of Pella, Demetrias, Vergina, Sindos and Derveni. And already in the 5th century BC, in places as far apart as Syracuse and Athens, Camarina and Macedonia, renowned engravers such as Evenetes were carving minting dies for gold and silver coins: masterpieces in miniature, low relief that incorporated the genius of the most celebrated works of Greek plastic art.

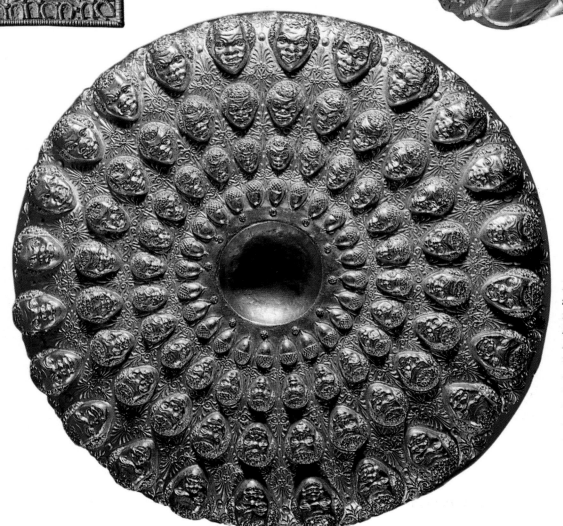

79 (right) The famous phiale of the Panagurishte hoard (Thrace, c. 310 BC) is a magnificent goblet for libations made by a Greek artist. Three concentric circles of heads of Africans, delicately and realistically portrayed despite the gradual reduction in size, surround an inner one of acorns, with lotus flowers between – a motif perhaps of Egyptian origin.

79 (above) One of the splendid gold rhyta of the Panagurishte hoard represents the head of an Amazon wearing a helmet. It has an unusual handle shaped like a winged sphinx. Given its preciousness, it is probable that it belonged to the reigning family of the Odrysai (4th–3rd century BC).

CULTS AND RELIGION OF THE GREEKS

80 (below) A masterpiece of the final stages of Archaic art, this rare bronze original, the so-called Piraeus Apollo (500 BC), may portray the god in the act of receiving an offering.

80 (right) A bronze head of the early 5th century BC provides a typical portrait of the father of the gods of Olympus – Zeus, the powerful lord of lightning, the tireless seducer of goddesses, nymphs and, less often, mortals.

The polytheism of Greek religion was shaped by a number of factors. First, the relatively few Olympian deities (named after Mt Olympus, the 'roof of Greece', where they were thought to live) shared by all Greeks co-existed with numerous lesser gods, deified heroes and demons. Also, the fact that divine omnipotence was limited by Fate and that the gods resembled humans, assumes a highly developed (and anthropocentric) concept of superhumanity and an automatic limit to mysticism. There was also no organized clerical order – priests and priestesses merely handled cult manifestations and did not form a class designated to impose orthodoxy. Above all, the Greeks conceived religiousness as respect for the gods and for the moral values of the community, not as a matter of personal conscience. There were some mystical elements of clear Oriental derivation and occasional evidence of 'deviations', for instance in the chthonic cults of Dionysus, Demeter, Kore-Persephone and Hades, in philosophies like Pythagoreanism and Platonism and in the later diffusion – from the Hellenistic period – of cults of gods such as Hermes Trismegistos, Isis and Mithras. The lack of sacred texts was compensated for by an immense mythological legacy, which writers, poets and philosophers drew on freely.

Foremost among the many deities was Zeus – father and brother of all the gods, god of the sky and of light, ruler of the cosmos, protector of all legally constituted power and rights – venerated by all Greeks. Hera, his hot-tempered sister and unhappy bride (fidelity was not a strong point of the lord of Olympus), was protectress of marriage, maternity and domestic life; she was worshipped particularly in

80 (below) On the west pediment of the temple of Athena Aphaia on Aegina (510–500 BC), this beautiful statue of the goddess rose in divine epiphany in the tumult of a battle between the Greeks and the Trojans.

81 (opposite) A painted clay plaque of the first decades of the 5th century BC from Locri (Calabria) depicts a scene of an offering of ritual gifts (vine shoots, a kantharos and a cock) to the infernal couple, Kore and Hades.

Argos, Olympia and Samos. Poseidon, daring and impetuous lord of the forces of earth and water, instigator of tempests and earthquakes, was revered in the coastal town of Isthmia, near Corinth. Athena, the warrior virgin, was protectress of the city that bore her name; she presided over craft activities and encouraged civilized behaviour, guaranteeing law and order against barbarism; her cult was devoutly observed in Aegina and Tegea, as well as Athens. Apollo, a handsome and ambiguous god, was bringer of health and terrible epidemics, patron of music and letters; his wishes were made known through the enigmatic responses of oracles. He was worshipped mainly at Delphi and Delos, but temples dedicated to his cult were also erected in Corinth, Phigaleia, Thermos and Didyma. His sister Artemis – goddess of hunting and related to two eastern deities, the 'Mistress of Animals' and Isis – was protectress of wild nature and monitored the dividing-line between the primordial human condition and civilized society; sanctuaries were dedicated to her at Ephesus and on Kerkyra (Corfu). The cult of Aphrodite, goddess of love in all its manifestations, originating from the Semitic Astarte-Ishtar, centred on Paphos, Cyprus, and Kythera. Many other divine figures were important: Hermes, messenger god, protector of merchants, heralds and thieves, guide of souls to the Underworld, guarantor of frontiers and a healer; Demeter, protectress of land and agriculture, object of the Eleusinian mysteries, linked with Kore-Persephone, her daughter, and Hades; Dionysus, god of wine and ecstasy, guardian of man's capacity to let his mind escape from the burden of everyday reality and act out life's dramas in the theatrical dimension of tragedy and comedy; Hephaestus, smith of the gods, lame and devoted husband of the beautiful Aphrodite; Ares, mysterious god of the warrior spirit; Heracles, symbol of the semi-divine man who, following his Labours and other arduous tasks, rose to immortality; and Asclepius, god of medicine, venerated at Kos, Pergamum and Epidaurus.

THE GREEK TEMPLE AND ARCHITECTURAL ORDERS

There is an important difference between the Greek temple and sanctuary. Sanctuaries were built in places 'appropriated' by a deity following a manifestation or apparition; temples were erected after a human decision was made to consecrate a site to a god (who thus became its 'owner') and construct a place of worship within the sacred precinct (*temenos*). The earliest temples – known to have existed from the 10th to 8th centuries BC – ranged from simple huts to more elaborate structures. But before long they were replaced by much larger and finer buildings. This evolution was made possible, in part, by developments in construction techniques and materials: stone took the place of wood and unbaked bricks, and structures became more stable and longer-lasting. These changes do not have to be explained by trade and cultural contacts with Egypt and the Middle East, since there is plentiful evidence of Minoan and Mycenaean monumental architecture.

The first phase in the evolution of the Greek temple took place in the 8th and 7th centuries BC, as shown by excavated examples at Thermos, Isthmia and Olympia, and clay models from Argos and Perachora. These early temples were built with stone foundations, timber frames, posts and lintels, and plastered unbaked brick walls. The roof and facings – the latter to protect the wooden upperworks – were of brightly painted clay, sometimes with ornamental figures in relief. Great attention was paid to decorating other prominent structures, such as the columns of the peristyle. These columns, surrounding the building on at least three sides and helping support the roof, were probably finished with decorative fluting, even in this earliest phase. The influence of these aesthetic canons is visible in the stone temples of later centuries: the traditionalism of religious rituals also affected architects and artists, as is evident from the early codification of the orders of classical architecture.

Greek temples functioned differently from, to us, more familiar places of worship. The *cella* or *naos* contained the cult statue of the deity and it was here the priests performed rituals; sometimes there was an adjoining *adyton*, accessible only to the priests, where an ancient cult image was venerated and the god might make his will manifest. Temples often included a *pronaos*, giving access to the *cella*, and

82–83 In this artist's reconstruction all the basic architectural components of the elevation of a typical Greek peripteral hexastyle (six columns at each end) temple of Doric order are visible (plan below). It also restores decorative features that are often lost, such as the brightly coloured paintwork. The modest size and relative simplicity of the rooms is also evident, since cult activities mostly centred on the altar which was usually in front of the building.

an *opisthodomos* – a rear chamber, symmetrical to the *pronaos* – whose functions are not entirely clear. Perhaps as a tribute to the early tradition of cult rituals performed in the open air, the altar stood outside the temple, generally in front and at the foot of the stylobate on which the temple was built. Greek temples are always

83 A rare pictorial document from the 6th century BC: this scene of a sacrifice on a painted wooden tablet was found in miraculously good condition in a cave at Pitsa, near Sicyon, in Corinth.

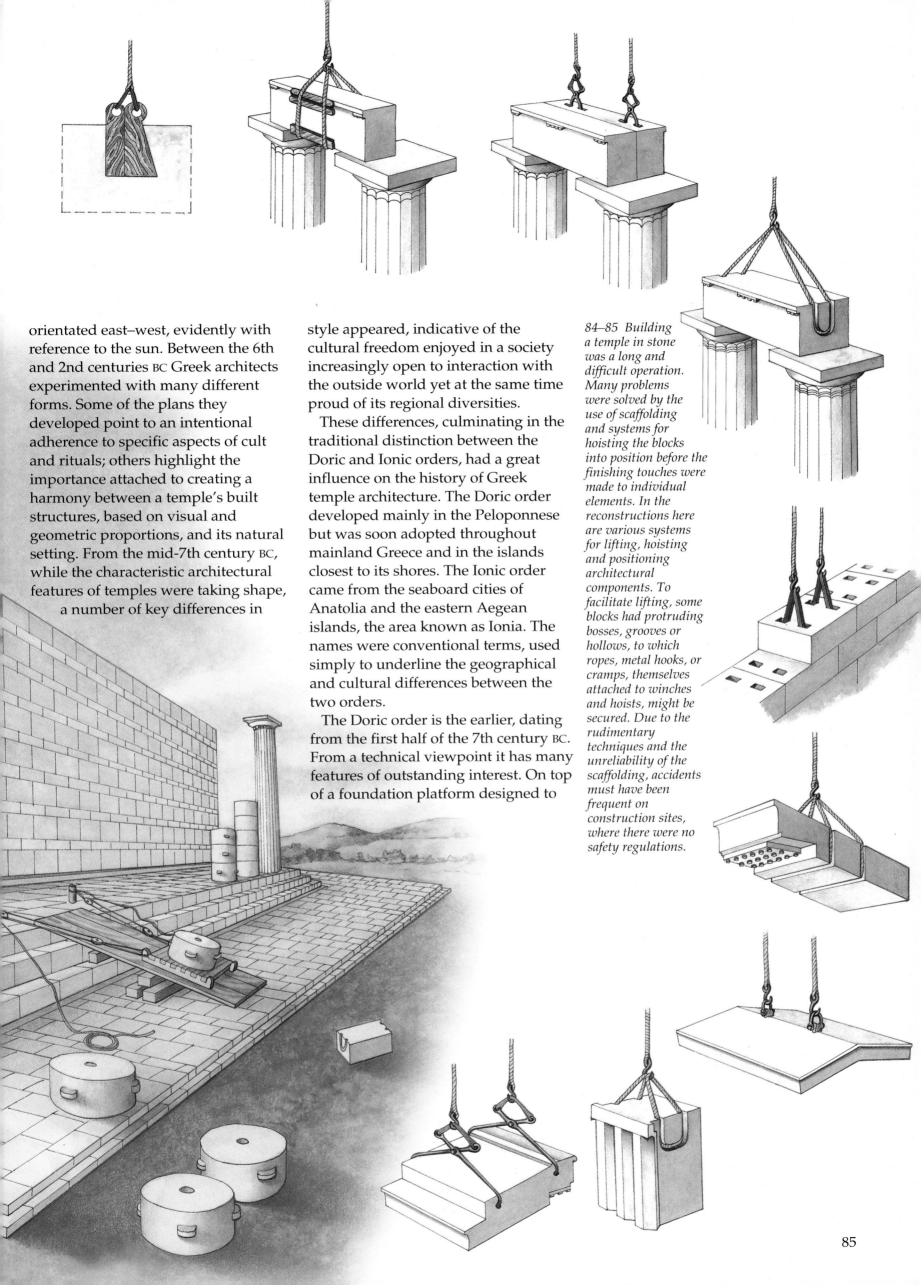

orientated east–west, evidently with reference to the sun. Between the 6th and 2nd centuries BC Greek architects experimented with many different forms. Some of the plans they developed point to an intentional adherence to specific aspects of cult and rituals; others highlight the importance attached to creating a harmony between a temple's built structures, based on visual and geometric proportions, and its natural setting. From the mid-7th century BC, while the characteristic architectural features of temples were taking shape, a number of key differences in style appeared, indicative of the cultural freedom enjoyed in a society increasingly open to interaction with the outside world yet at the same time proud of its regional diversities.

These differences, culminating in the traditional distinction between the Doric and Ionic orders, had a great influence on the history of Greek temple architecture. The Doric order developed mainly in the Peloponnese but was soon adopted throughout mainland Greece and in the islands closest to its shores. The Ionic order came from the seaboard cities of Anatolia and the eastern Aegean islands, the area known as Ionia. The names were conventional terms, used simply to underline the geographical and cultural differences between the two orders.

The Doric order is the earlier, dating from the first half of the 7th century BC. From a technical viewpoint it has many features of outstanding interest. On top of a foundation platform designed to

84–85 Building a temple in stone was a long and difficult operation. Many problems were solved by the use of scaffolding and systems for hoisting the blocks into position before the finishing touches were made to individual elements. In the reconstructions here are various systems for lifting, hoisting and positioning architectural components. To facilitate lifting, some blocks had protruding bosses, grooves or hollows, to which ropes, metal hooks, or cramps, themselves attached to winches and hoists, might be secured. Due to the rudimentary techniques and the unreliability of the scaffolding, accidents must have been frequent on construction sites, where there were no safety regulations.

provide a level, solid surface a *crepidoma* (platform) of three high steps was laid. The top one was the stylobate, which formed the floor of the temple and which supported the columns. Doric columns have no base, perhaps a survival from earlier, wooden temples, where pillars were fixed straight into the ground. Column shafts were fluted and robust, with a slight bulge near the middle. This is known as *entasis* and is designed to emphasize the strength of the supporting structure but also to compensate for an optical illusion which makes the columns seem more slender than they in fact are. At the top

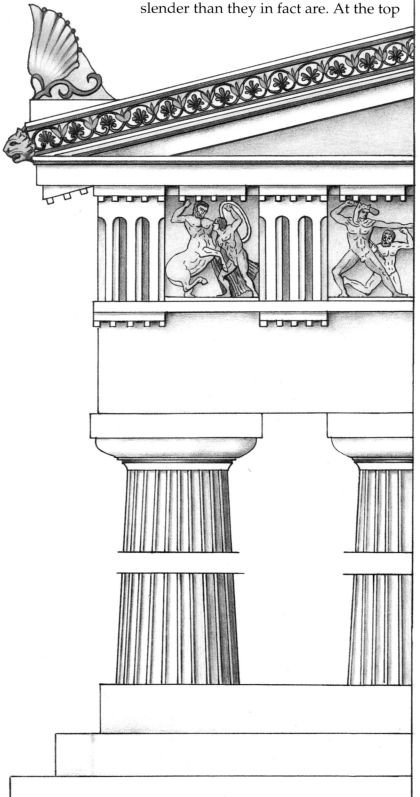

of the column was the capital, comprised of an *echinus* shaped like an upturned truncated cone, initially rounded and flattened, but later more streamlined, and an *abacus*. The influence of wooden Archaic models is particularly evident in these elements. On the capital rested the architrave, which was divided into a plain *epistyle*, and a frieze decorated with metopes separated by triglyphs, also derived from earlier decoration carved in wood. At the ends of the building the two sides of the sloping roof delimited a triangular space known as the pediment. This was soon occupied by imposing sculptures. Finally, decorated gutters and antefixes were mounted along the eaves and cornices of the pediments, while *acroteria* – inspired by natural motifs or depicting gods or demons – projected from the corners.

Early in the 6th century BC the Ionic order was developed by architects in Greek colonies in the eastern Aegean and Asia Minor. The structures and building techniques of Ionic temples clearly evolved in much the same way as Doric; however, the change from wood and unbaked brick to stone was slower than in the Doric area. Some characteristic features of the Ionic order can be attributed to the area's cultural contacts with the Near East and its architecture. The imposing forms of the Ionic order bear the stamp of monumental complexes of Mesopotamia and Persia. Harmonious proportions and ornate architectural decoration evoke the elegance typical of the palaces of great oriental kings. With the introduction of the dipteral plan – with a double row of columns – the temple was surrounded by a regular and imposing 'forest of stone', reminiscent of the vast hypostyle halls crowded with massive columns in sanctuaries of Egypt and the Near East, designed to emphasize the immense gulf between mortal and divine.

Two structural elements – column and frieze – differentiate the two orders. The Ionic column did not rest directly on the stylobate but on a moulded 'cushion' base, which accentuated the clean lines of the tall, fluted shaft with no *entasis*. At the top was a delicate capital, formed of two generously proportioned volutes. The base perhaps derives from the introduction of stone at the bottom of wooden columns to separate them from the damp ground; the capital would appear to have originated from wooden prototypes.

The frieze was now no longer comprised of alternating triglyphs and metopes; instead it was a continuous series of large slabs forming long, carved narrative panels, also more oriental than Greek in taste. Closely related to the Ionic capital was the so-called Aeolic capital, found in areas where this Greek dialect was spoken (Boeotia, Thessaly, part of Asia Minor and islands of the northeastern Aegean). Its most characteristic features were large stylized volutes which sprang from the shaft and had openwork carvings. Following Vitruvius, writing in his *De Architectura* (1st century AD), the Corinthian order has traditionally been included among the Greek architectural orders. In fact this is chronologically and historically incorrect since the Corinthian capital, reputedly invented by Callimachus in the last quarter of the 5th century BC, was rarely used in the Greek world and did not constitute a new architectural order. Until it became popular in Roman times, it was merely adopted as an alternative to the Ionic capital. Roman architects working in the Hellenistic tradition developed a Corinthian 'order' inspired by the Doric and Ionic orders, which by that time had largely fallen from use. The plans, structures and proportions they created were often new, with variants and combinations that reveal the underlying eclecticism of their artistic philosophy.

The Corinthian capital is characterized by a huge inverted bell shape, surrounded by acanthus leaves bent over backwards, with the flower on the *abacus*. It is a triumph in miniature of gently curving lines and surfaces which offered skilled craftsmen scope for creating chiaroscuro effects. The shaft of the column and its base followed the Ionic model, albeit with variants.

GREEK THEATRE

88 An Archaic relief of the Ionic school shows two dancers performing to the sound of a double flute. The tradition of accompanying the actors' performance on stage with intermezzi sung and set to music, or interludes of dancing and miming is documented for Greek tragedy and other plays. Modern stagings of ancient plays also use similar sequences of dancing, singing, music and miming.

The origins of western theatre coincided with the birth of Greek civilization. After a brief process of evolution, it existed in an already developed form by the end of the 6th century BC. Drama differed from other forms of expression based on sight, sound and gesture used to portray reality to an audience. This difference stemmed from the fact that drama was much more than mere description and narrative. It offered new dimensions compared with sterile, religious ceremonies and rituals which were intended as displays of personal status or statements of clan, caste or religious identity.

In Greek theatre dramatist and actor – through their ideas and performance respectively – escaped from the subjective dimension and assumed a different identity and destiny. Drama is not simply a portrayal of everyday life, current events or myths and legends: it is action, the realization of facts, meant not merely to 'entertain' spectators but to involve them on ethical, spiritual, political, psychological and existential levels. Behind the metaphors of theatrical space, time and action lies the real spectacle, be it tragic or comic, of the human condition and the questions it poses. In ancient Greece and particularly in democratic Athens, from Cleisthenes to the battle of Chaeronea, this was the real significance of the genres we call 'tragedy' and 'comedy'. These genres are not far removed from modern theatre: indeed many of the finest Greek plays are still performed. We have no precise knowledge of how the two genres initially evolved: the few pieces of information left by Herodotus, Aristotle and others are contradictory. Only odd fragments of the earliest known tragic poets or comic playwrights have survived. The oldest works passed down to us offer examples of an already defined literary genre, with established (and respected) conventions, internal structure, language and metre. Only 33 tragedies and 18 comedies – not all complete – have been preserved in medieval codices and a few rare fragments of papyrus texts.

As well as the illustrious tragic poets Aeschylus, Sophocles and Euripides and the great comic playwrights Aristophanes and Menander, others, such as Phrynichus, Eupolis and Cratinus, deserve mention. Between the late 6th and the 4th century BC hundreds of competitions and performances took place before enthusiastic audiences, not only in Athens but in the countless theatres that had sprung up in cities and sanctuaries throughout the Greek world. But the theatrical performances staged in Athens were pre-eminent. They were mounted as part of festivals involving rituals and sporting contests held periodically in honour of a particular deity, most often Athena and Dionysus. The festivals were organized by the state, and the funds were contributed by Athens' wealthier citizens. The Great Dionysia, celebrated in honour of

89 This strange terracotta comic mask was discovered in Tarentum and dates from the 4th century BC. It demonstrates the tradition of acting with the face covered by stylized features, as if emphasizing the estrangement of man from himself in the process of acting. The mask also has similarities with comic types depicted on Apulian painted vases of the same period.

Dionysus in the month of *Elaphebolion* (March/April), was undoubtedly the most important festival. It lasted six days, involved the whole population (everyday activities came to a standstill) and attracted many foreigners to the city – thousands of spectators gathered in the Theatre of Dionysus, on the southern slopes of the Acropolis.

The theatrical events took the form of competitions in which, after an initial selection, three dramatists could take part, each of them presenting four works in the course of a day: a trilogy of tragedies and one satyr play. With its burlesque plot and characters, often liberally sprinkled with trivia and obscenities, this 'opera buffa' must have stimulated a liberating explosion of mirth and sensuality after hours of concentration and anguish during performances of the tragedies. On one of the following days the works of comic playwrights occupied the stage. From morning till dusk the Athenians crowded the auditorium, rowdily expressing their enthusiasm or displeasure, overcome by boredom or engaged in vociferous argument with fellow spectators.

The panel of judges was formed of ten people picked at random, one from each of Athens' electoral constituencies. At the end of the performances, each judge wrote the titles of the three competing tragedies in order of preference on a tablet. Only five of the ten tablets were selected and counted, and their votes decided the winner, who was duly acclaimed.

Theatre buildings were also a Greek invention. Already in the Minoan palaces and in a number of centres founded soon after the Helladic Dark Ages, there appear to have been open-air public spaces set aside for performances. Tiered seating allowed spectators to participate in rituals that also had religious connotations. But it was not until the 6th and 5th centuries BC that this most celebrated of Greek secular structures acquired its conventional form (which probably developed from an earlier wooden version, converted into stone). A fundamental requirement was the setting – in a hollow, enhanced for the purpose or created artificially, situated on high ground, preferably in a prominent or spectacular position. The theatre was a meeting-place for thousands of citizens, who gathered to watch plays created by the genius of the tragic and comic poets. It was also

90 This painted clay model represents the backdrop of a theatre and provides a good picture of such a structure in the 3rd century BC.

a venue for leisure pursuits and for debates on countless topics – politics, customs, fashions, historic events, myths, religion and moral issues. It thus became a characterizing feature of the Greek city and by the 4th century BC its architectural form followed a precise code. Its structural components were the *orchestra*, a circular or semicircular space occupied by the chorus during the action on stage; the *scene*, a stage with an architectural backdrop with three doors and spaces for simulated panoramas and mobile 'pictures', according to the demands of the script; and the *koilon* – now better known by the Latin term *cavea* – practically carved out of the hillside, semicircular in shape and consisting of vertical tiers of steps cut by radial

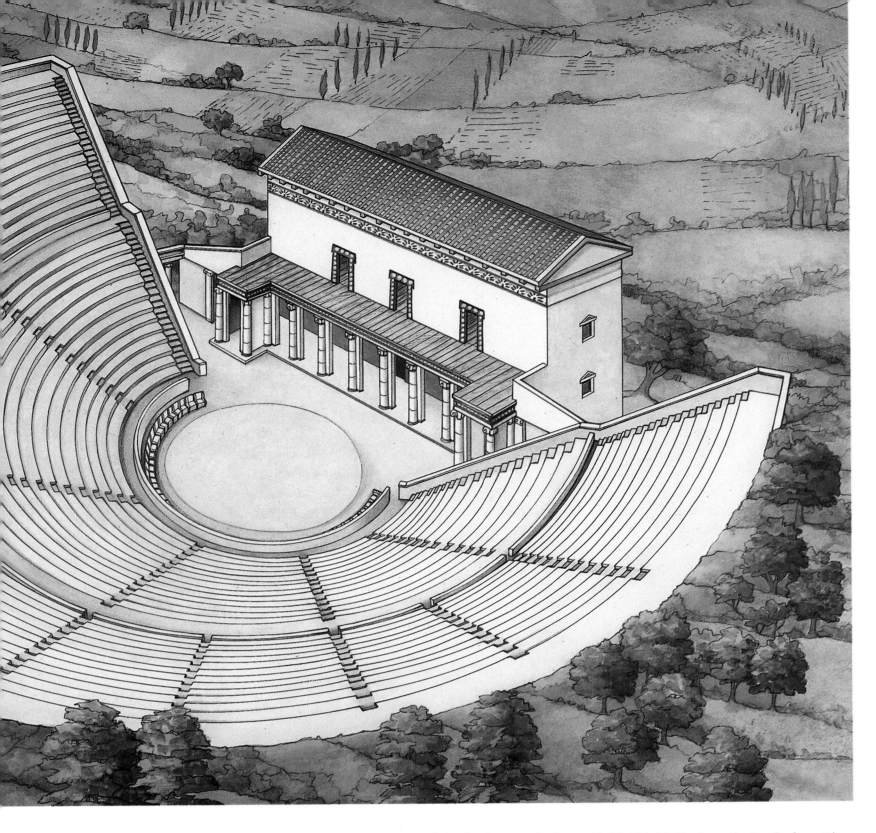

stairways to allow access for the thousands of spectators. The *cavea* was sometimes divided horizontally into two or three sections by corridors called *diazomata*. Its first row, next to the *orchestra*, was normally occupied by seats of honour, often decorated – the *proedria*, reserved for priests and public magistrates, as shown by the inscriptions frequently found on the seats. The audience entered the auditorium along two wide corridors, the *parodoi*, between the *cavea* and the stage, at the sides of the orchestra.

One of the most amazing aspects of Greek theatres is their perfect acoustics: sounds carry from the stage to the very top row of the *cavea* without variation in pitch, intensity or length. A fine example – perhaps the finest – is at Epidaurus in the Argolid,

in the sanctuary of Asclepius, god of healing. This was already famous in ancient times for its imposing dimensions, harmonious proportions and splendid acoustics. A coin dropped on the stone at the centre of the *orchestra* can be heard perfectly at any point of the *cavea*, which extends far up the hillside and has seating for around 15,000 spectators. This amphitheatre was built around 350 BC by the architect known as Polyclitus the Younger (to distinguish him from the sculptor of the same name). What strikes visitors most is the overall harmony of the theatre's design, giving the impression of a project which set out – and this was surely the intention – to bring together actors and audience, dramatists' texts and spectators' ideas and thoughts.

90–91 This idealized reconstruction of a typical Greek theatre highlights one of the important elements of Greek theatral architecture: the search for a panoramic site which utilized the surrounding landscape as an integral part of the theatre. Such a setting could better dissolve the boundaries between the stage and the external universe, enabling spectators to enter a dimension beyond their daily lives and become totally immersed in the space and time of the action.

SPORT

92 (top) Three youths compete in a race in a relief decorating one side of a base of a funeral statue belonging to a young Athenian man (510 BC), now in the National Museum of Athens.

92 (centre) This lekythos with black figures on a white ground by the Edinburgh Painter dates to the late 6th century BC and shows young javelin throwers training.

92 (below) A Panathenaic prize amphora with black figures (dated to 525 BC) documents one of the most widespread sporting competitions of ancient Greece – the horse race with a quadriga, generally within the reach only of aristocrats. The vase is now the National Museum of Taranto.

No people of antiquity attributed as much importance to sport as the Greeks. Gymnastics – physical exercise carried out by males only, completely naked – were an integral part of the education of every young man and one of the distinguishing factors that the Greeks believed set them apart from barbarians. Every city invested substantial resources in the construction of a *gymnasium*, a complex similar to a present-day campus and including a *palaestra* for physical education. This structure normally consisted of a square court, with porticoes offering shade, service facilities, changing rooms and fountains. Around it were tree-lined avenues, baths and rooms for teaching. The teaching was left to the personal initiative of philosophers and experts in various disciplines; pupils of the practical arts, including fine arts, got hands-on experience in workshops.

Sport necessarily meant competitive sport, considered both part of a young man's education – perhaps a remnant of ancient initiation rites designed to instil courage, virtue and military skills – and a cultic offering. It had been the custom among the aristocratic élites of the Mycenaean and Homeric world to hold sporting contests in honour of the dead.

A link was thus established, very early in Greek history, between religious festivals and competitive sporting events held in the great sanctuaries both outside cities and in the principal *poleis*.

Literature provides references to some of the great sporting events of the ancient Greek world: the celebrated Olympiads, according to legend initiated by Heracles in 776 BC; the Pythian Games, held in Delphi in honour of Apollo; the Nemean Games, celebrated at Nemea in honour of Zeus and recalling one of Heracles' Labours; the Isthmian Games, held in the sanctuary of

Poseidon on the Isthmus of Corinth; and the Panathenaic Games, part of the great festivities organized in Athens to honour Athena. Any departure from fair play was severely punished and the only prize besides the purely symbolic laurel wreath was the glory which the winner basked in and which reflected on his people and native city-state, thus honoured in the eyes of all Greece.

The most important athletic disciplines were running, with races

92–93 and 93 (right) The same statue base with the three young men in a running race also shows this scene of an ancestor of hockey (right) and (below) an intense moment in the midst of a wrestling match. The athletes' taut bodies are shown engaged in the struggle, emphasizing their muscles, depicted according to the conventions of ancient Attic art.

over different distances and even in armour (*hoplitodromeia*), discus and javelin throwing, long-jump, boxing, wrestling and *pancration* – a contest involving boxing and wrestling. Restricted to the wealthy were disciplines involving horses, including chariot racing. Musical, vocal and poetry contests were commonly associated with the athletic events, further evidence of the idea of unity that characterized the education of young Greeks.

Before training, under the eye of his coach, or taking part in a contest, the athlete performed a preparatory ritual consisting of covering his body with perfumed oil from a leather *aryballos*. When his strenuous physical exertions were over, and before taking a relaxing bath, he then scraped his skin clean of dust, oil and sweat with a *strigil*, a curved instrument designed for this purpose.

The popularity of sport among the Greeks is amply attested by finds of athletes' equipment (*strigils, halteres* – weights used in jumping – bronze replicas of *aryballoi*, javelins), and by the frequent choice of sporting events as a theme on huge numbers of Attic vases produced in the 6th and 5th centuries BC. Many of these vases were tributes to the youth of a city, to military valour exalted by sport and perhaps – if the vase is found among grave goods – to the premature death of a young man, a metaphor of life as a contest fought against death.

94 (top) A fine example of a bronze helmet in the Corinthian style, found in Ruvo di Puglia, equipped with cheek and nose guards, and decorated in relief on the front.

94 (centre) The front of a bronze cuirass of the late 4th century BC, embossed with anatomical details by a skilful craftsman of Magna Graecia.

94 (right) The famous statue of a cavalryman from Grumentum (Basilicata), a bronze of around 550 BC. It shows a warrior in fighting trim, protected by a helmet and cuirass.

Countless ancient literary sources referring to the 'art' of warfare, together with archaeological finds, give a clear picture of developments in ancient Greece in man's most inhumane activity – from the heroic deeds of Mycenaean warriors immortalized in the poems of Homer to the great military exploits of Alexander the Great and Demetrius Poliorcetes, and the inventions of Archimedes. The clothing and armour worn by Greek foot-soldiers varied enormously, but were always essentially practical. Helmets were generally made of bronze, lined with leather and sometimes padded. Whatever the style (Corinthian, Illyrian, Macedonian, Thracian), the common aim was to afford maximum protection against small missiles hurled into the advancing rows of hoplites, as well as against blows received in hand-to-hand fighting. With protection for the face, nosepieces and thick, sometimes decorated, coverings wrapped around the head and tied with laces, only the eyes, tip of the nose and mouth were left exposed. Corslets and breastplates were generally made of thick, lined leather, reinforced – in less sophisticated versions – with metal strips. Better-quality examples were entirely covered with metal. Completing the infantryman's outfit were arm-guards and greaves, as well as the shield. The cavalry, comprised of aristocrats and the wealthy, paid for

95 Also from Ruvo di Puglia, this frontal (right) and breast-strap (bottom left) are from the trappings for war or parade horses. They probably date to the early 5th century BC.

the advantage of greater speed and mobility with less effective protection for both horse and rider.

Weapons took many forms: the most lethal were long spears designed for thrusting rather than throwing and capable of inflicting deep wounds, and even worse lacerations when they were pulled out. Also frequently used were light throwing spears, arrows with tremendous impact and smaller missiles like lead pellets and stones thrown with catapults. Weapons with sharp cutting blades, like swords, were also used. All weapons were made more lethal because even if the wounds they caused were not fatal, they often led to death from infection. Military tactics centred on use of massed formations of which the Macedonian phalanx was the best and most flexible unit prior to the advent of the Roman legion. Techniques changed through the centuries and according to whether fighting was on land, at sea or in a siege. In sieges, war machines came into play, or defensive systems like those made famous in the Hellenistic period, ranging from mobile towers to catapults.

96 (top) A detail from the base of an Attic kouros of 500–490 BC preserves an image of a marching hoplite, with his Corinthian helmet raised on his head, his lance, shield, cuirass and shin guards – all in accordance with literary epic tradition.

96 (centre) A dramatic scene from a siege, with hoplites in front of the walls of a city with bastions. This slab comes from famous Ionic frieze of the Nereid Monument at Xanthus, in Lycia, dated to the early 4th century BC.

96 (right) A duel between fully armed hoplites is shown on this black-figure, skyphos of the Chalcidian type, dated to the mid-6th century BC, in the National Archaeological Museum of Naples.

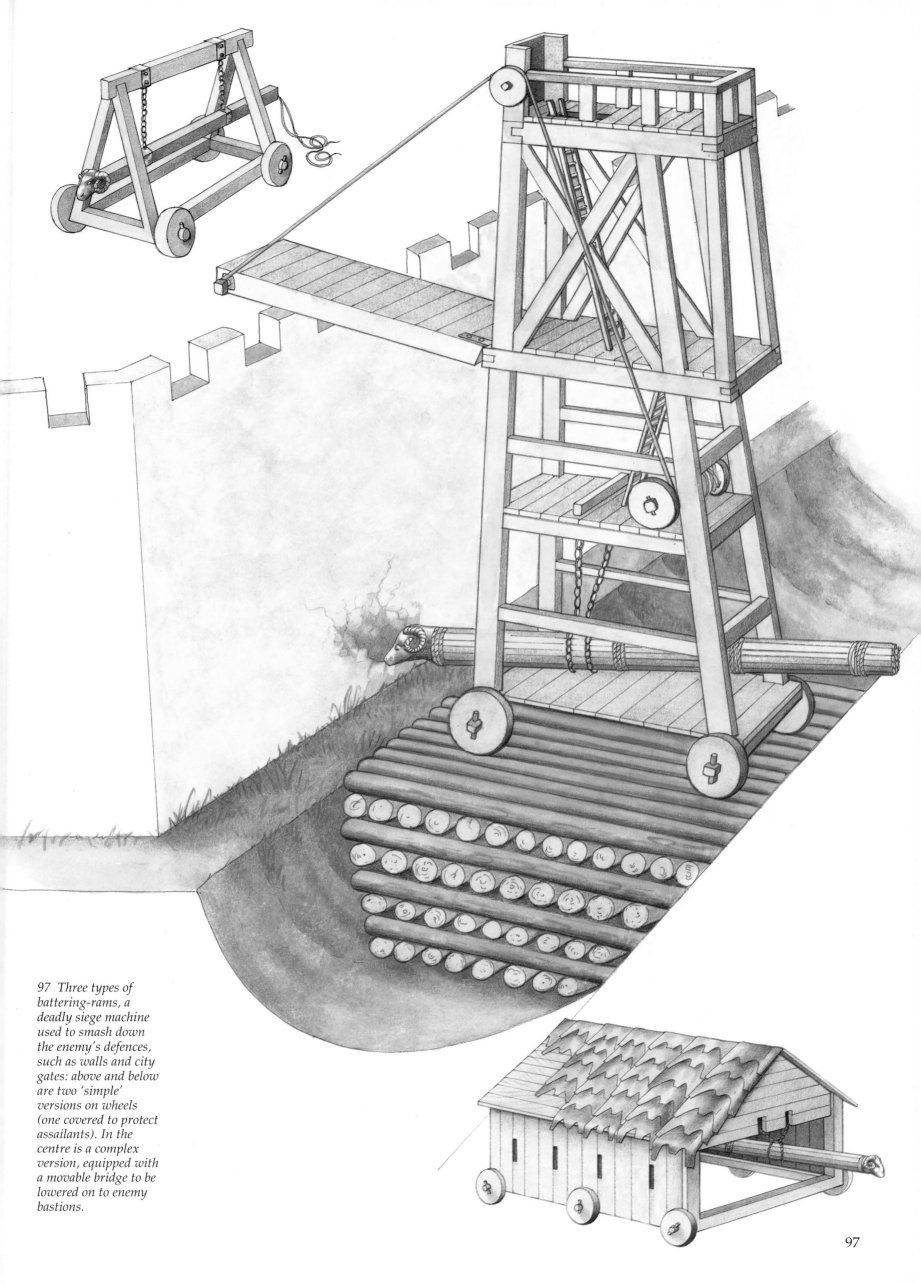

97 Three types of
battering-rams, a
deadly siege machine
used to smash down
the enemy's defences,
such as walls and city
gates: above and below
are two 'simple'
versions on wheels
(one covered to protect
assailants). In the
centre is a complex
version, equipped with
a movable bridge to be
lowered on to enemy
bastions.

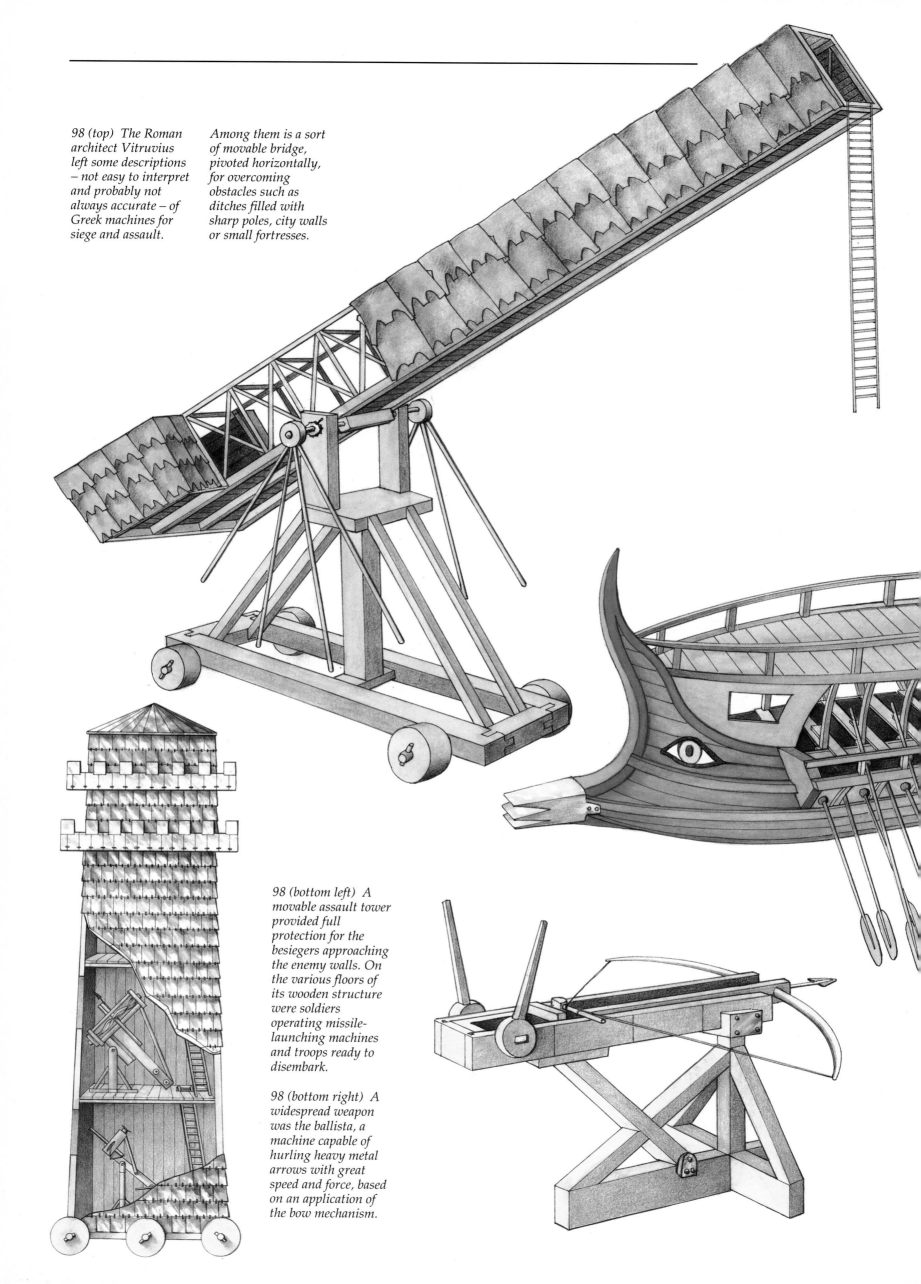

98 (top) The Roman architect Vitruvius left some descriptions – not easy to interpret and probably not always accurate – of Greek machines for siege and assault.

Among them is a sort of movable bridge, pivoted horizontally, for overcoming obstacles such as ditches filled with sharp poles, city walls or small fortresses.

98 (bottom left) A movable assault tower provided full protection for the besiegers approaching the enemy walls. On the various floors of its wooden structure were soldiers operating missile-launching machines and troops ready to disembark.

98 (bottom right) A widespread weapon was the ballista, a machine capable of hurling heavy metal arrows with great speed and force, based on an application of the bow mechanism.

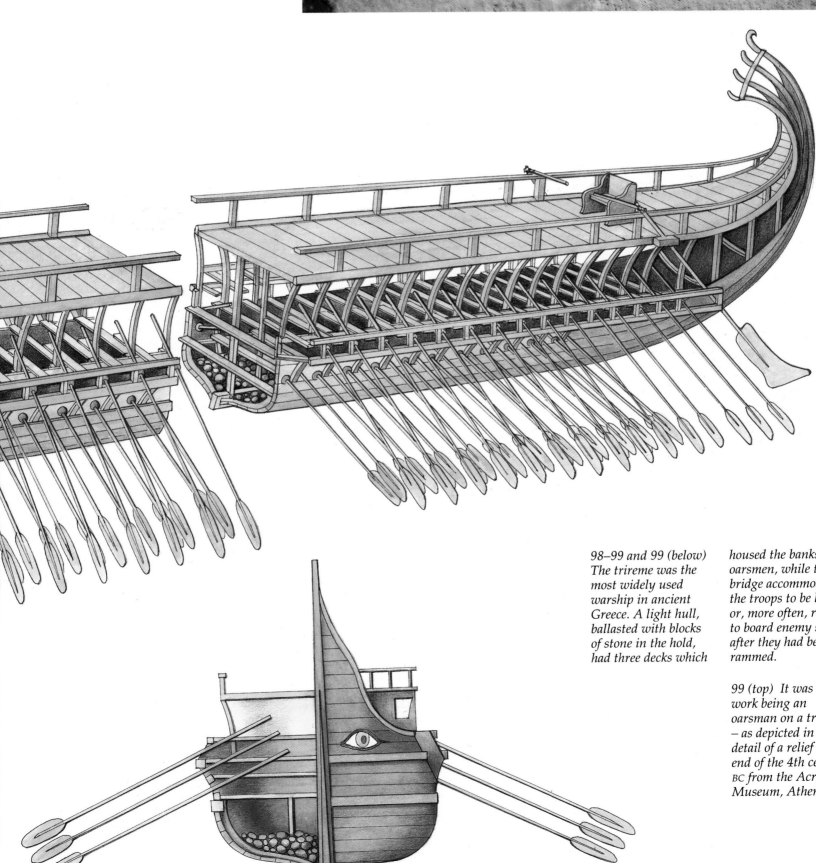

98–99 and 99 (below) The trireme was the most widely used warship in ancient Greece. A light hull, ballasted with blocks of stone in the hold, had three decks which housed the banks of oarsmen, while the bridge accommodated the troops to be landed or, more often, ready to board enemy ships after they had been rammed.

99 (top) It was hard work being an oarsman on a trireme – as depicted in this detail of a relief of the end of the 4th century BC from the Acropolis Museum, Athens.

GREEK ART THROUGH THE CENTURIES

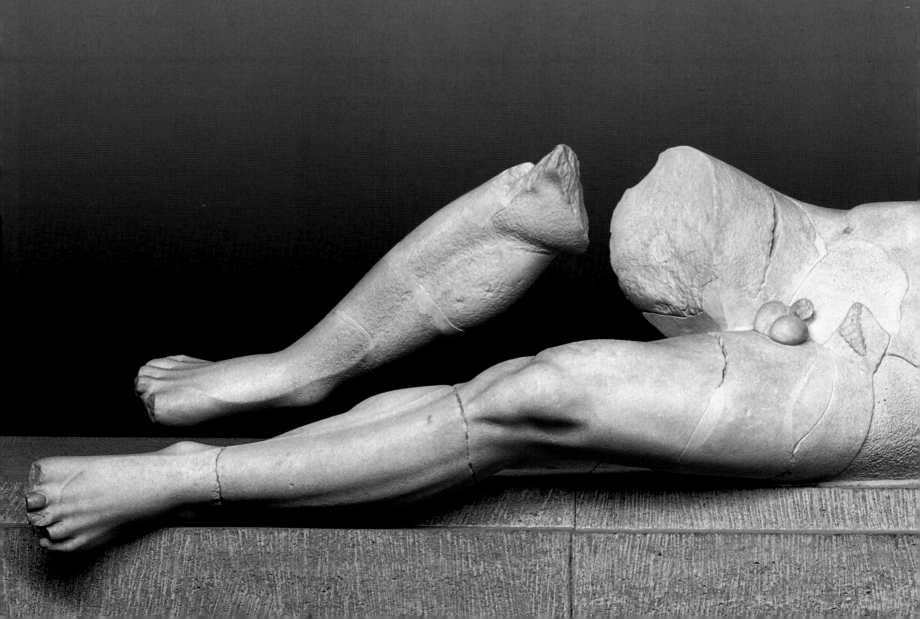

100–101 The Dying Warrior from the west pediment of the temple of Athena Aphaia the island of Aegina. This poignant statue marks the end of Archaic conventions in Greek sculpture at the beginning of the 5th century BC.

IN PURSUIT
OF PERFECTION

Greek art, in the strictest sense of the term, dates from the 10th to the 1st centuries BC. Its course was characterized by great unity, range and depth and – like the rest of Greek culture – it had a determining influence on the entire development of western civilization. Its beginnings coincided with the economic, demographic and cultural recovery that began around 1000 BC, at the end of the so-called Helladic Dark Ages, following the destruction of the Mycenaean kingdoms and the interruption of Mediterranean trade. From the Aegean to the shores of Anatolia, migrations triggered a diaspora of Ionians and Aeolians, peoples who belonged to the race of the Hellenes, as proved by their close linguistic affinities, source of the Greek spoken by all Greeks.

As early as the 9th–8th centuries BC it is evident that a truly innovative concept of art was advancing within the emerging culture.

Several themes were of key significance. One was the search to understand the essence of the universe and the harmonious and perfect mathematical laws by which it is governed. Another was the desire to represent not only the exterior form of reality but also its intricate philosophical, ethical and political values, without letting spirituality slide into mysticism. The exaltation of *logos*, reason, as the ultimate dimension of the human mind, serving to determine man's relationship with the Absolute through knowledge and love of reason – *philosophia* – was influential, as was an elaboration of an artistic language in perfect synthesis with content, expressing the interior rather exterior reality of things.

This process of exploration and discovery reached its climax in the 5th century BC, the most splendid in the cultural and political history of Greece, as was later acknowledged by the Romans, who introduced the term 'classical' to describe it. The art of this period – subsequently further enriched by innovative ideologies, subject-matter and styles of the 4th to 1st centuries BC – has had an immense impact on the art of the western world. It has been a constant point of reference, at times inspiring imitations, revisitations, revivals, and at others a total rejection of 'classical' tenets.

We will now journey along this amazing path, but we must first consider its remarkable foundations, laid in the 3rd and 2nd millennia BC in the Cyclades, Crete and the Mycenaean kingdoms, civilizations whose artistic development already differed from the artforms of Egypt, Mesopotamia and Asia Minor.

102 and 103 A masterpiece of mature Classical art: the so-called Kaufmann Head of Aphrodite. This beautiful head of the goddess of love and beauty emphasizes the very varied but also canonical character of the artistic language which reached its highest level with the artists of the 4th century BC. The original, attributed to the young Praxiteles or one of his followers, is among the best expressions of the quest for beauty in Greek sculpture.

Prehistory and protohistory
(*c.* 45,000–1220 BC)

The Helladic Dark Ages
(*c.* 1220–900 BC)

The Geometric Period
(*c.* 900–700 BC)

The Orientalizing Period
(*c.* 700–610 BC)

In the Neolithic, around the 7th millennium BC, advanced forms of settlement are attested by the 'proto-urban' structures of Sesklo and Dhimini (Thessaly). Following the diffusion of metallurgy in the 5th and 4th millennia BC, the first evidence of Indo-European civilization in the region is the Aegean culture of the Cycladic islands (3rd millennium BC). Its art, characterized by linear elegance and harmonious geometric forms, is exemplified above all by the production of statues and statuettes in local marble (the so-called 'idols'). The highly sophisticated Minoan civilization blossoms on the island of Crete: many imposing palace-settlements are built and a palatial brand of figurative art is developed, marked by linearity, colour and vitality of expression. The almost contemporary rise of the Mycenaeans in the Peloponnese and Aegean brings a new culture to the fore: pomp and splendour pervade its art, conceived as a celebration of its warrior aristocracy; its boldest innovations are seen in gold jewelry, pottery and architecture (fortified settlements and tholos tombs, using the megalithic technique).

Cycladic art
(*c.* 2800–2000 BC)

Minoan art
(*c.* 2100–1450 BC)

Mycenaean art
(*c.* 1700–1220 BC)

The demise of the Mycenaean culture is followed by a troubled period in the Mediterranean, with further Indo-European (Dorian) invasions and consequent turmoil on the Greek mainland. Scattered surviving communities produce simple forms of figurative and decorative art in late-Mycenaean style; their settlements are mere shadows of the earlier palaces (Dreros, Karphi, Kavousi). Slow economic and demographic recovery in the 10th century BC brings new forms of art, reflecting a new attitude to the complex but orderly pattern of the universe: this art is rigorously abstract and geometric, as displayed by ceramic products from all parts of Greece, with Athens in the forefront. Agglomerations of settlements create urban centres, where burgeoning trade stimulates new forms of artistic language.

Sub-Mycenaean art
(*c.* 1220–1000 BC)

Proto-Geometric period
(*c.* 1000–900 BC)

Throughout Greece, and particularly in Athens, the geometric approach to artistic expression evolves in increasingly sophisticated forms, with infinitely varied decorative motifs and the eventual re-introduction of occasional figurative scenes, still essentially angular in style. The cohesive focus of 7th-century Attic vase-painters, masters of ornamental balance, is replaced by more widespread presence of figurative themes, inspired by the heroic culture of the patrons of art, the ruling aristocracies. In architecture, new plans of temples and houses emerge, these too marked by geometric rigour and rationalism. Sculpture re-appears, in wood and ivory and in the form of small bronzes, again with a strong geometric influence.

Early Geometric period
(*c.* 900–850 BC)

Middle Geometric period
(*c.* 850–750 BC)

Late Geometric period
(*c.* 750–700 BC)

With colonization in full swing and close and enriching commercial and cultural contacts established with the rest of the Mediterranean, Anatolia and Mesopotamia, the abstract geometric style gives way to the figurative naturalism of Oriental art. But Greek artists soon abandon its age-old conventions and elaborate their own style, as seen in beautiful pottery (Corinth, the Cyclades, Ionia, the Dodecanese), the first monumental stone sculptures and elegant gold jewelry. Oriental influence is seen in architecture too – most evident in the preference for imposing constructions and chiaroscuro effects, rich ornamentation and the self-aggrandizing largesse of patrons – the ruling tyrants and aristocrats. In Magna Graecia innovative urban planning schemes are introduced.

Early Orientalizing style
(*c.* 700–675 BC)

Middle Orientalizing style
(*c.* 675–640 BC)

Late Orientalizing style
(*c.* 640–610 BC)

The Archaic Period
(*c.* 610–490 BC)

The progressive abandonment of the figurative repertoire and Orientalizing style signals the now total autonomy of Greek art and its first steps towards Mediterranean supremacy. In architecture the orders and the form of the temple are codified, with much more frequent and imposing use of stone. Corinth and Athens inundate markets with figured ceramic vessels, decorated with theological, mythological and epic scenes (often with topical references); Athens is dominant until the end of the 5th century BC. Throughout Greece – but especially in Athens, the islands and Ionia – life-size or larger stone statuary makes its mark, ushering in a truly distinctive style. Already implicit is an awareness of art's communicative, propaganda and celebratory functions, and a major goal is the perfected representation of the human figure.

Early Archaic
(*c.* 610–570 BC)

Middle Archaic
(*c.* 570–530 BC)

Late Archaic
(*c.* 530–510 BC)

Final Archaic
(*c.* 510–490 BC)

The Classical Period
(*c.* 490–323 BC)

After a rejection of Archaic conventions and a transitional phase characterized by stylistic calm and balance, Greek art attempts to represent the dynamism of the human body in space, with idealized beauty and interior emotions, interpreted as positive or negative manifestations of man's relationship with the deities, laws, community and the ethical values championed by Athenian democracy. Sculpture and vase-painting offer good examples. Architecture attains maturity with exceptionally harmonious forms and structures; the apex of decorative elegance and grandeur is reached in increasingly ornate and complex pedimental compositions. Philosophy is an influence on artists such as Polyclitus, Phidias, Ictinus and Callicrates, as well as many famous painters of the period. It also influenced 4th-century architectural and artistic developments, characterized by an emphasis on emotions and relativity which conveys the feeling of crisis experienced by the Greeks between the Peloponnesian War and the death of Alexander the Great.

Severe Style
(*c.* 490–450 BC)

High Classical period
(*c.* 450–400 BC)

Late Classical period
(*c.* 400–323 BC)

The Hellenistic Period
(323–31 BC)

The immense empire of Alexander the Great is split into kingdoms, leagues and minor states but the diffusion of Greek artistic culture, even in places beyond the Hellenic world, inspires artistic styles and trends of the highest level. No longer dominated by Attica, art comes from many centres, and the cities of Pella, Rhodes, Alexandria, Pergamum, Athens, Tarentum and Syracuse are its new capitals. Once more under the patronage of kings and aristocrats, art and architecture are used to convey emotion, narrative and the magnificence designed to add prestige to power. Greece and Greek art maintain their hold even after conquest by Rome (146 BC) – the language of Hellenism is destined to survive until Augustus comes to power, and even then to make a significant contribution to Roman art.

Early Hellenism
(*c.* 323–220 BC)

Middle Hellenism
(*c.* 220–100 BC)

Late Hellenism
(100–31 BC)

106 Cycladic marble figurines take several forms. The earliest are the so-called 'violin-' or fiddle-shaped idols, sometimes with indications of sexual characteristics (below left). There are also more anthropomorphic types, though they are still schematic. As seen in the figurine (top) and the head (below right), they are usually standing figures, with stiff postures, a reduced profile and arms often folded on the breast.

ART IN THE THIRD AND SECOND MILLENNIA BC: CYCLADIC, MINOAN AND MYCENAEAN

107 (above) This clay vessel engraved with spiral motifs and a stylized boat comes from the island of Syros. The function of these vessels is not certain, though they may have been filled with water and used as mirrors.

107 (below) A Cycladic figurine representing a musician intent on playing the lyre, from the island of Syros, in the heart of the Aegean, a thriving commercial centre between the 3rd and the 2nd millennia BC.

107 (below) A painted ceramic pedestal or lampstand is an interesting document of the first close relations between the island of Melos, where it was found at the important site of Phylakopi, and Crete during the 2nd millennium BC. It is an early, and rare, example of the human form depicted on pottery and shows fishermen carrying their catch.

The Cyclades in the Middle Bronze Age (2800–2200 BC) provide some of the earliest artistic representations from the period when Greece was being extensively settled. Here the first buildings made of stone and unbaked brick were erected in flourishing villages on Syros, Keros, Amorgos, Naxos, Melos and tens of other islands dotted about the Aegean. These buildings can be considered the archetype of the characteristic Cycladic architecture that modern tourists still find so fascinating. And it was in these villages that the typical Cycladic pottery was produced – burnished wares with intricate incised non-figurative patterns – as well as remarkable statuary in local marble, together considered the finest and most significant products of the artistic skills of the peoples of the Aegean at this time. The human figure was simplified to the extreme, with a rigorous sense of form and proportion: both males and females are depicted, usually standing, with a slight groove to distinguish the legs, a profile reduced to the essentials, smoothed head and shoulders, breasts and a barely discernible nose. This extreme simplification points to a remarkable ability to capture the essence of form.

The celebrated 'flute player' and 'lyre player' statuettes, for example, have an amazing capacity to express the complexity of the human figure in action in space, achieved through the pure geometry of harmonious lines. But their significance goes far deeper – as a portrayal of an aristocratic world where banquets were accompanied by the uplifting notes of the flute or by bards reciting poetry set to music. By around 2200 BC, however, the focal point of trade had shifted to the southern Aegean. Crete had established its great maritime hegemony, thanks to the island's exceptional resources, the business acumen of its merchants and its position as a geographical 'bridge' between Egypt, Anatolia and Greece.

Before long Crete was also preeminent in the Mediterranean as a centre of artistic development. By 2100 BC the network of Minoan *emporia* extended as far as Samothrace, in the northeastern Aegean. On Crete itself, in the space of two centuries, the island's 'princes' turned prehistoric village settlements into 'palaces': an architectural and urban model never before seen in the western world and, in terms of luxury and splendour, worthy of the monarchies of Egypt and the Near East. The surviving structures of the great palaces of Knossos, Mallia, Phaistos and Zakros and the villa of Hagia Triada – for the most part rebuilt in the 17th century BC – point to outstanding skills in the design and organization of these colossal complexes. With many hundreds of rooms, often built two or three storeys high, their amenities included staircases, corridors, porticoes and ramps, all arranged around a huge central court.

Among their significant features are the absence of fortifications, a combined use of wood and stone for load-bearing structures and a logical distribution of facilities between the various wings of the palace – in spite of the appearance of an unplanned sprawl of rooms. A rational approach to planning is seen in the position of storerooms and the grouping of workshops used by craftsmen in the service of the ruler. Particularly striking is the elegance of architectural and pictorial decoration in living quarters, throne rooms, reception rooms and porticoes, revealing a sense of colour which attests to the pleasure-loving lifestyle of the Cretans. The palace of Knossos was excavated over a period of around thirty years from 1899 onwards by Arthur J. Evans. He partly restored the site, based on sound archaeological evidence, though perhaps not in the way it would be done today. It now has a somewhat curious Edwardian appearance, with picturesque ruins in painted concrete, which at least assist the modern visitor to imagine what the palace looked like in its former glory. At Phaistos, meticulously excavated by the Italian School of Archaeology in Athens, it has been possible to determine the fundamental scheme and technical solutions adopted by the Cretan architects.

Naturalism was undoubtedly the unifying element of Cretan art: colour in painting and delicacy of pattern and line in metalworking and jewelry were used to heighten the descriptive and narrative expressions of the artist's almost tangible delight in the world around him, perceived through facets of everyday life or the wonderful variety of nature.

The frescoes which decorate the palace of Knossos and, to a lesser extent, other royal residences are works of exceptional beauty: reduced to tiny fragments by earthquakes and devastation in the second half of the 2nd millennium BC, they have in many cases now been restored and give a fairly good idea of the skills of Minoan artists. Outstanding works like the 'Priest-King', 'Dancing Lady', 'La Parisienne' and others depicting bulls sports and dolphins, or the

108 (opposite) Both elegant and solemn, the 'Priest-King' is one of the most famous figures from the large frescoes which once decorated the rooms and corridors at the palace of Knossos. It is typical of the vivid naturalism of Minoan art between 1700 and 1400 BC, with its smooth lines and grasp of detail that go beyond the formal conventions of ancient Egyptian painting. Recent research has suggested that the fragments restored as one figure in fact originally came from three different figures.

109 (right) It was the excavations by the Greek archaeologist Spyridon Marinatos at the site of Akrotiri on Thera (Santorini) that brought to light the breathtaking frescoes that once decorated the houses of the town there. The site was engulfed by a violent volcanic eruption, probably in the 16th century BC. Here we see a scene of two young boys boxing, found in Room Beta 1 and now housed, as are other frescoes from Akrotiri, in the National Museum of Athens. The artist has portrayed the action of the two young men naturalistically and realistically, through the exchange of blows. The figure on the right, with his guard down, has just landed a blow, but has exposed himself to the jab of his opponent.

110 (right) The well-preserved sarcophagus from Hagia Triada on Crete provides good evidence of the bright colours favoured by Cretan artists. On the side shown here is a scene of preparations for a religious rite, culminating in a sacrifice, perhaps an offering to the dead man, and thus relating to the object's funerary purpose. Stylized floral friezes frame the scene. Note the typical Cretan costumes worn by the participants and the details of objects and vessels, actual examples of which have been found in excavations.

sarcophagus from Hagia Triada, show how different the Minoan artists' approach is from their Egyptian counterparts. Lines do not confine figures to two-dimensional forms but provide fluidity and dynamism; gestures become more lively, composition breaks away from rigid conventions and colours have a luminous quality that is unknown in the East.

A marvellous anthology of Cretan painting is to be found in the town of Akrotiri, on the island of Thera (Santorini), known as the Pompeii of the Aegean. Here naturalism reached great heights in dynamic scenes of ships and ports, probably celebrating the trading supremacy of the Minoan rulers, with exotic touches – such as the famous 'Blue monkeys' fresco – alternating with sporting events, possibly forerunners of the sacred contests of the Homeric and classical age – for instance the 'Boxers'.

Jewelry, metalwork, figurines, pottery – all express the vibrant naturalism that pervades Minoan art. Examples are numerous: the beautiful gold pendant from Mallia, on which two wasps heraldically cling to a flower; the exquisite steatite and gold bull's-head rhyton from the Little Palace at Knossos, used for sacred libations; gold cups – found at Vapheio, in Mycenaean Laconia, but the work of Minoan artists – with wonderful scenes of country life and bull hunting; the famous faience 'Snake Goddess', a prototype of Artemis *Potnia theron* of the Greeks, with her small, slender body and full breasts, an irrepressible symbol of fertility, like the bull, sacred animal of the Cretans. And potters moved on from the non-figurative motifs of the past to experiment with naturalistic imagery: the sea and marine creatures are much in evidence, as are plants and flowers, as attested to by finds at Gournia and Kamares.

110–111 (left) This outstanding image is a detail from a fresco from Knossos showing an exciting moment in the bull sports – a sort of bloodless bullfight in which both young men and women took part. These dangerous and acrobatic games were perhaps part of initiation rites or ritual celebrations. The Cretan artist has attempted to go beyond two-dimensional space, which reached Crete from Egyptian art. Bull and acrobats are not on the same level and the method of outlining the body suggests three-dimensional figures.

111 (Above) This example of the remarkable frescoes from Akrotiri on Thera (Santorini) comes from the West House (16th century BC). It shows a richly dressed young woman, probably a priestess, holding an incense-burner with a flared shape.

112 (below) and 113 From the outstanding tholos *tomb of Vapheio, most probably belonging to a Mycenaean 'prince', came rich gold objects, including these two beautiful gold cups decorated in repoussé (15th century BC). One is a masterpiece by a Cretan goldsmith, working in the exquisite naturalistic style typical of Minoan art. It depicts the capture of a bull, drawn to a luxuriant olive grove and quickly trapped after being deceived by the decoy cow used by the hunters.*

112 (above) Perhaps the work of a Mycenaean goldsmith, this cup from Vapheio has a more vigorous and less refined style, well suited to the subject: a bull runs through trees, while another struggles in the hunters' net and a third launches a furious charge against the hunters.

Mycenaean civilization became the centre of artistic initiative from the 14th century BC on (although some important examples of Mycenaean art date from the previous two centuries). By this time the aristocracies of the Peloponnese and other areas had gained political, commercial and economic control over the Aegean and their influence spread over the entire Mediterranean. Centres perched on natural acropolises from the 17th century BC now evolved towards an urban model that had much in common with the palaces of Crete. In many respects they also resembled medieval walled towns, huddled around the castle of a feudal lord. Examples include Mycenae, Argos

and Tiryns and others in the Argolid, Laconia and Messenia, but they were also sited in Attica, Boeotia and Thessaly, where there are many places celebrated in Homer's epic poems.

The Mycenaean palaces grew in size and number of rooms (while still adhering to the ancient *megaron* model). Courts surrounded by colonnades were added, together with monumental gateways and service facilities. Around the main structures were houses, probably occupied by dignitaries with political and military functions. The palaces were protected by immense walls, constructed using the megalithic technique. Along the walls were bastions, passageways, galleries, posterns and gates. Palaces were built on two floors with a vast, central *megaron* surrounded by living quarters and service facilities; the focal point was the throne room where a huge hearth was the most prominent feature (a fine example has been excavated at Pylos). Other buildings inside the walls included cult areas, craftsmen's workshops and houses of the aristocratic warrior class and in some cases merchants too.

Decoration appears to have been influenced by the luxury of the Cretan palaces: wall paintings embellish the most important rooms, and there are some of the amenities already found at Knossos (bathrooms and elegant, porticoes for strolls in the shade).

Archaeology has brought to light Mycenaean art of exceptional quality: fragments of frescoes from Mycenae, Tiryns and Pylos give only a glimpse of the brilliant colours that once embellished the palaces, even with the Myceanean painters' more restrained style compared with their Minoan counterparts. Splendid objects were created in gold and silver, for instance the famous burial masks (including one wrongly attributed to Agamemnon, but datable to the 16th century BC), niello-inlaid daggers, ritual vases shaped like animals, jewelry found in the tombs of kings and aristocrats and elegant pottery, with ornament now abandoning Minoan naturalism in favour of increased stylization.

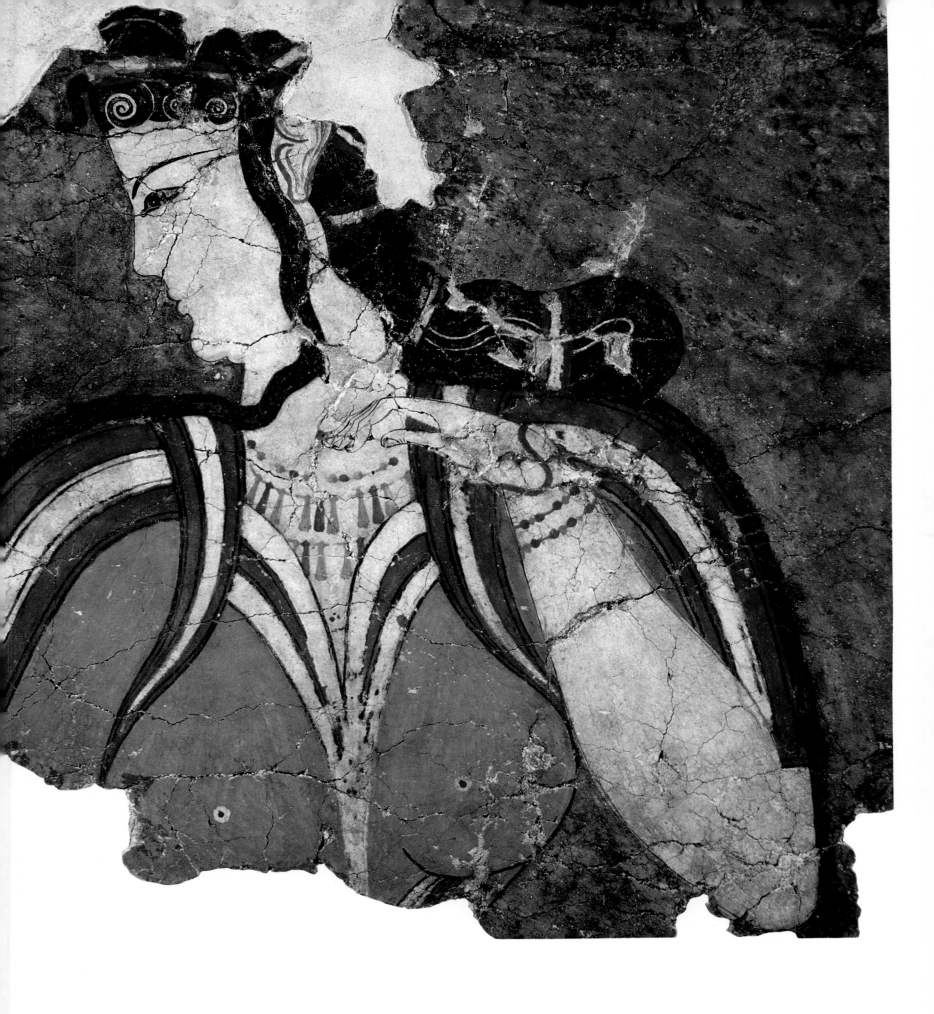

114 (opposite, left) A female painted terracotta figurine from Mycenae in the typical stance of a supplicant, with arms upraised and a stylized shape reminiscent of the Greek letter phi.

114 (opposite, below) A characteristic example of Mycenaean painted pottery of the 13th century BC. In the so-called Palace Style natural motifs became more stylized, stately and monumental, as seen in the floral elements covering the surface of the vase. The range of shapes was quite limited, and this type of decoration was frequently used on large vessels, especially jars such as this one.

114–115 This fresco dating from the 13th century BC, found at Mycenae and now in the National Museum of Athens, is an extraordinary document of the remarkable influence of Minoan painting on Mycenaean art after the Mycenaean conquest of Crete. It portrays a splendidly dressed young woman, rendered with clear lines and bright colours, with many fine details added by the skill of the painter.

116 (top) A precious diadem of gold leaf decorated with stylized flowers comes from Shaft Grave III of Grave Circle A at Mycenae, excavated by Schliemann. It dates to the 16th century BC.

116 (centre) A casket made of wood covered with gold leaf. The panels of repoussé decoration show lions, in the so-called 'flying gallop', attacking their prey. It comes from Shaft Grave V of Grave Circle A.

116 (below) Less well-known than the funeral mask of Agamemnon, this stylized mask of gold is from Shaft Grave IV of Grave Circle A at Mycenae, and dates from the 16th century BC.

117 The famous gold funeral mask 'of Agamemnon' from Shaft Grave V of Grave Circle A at Mycenae actually belonged to a Mycenaean prince who lived at least three centuries before the leader celebrated in Homer's poems (16th century BC). It is probably not a portrait, but is interesting because it documents the Mycenaean artistic conception of the human figure. Marked by a simplified naturalism, the dead person's face is characterized by a few details – the beard denoting old age, the eyes tightly shut in eternal repose.

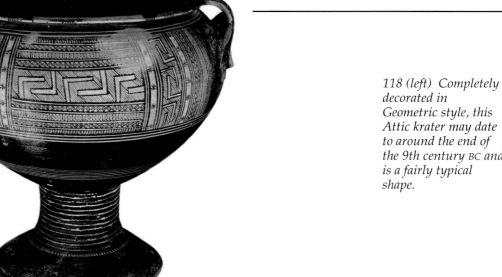

THE GEOMETRIC STYLE

With the instability of the 12th and 11th centuries BC came the decline and disappearance of Mycenaean civilization and its art. In Attica and other areas untouched by the turmoil – such as Ionia, the Cyclades and Euboea – and also in the Dorian regions of the Argolid, Laconia and Crete, the 10th century BC saw the cautious beginnings of an economic and demographic recovery which led to the formation of proto-urban communities. These were an early, tentative progression from the palace-settlement model. Towns such as Karphi, Dreros and Emporion provide good evidence of this trend. In art, Greek ceramic workshops

118 (left) Completely decorated in Geometric style, this Attic krater may date to around the end of the 9th century BC and is a fairly typical shape.

were producing new and more functional types of vases, with a decorative style that, from the very start, was radically different from the naturalistic motifs favoured by Minoan and Mycenaean artists. With a remarkable sense of compositional balance, vase painters used sinuous bands, concentric circles and semicircles. This was the beginning of the so-called Geometric period (10th–8th centuries BC). Vases were decorated with increasingly delicate and ornate abstract designs, based on linear and geometrical elements and motifs. Within the rigorous respect for symmetry, artists showed outstanding invention in creating countless variations. Geometric art reflected a new perception of things. Nature was no longer viewed simply as a universe to represent, but rather a complex and infinite reality governed by its own laws. It was this order that the artist set out to portray, rather than nature's plethora of deceptive and constantly changing forms.

Recovery continued slowly but steadily throughout the 9th century BC. By the 8th century the Dark Ages were long forgotten. Small communities disappeared, replaced by a single dominating centre.

118 (centre) In the last quarter of the 8th century BC Corinth produced large numbers of vessels in the late Geometric style which were widely exported. Typical shapes were kotylai *and* skyphoi *– drinking vases used in banquets.*

118 (below) In the first half of the 8th century BC Greek potters, especially in Athens and Euboea, introduced figurative motifs in the complex weave of geometric decorations that covered vases. Funerary scenes were frequent, alluding to the purpose many of these vases were intended for, as part of the burial assemblages of persons of high social standing. This is demonstrated by the scene shown here, in which we see the lying-in-state of the dead person and the funeral lamentations, in accordance with a tradition throughout the Mediterranean.

Alternatively, villages gravitated towards a single site, chosen for its pre-eminence or favourable position: the resulting *synechiae* were the forerunners of the *poleis*. We have little evidence to reconstruct the layout of important centres like Athens, Sparta and Corinth. Over the centuries these prosperous cities have been rebuilt over and over again, and traces of previous levels have been lost. We can identify little more than the land they occupied, their public areas and cemeteries. More plentiful remains of have survived in Eretria and Knossos.

The architecture of this period appears to have been characterized by a certain poverty of materials and forms. Most buildings have stone foundations, a wooden frame and walls of unbaked brick. They vary from the late Mycenaean *megaron* to new plans, based on a small number of square or rectangular rooms. Simple forms and materials were used for temples and sanctuaries of which there were many, evidence of the importance attached to cult. Significantly, they are often found in places connected in some way with Mycenaean civilization or with mythical 'heroes' celebrated in the Homeric poems or in epic poetry of local origin. Cult places were endowed with precious votive offerings, in particular bronze tripods decorated with stylized horses or geometric patterns.

The pottery of the Middle and Late Geometric periods combined rectilinear motifs in infinite ways. A bold innovation in the first half of the 8th century BC was the introduction of spaces in which artists painted scenes with stylized and geometric human figures or tiny animal friezes. Towards the end of the 8th century BC Attic pottery entered a new phase, breaking away from the rigidity of geometric patterns to favour a more prominent presence of human figures and epic and mythological themes. Decorations on kraters and large amphoras, often used as markers over the graves of men and women respectively, convey an impression of disorder indicative of the desire now to move on from abstract art.

119 A masterpiece of Geometric vase painting – the large Dipylon amphora (760–750 BC) is over 1½ m (5 ft) high and was originally placed as a tomb marker over a female grave. The unity of its decoration is perfect and its representation of a scene of a funeral with mourners has an emotional depth.

119

THE ORIENTALIZING PERIOD

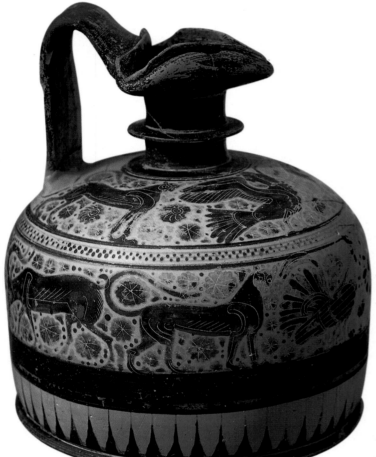

120 (centre) A small oinochoe, *typical of the rich figured production of Corinth in 7th century* BC. *The surface of the vessel is filled with with animal friezes and geometric motifs.*

120 (right) A masterpiece of Orientalizing style from Paros (Cyclades), this oinochoe *has a mouth in the shape of a griffin head, using iconography of Near Eastern origin. It dates to the first half of the 7th century* BC.

120 (left) A small vase for ointment, this lovely Corinthian alabastron *is decorated with the sinuous figure of the demon Typhon and with animal figures in black paint, with finishing touches in red and incised details.*

Between around 725 and 675 BC, Oriental works of art were imported to the west in huge quantities. The result was the widespread penetration of a new artistic, iconographic and, in part, ideological language. Its impact was felt throughout the Mediterranean, both in the Levantine regions, increasingly coming under Assyrian hegemony with the decline of the Egyptian and Hittite empires, and in the west where, after the upheaval of the Dark Ages, Greek and Phoenician colonialism was dominant and trade was re-emerging on a vast scale. But its most profound influence was seen in Greece, which is why the 7th century BC is known as the Orientalizing period of Greek art.

It was in the 8th century BC that Greece and its oldest western colonies had first discovered the art of cultures of the east – from the age-old and now declining Egyptian empire to the shorter-lived kingdoms of Anatolia, Mesopotamia and Syria. The routes travelled by Phoenicians, Greeks and Etruscans were also taken by exquisitely crafted products, exported to meet the growing demands of Mediterranean aristocracies, who were fascinated by the elaborate and exotic products of Oriental art. The high quality of these objects and their innovative features when compared with the austere Geometric style – whether Greek, Villanovan/Etruscan or Iberian – meant that Oriental art was soon adopted as a model. To the west came objects of outstanding artistic quality: beautiful tablewares of precious metals, skilfully embossed and incised, bronze cauldrons from northern Syria and Urartu, jewelry, carved ivory, 'exotic' items to be displayed as a sign of prestige and power. For these products arrived as gifts to seal trade alliances between the western aristocracies, who controlled of raw materials (primarily metals) in their territories, and their far-off Oriental or Greek partners from whom they acquired finished products. Local artists and craftsmen borrowed from the vast pictorial corpus – both figurative and naturalistic – offered by the east.

Thus Oriental art had a significant general influence on the re-awakening west. Greece was the first politically advanced and culturally developed civilization to be influenced by the Orient. However, it quickly assimilated the techniques and ideologies offered by eastern cultures and re-invented them in its own way. Pottery shows evidence of this process most clearly. Corinth had gained supremacy as a trading power,

121 This spectacular large krater is in the Corinthian style. Both sides are shown here, above is a scene of a banquet of Heracles and Eurytos, below is a frequent motif – fighting hoplites.

exporting its fine-quality pottery far and wide. This wide distribution demonstrates that the Mediterranean was by no means the exclusive trading arena of the Phoenicians; it was instead divided into freely accessible areas of influence. The craftsmen of the Mediterranean borrowed from each other frequently: the Carthaginians, for example, copied designs and decorative motifs of Greek pottery from imported originals. During this period Greek vases were themselves characterized by a mix of forms and motifs, as were the Oriental products that inspired them.

By the early 7th century BC new developments in iconography had been fully assimilated, although differences existed from region to region. In areas like Attica, where the old aristocracies clung to tradition as well as to their privileges, there was greater reluctance to abandon the old Geometric style and adopt the more fanciful patterns of Oriental models.

The Orientalizing style advanced everywhere, although it never replaced the fundamentally rationalist spirit in design introduced in the Geometric period. The new motifs – exotic creatures and monsters, royal hunts and processions, symbols and purely ornamental patterns – were soon re-elaborated as artists searched for an equilibrium, a synthesis between form and content, not evident in the products of the east. For example, the shapes of vessels retained their functional and practical aspects, which were even improved, but themes and decorative elements changed; imaginative design was made to follow orderly composition more closely; the repetitive flatness or 'unrealistic naturalism' of Oriental

122 (below) This bronze plaque, embossed and engraved with the killing of Cassandra by Clytemnestra, comes from the Heraion of Argos and dates to the first half of the 7th century BC.

122 (right) Cast bronze griffin heads such as this were attached to bronze cauldrons imported from Urartu in the first half of the 7th century BC. *This one was dedicated to Apollo at Delphi.*

art was replaced by attempts to create coherent forms and greater narrative expression. More importance was attributed to ideas than to symbols – this was, after all, the century that saw the birth of philosophy in the Greek settlements in closest contact with the east, the Ionian colonies of Asia Minor. The effects of these developments can be clearly seen in the remarkable pottery of Corinth, as well as in proto-Attic and Graeco-Oriental pottery.

The work of western craftsmen is easily distinguished from Oriental equivalents in the production of cauldrons and tripods. Until the 9th century BC these large vessels of sheet bronze or precious metal were used mainly at sumptuous aristocratic banquets, in keeping with traditional Mycenaean practice. From the 8th century BC onwards they were increasingly dedicated in cult places as votive offerings for gods or heroes. Their widespread distribution points to the progress made by western metalworkers whose methods were influenced by Near Eastern technology, primarily from the Syro-Hittite area and Urartu in the 8th and 7th centuries BC.

The earliest major statuary in Greece was also influenced by the east, as is evident from the preference for imposing, stiff figures, represented

123 (left) This attachment in the shape of a winged siren belonged to a orientalizing cauldron produced in Greece and offered as a dedication in the sanctuary of Olympia around the mid-7th century BC.

in the conventional frontal pose. However, the Greeks very quickly broke away from Egyptian and Mesopotamian models, both in the representation of the human figure and small bronzes (with a 'poorer' version in terracotta). Frontality was simply seen as a convenient solution which sculptors soon strived to modify to achieve greater realism. Notable efforts in this direction are seen in the greater attention to proportions in Greek statues. Greek architects were more independent of outside influence, as seen in temple architecture, although even here there are occasional references to the east: for example, the decoration of wooden structures with polychrome terracotta, adding a vibrant note to buildings. This period also saw the emergence of the whole concept and structure of the Greek temple, and the Doric and Ionic orders; sanctuaries also developed a richer and more monumental dimension.

123 (above right) A masterpiece of the orientalizing style from Rhodes, this is the famous Lévy oinochoe, which may date to around 640 BC. It is decorated all over with a sequence of very fine friezes with lines of wild goats and is completed by a series of imaginary animals and bands of geometric decorations.

123 (right) The delicacy of orientalizing art is revealed in this gold sheet, decorated with a series of metopes depicting examples of the rich Oriental repertory. It is from the sanctuary of Apollo in Delphi.

THE ARCHAIC STYLE

In the 6th century BC the east was in the hands of great empires – first Assyria, later Persia – and its cultural and artistic supremacy was a thing of the past. Greece now occupied the dominating place on the cultural scene. In the 6th century BC the Greeks competed for trade on an equal footing with their Phoenician rivals and their art no longer bowed to the Orient. These new developments did not merely stem from a change in taste. The Greeks had consolidated their own cultural characteristics, already evident in politics and literature at the end of the 7th century BC. An artistic renaissance soon followed and its products invaded Mediterranean markets.

From this point on Greek culture was the frame of reference for western civilization. Its success derived from its ability constantly to re-shape forms of expression, in a dialogue conducted both at home and with the non-Greek world, in theory and in practice, in organized according to function but with regard paid to aesthetic considerations. This is borne out, for example, by the search for suitable sites for temples. In Greece itself the tumultuous growth of large city-states between the 9th and 7th centuries BC had delayed the emergence of urban planning schemes. A limited plan was implemented in Athens during the rule of the tyrants (c. 560–510 BC).

For the benefit of worshippers and the community at large, the tyrants spent lavishly on numerous buildings

124–125 The frieze on the north side of the Siphnian Treasury at Delphi (c. 525 BC) depicts the battle between the gods and the giants and is a masterpiece by a late Archaic Ionic artist. The balance of light and shade in the tumultuous struggle of the giants, who rebelled against the power of the gods and the established order of things, is remarkable. The bodies dramatically confront each other – the gods are recognizable by their characteristic features (the lion skin on the shoulders of Heracles, the cuirass with the head of Medusa for Athena); while the giants are so standardized as to be indistinguishable, hidden under heavy armour and helmets, a shapeless amalgam of evil. The artist has also attempted to express movement and depth of space by the division of planes and differences in relief, revealing a desire to investigate the third dimension to the full.

abstract concepts of design and in practical, creative aspects of everyday life. Developments in Greek urban planning certainly diverged from Oriental models. Already in the 9th and 8th centuries BC a number of *poleis* had applied rational criteria in the distribution of urban spaces and their functions. By the end of the 7th century, while the problem of urban planning was ignored in the east, colonial settlements like Metapontum, Megara Hyblaea, Poseidonia (Paestum) and Selinus offered examples of the systematic planning of towns and their outlying territory on a grid layout. Areas were and works of art in the most important Panhellenic sanctuaries, on occasions constructing cult centres of monumental dimensions. This phenomenon was particularly evident in Greek settlements in the eastern Aegean and Asia Minor, with the perfection of the Ionic order and its use in grandiose forms, such as the Third Temple of Hera on Samos and the Temple of Artemis at Ephesus. Meanwhile, the Doric order was developing in western colonies: it first appeared in several variants, which shared the same imposing forms and harmony of proportions, and often incorporated elements of the Ionic

style and local tradition. Sanctuaries are of particular interest in this period because of the 'ritualized disorder' that characterized their layout.

Delphi and its celebrated sanctuary and oracle of Pythian Apollo is typical. No planning regulations existed in this sacred site but whatever occupied the space inside the *temenos* – the sacred precinct – remained untouchable. Here there was greater scope than elsewhere for innovation and experimentation, and architectural and artistic ideas from all over Greece were put into practice. A good demonstration is provided by the frieze of the Siphnian Treasury, which is considered as the culmination of Archaic Ionic sculpture.

The term 'Archaic' is used to designate Greek art of the 6th century BC and refers to its 'old' look (*archaios*) compared with art of the following century, which the ancients themselves saw as the climax of their search for perfection. Artists keen to experiment with style and form often

125 (top) The earliest known equestrian statue is the 'Rampin Horseman', perhaps representing a son of Pisistratus, the Athenian tyrant (550 BC), or one of the Dioscuri. It is a fine example of Archaic Ionic sculpture in Cycladic marble, with delicate modelling of the limbs and face, relaxed in the Archaic 'smile'.

125 (right) The splendid calf-bearer (moscophoros, 570–560 BC) is an early, large-scale statue, found on the Acropolis of Athens where it was dedicated to the patron goddess of the city by a certain Rhombos. It represents a man carrying a calf on his shoulders as a sacrificial offering.

The sculptor has broken away from the rigid convention of frontality of archaic kouroi *and has also attempted a higher level of definition of anatomical detail. His representation of the transparent effect of the light ritual dress worn by the young man is also noteworthy. The eyes were originally inlaid.*

chose sacred sites, consecrated to a particular god or goddess, as their testing ground, possibly an acropolis or sanctuary, and sometimes burial places, where monumental tombs left evidence of their noble owners' existence for posterity.

Pediments with relief sculptures were a further important element of Archaic temple architecture. Mythological themes dominate these sculptures – religion's figurative representation of the universe, to which philosophers were then devoting their more rational enquiries. Life-size statues of the human figure first appeared in Greek art in the 7th century BC.

126 (right) This fragmentary statue from the Acropolis of Athens depicts a Sphinx – with the typical features of a winged lioness with a woman's head – and dates to the third quarter of the 6th century BC. The Archaic characteristics are most evident in the face, with its smile, the sharply defined eyes and in the repetitive, flat waves of the hair.

126 (centre) A series of painted clay antefixes comes from the important Archaic temple of Thermos, in Aetolia, dating from the mid-6th century BC. This is a head of a Satyr, one of the half-human, half-animal creatures of Dionysus' retinue, which has here become a grotesque image of great expressive intensity.

126 (right) An early masterpiece of Attic ceramic painting, the famous François Vase was made by the great ceramist Ergotimos and painted by the Greek painter Kleitias in about 570 BC. A large krater (wine-mixing bowl) with volute handles, it was found in a tomb at Chiusi (Etruria). The decoration takes the form of six registers with mythological and epic scenes, with a total of 270 figures and 121 inscriptions.

127 (opposite) This kore from the Acropolis of Athens is one of the last examples of Archaic Attic sculpture (530–520 BC). The white insular marble was enriched with colours for the dress and jewels (diadem and earrings). Her form is both revealed and veiled by the drapery, which absorbs light due to the soft shifts of plane and deep folds.

Throughout the next century the initially static and rigid forms of young women (*korai*) and young men (*kouroi*) moved towards a more idealized representation. Statues of the Archaic period do not portray individualized features or emotions – nothing about age, condition or personal history is revealed by facial expression or posture. While the *korai* wear traditional, elegant garments, the *kouroi* are shown completely naked, their nudity intended to highlight the perfection of the human form, regarded by philosophers as indissolubly combining visible and invisible, material and abstract.

The statues often depicted young or not-so-young aristocrats, entrepreneurs, warriors, athletes, physicians, politicians, priests and priestesses. But this was of no interest to the sculptors, their patrons or the public. The intention was simply to offer to the gods and posterity an image of the splendour of youth, a supreme expression of Being materialized in humans, for votive and funerary use.

The first *kouroi* had a stiff and heavy look and the *korai* were like cylinders, with practically no resemblance to natural form. Around 560 BC attempts were made to reproduce a type of beauty that was both ideal and real. Anatomy was studied in greater depth, plasticity improved, drapery became softer, there were the first signs of movement,

128 (top left) One of the last masterpieces of black-figure painting by the great Exekias is this famous kylix with Dionysus on a ship. The scene is taken from the myth of the abduction of the god by pirates, who were transformed into dolphins.

128 (top right) This red-figure krater with volutes, from the end of the 6th century BC, has a decorated band around the neck with the fight between Hector and Achilles.

128–129 A scene from everyday life rather than myth, this relief from a statue base from Piraeus (510 BC) shows two young men inciting a fight between a dog and a cat.

however slight. Only faces still had the fixed, expressionless look of the period, the so-called 'Archaic smile'. By the end of the 6th century, *kouroi* and *korai* had reached the highest point of their refinement; the new century ushered in changes which overturned existing conventions, as seen in the pedimental sculptures of the Doric Temple of Athena Aphaia, on Aegina.

These developments were influenced by regional styles, with a large degree of interaction and reciprocity: Doric-Peloponnesian was characterized by solid shapes, a skilful disposition of masses and powerful use of chiaroscuro; Ionic (from the islands and Asia Minor) was gloriously successful in its sensitive treatment of light and delicate use of relief, accentuating the natural slimness of male figures and the grace of the *korai*; Attic, reaching towards a synthesis of the two styles, toned down their excesses and enhanced their finer points to create the masterpieces of the early 5th century BC.

By the middle of the 5th century, Corinthian pottery had passed its peak and Mediterranean markets were flooded with vases from various centres of production. This was the period when figured Attic pottery was exported to the entire ancient world – especially Etruria – in large quantities. Workshops in the *kerameikos* quarter of Athens, where potters and vase-painters worked closely together, moved on from the animal-frieze motifs of the Orientalizing tradition to draw on an inexhaustible mine of Greek myths and epic tales. The great painters of black-figure pottery were Kleitias (whose signature appears alongside the potter Ergotimos' on the François Vase), Lydos, the Amasis Painter and Exekias. But within a half-century the new red-figure technique had been invented, allowing greater freedom of expression. Euphronius was one of its greatest artists. As well as vases created by famous potters and painters (the fact that they signed their work shows they were aware of their prestige), ordinary pottery was produced along semi-industrial lines for the mass market. Many of these vases have echoes of the fashionable styles and the great artists of the day. Whether they are products of art or craft is hard to say, but the importance of this production, in response to market demand, is undeniable.

THE 'SEVERE' STYLE
(500–450 BC)

130 Aegina was home to an important school of sculptors and its products can often be identified. This beautiful woman's head wearing a helmet (possibly Athena?) comes from the island and possibly dates to the first half of the 5th century BC.

In the first half of the 5th century BC developments in Greek art coincided with, and were influenced by, changes in philosophical thought and other areas of cultural expression. These developments were the outcome of intensive study by leading exponents of schools of philosophy that had sprung up throughout the Hellenic world, from Ionia to *Magna Graecia*, from the mid-6th century BC. In the first half of the 5th century BC the concept of Beauty acquired a new importance as an expression of inner beauty – implying that high spiritual and moral values result in an equally pleasing external appearance. As proposed by the great philosophers of the period – Parmenides of Elea and Heracleitus of Ephesus – the perfect harmony of forms and values was a demonstration of the unity of Being: an indivisible, eternal, dynamic and multiform reality.

In the arts, the sense of the 'oneness' of reality was reflected in the rejection of schematic conventions in representation. Greek artists searched for the ideal, perfect expression of the nature of 'Being' and tried to develop an artistic form in which reality was portrayed in all its significance and expressed coherently, beyond the limitations of time and space imposed by everyday life and sensory perception.

Writers of antiquity used the word 'severe' to describe the initial stages of this transitional phase in Greek art, in the first half of the 5th century BC. Their intention, with this term, was to underline the moderation and equilibrium of an artistic style that had made harmony and perfection its goal.

131 A magnificent detail of the river Cladeus, personified on the east pediment of the Temple of Zeus at Olympia. As if awakening from a deep sleep, he turns to the centre of the scene, where the chariot race between the cruel king of Elis, Oenomaus, and the young prince Pelops, after whom the Peloponnese would be named, is about to begin. The torsion of the body beautifully evokes the liquid nature of this spirit of the river which mixes its waters with those of Alpheus in the plain of Olympia.

132 (right) A masterpiece of the Severe style of sculpture, the famous Charioteer of Delphi was part of a votive group dedicated by Polyzalos, tyrant of Gela, to celebrate a victory in the chariot race in the Pythian Games of 478 BC.

132 (below right) The fine bronze head of the Chatsworth Apollo, was discovered in Cyprus and dates to around 460 BC, when the island was under Athenian rule. The look expresses a severe protoclassical dignity, which was enlivened by the eyes inlaid with glass paste.

133 (opposite) The proud head of the famous bronze statue of Zeus, or perhaps Poseidon, absorbed in hurling a thunderbolt or trident (470–460 BC). Because the statue was recovered from a shipwreck off Cape Artemisium (Euboea), its original context and function cannot be reconstructed. The dynamic force of the body, with a powerful and co-ordinated unity, was based on chiasmus – the counterbalancing of limbs under stress with those relaxed – which Polyclitus would often use in his works. The position of

the god in the space definitively breaks away from the single frontal view, typical of the statuary of the previous century. Trends in this direction were already evident in the subtle

dynamic restlessness that animated the Critian Boy or the Charioteer of Delphi. The significance of the Artemisium Zeus lies both in this and in the outstanding quality of anatomical definition.

Architectural production advanced apace throughout the Greek world in this period. From Sicily to Campania, from Attica to the Cyclades, fast-growing cities acquired a new and monumental aspect. But there were no significant changes to the models established after the experimentation of the previous century. The only evidence of real innovation comes from the mighty temple of Olympian Zeus, at the Panhellenic sanctuary of Olympia. Games held here every four years in the god's honour became an important event and an opportunity for political dialogue: during the Games a sacred truce was proclaimed to promote the peaceful settlement of conflicts, inspired by Zeus himself.

The temple in some ways echoes the gigantism of Ionic temples, which Siceliot architects had already experimented with, using the more restrained forms of the Doric order, between 530 and 480 BC.

Developments were seen instead in an aspect previously neglected in Greece proper: urban planning. Hippodamus of Miletus devised a rational code for the layout of towns, which by now had larger populations and consequently more complex functions and needs. Cities were set out on a rectangular grid system, with

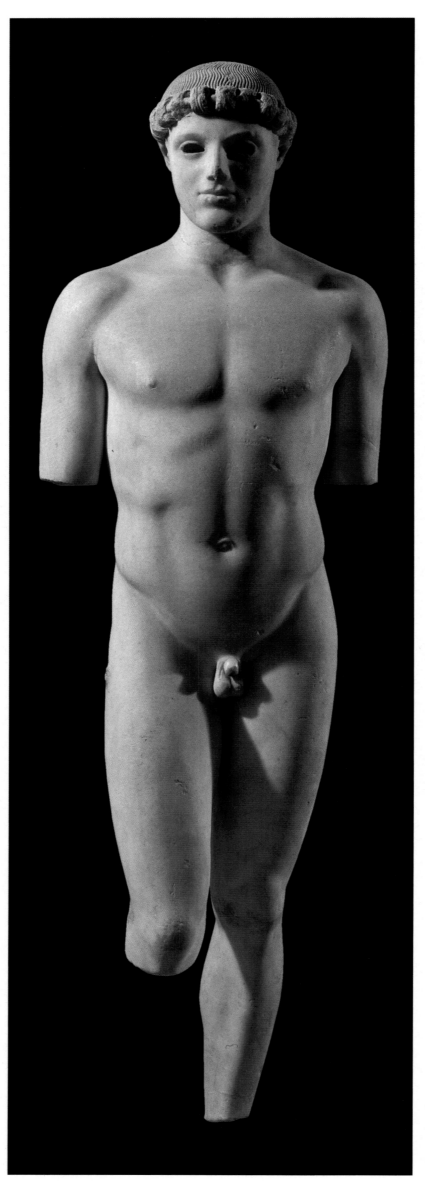

134 Critian Boy, a superb marble from the Athenian Acropolis of about 480 BC. It is so called because of the resemblance to the work of Critios, though it is not known for certain who the sculptor was. This is the first statue of a young man to go beyond the rigid frontality of Archaic kouroi, breaking the rules of artificial symmetry and moving towards the expression of movement, and, through the shifting of weight, suggesting a subtle interior tension.

135 (opposite) The seeds of the 'Severe' revolution in sculpture are clear in the fine head of the Dying Warrior from the east pediment of the temple of Athena Aphaia on Aegina. There is no longer a psychological detachment: his lips are open in panting, his cheek muscles are contracted in a grimace and his face creases up with fatigue. The dying 'godlike' hero is here represented in a more authentic, painfully mortal condition.

land distributed according to function. Streets, defensive works and sacred, administrative and commercial areas were adapted to the site and terrain. The 'Hippodamian' scheme, as it was later known, owed much to experiments of the two previous centuries in the colonies of *Magna Graecia* and it was most successfully used in the layout of Miletus, Piraeus and the colony of Thurii, in Puglia.

More significant and complex developments took place in figurative art. The east pediment of Aegina marks the emergence of a new kind of expression, far removed from the conventional formulae of the 6th century BC. It was not long before Athenian sculptors produced masterpieces such as the celebrated Critian Boy and the Tyrannicides by Critios and Nesiotes (480–470 BC). Contemporary bronze sculpture reached exceptional heights in the Peloponnese, where there were flourishing schools in Argos and Sicyon, as well as in *Magna Graecia* (Tarentum especially). The tyrants of Hellenized Italy became major patrons of the arts, competing with the most prosperous cities of the Greek homeland to embellish the great Panhellenic sanctuaries with artworks of enormous value. One such offering was the famous Charioteer group, donated to Delphi by the tyrant Polyzalos of Gela.

The different intended uses of works of art often help explain the diversity of styles, as in the case of certain categories of products of *Magna Graecia* – for instance *pinakes* (plaques), clay metopes used in Locri as votive offerings to Demeter and Kore. Ionian forms of the late Archaic period were still prominent – as in the contemporary pottery of many Western Greek colonies.

136–137 Two of the most admired masterpieces of Greek art are the famous Riace bronzes, representing warriors or kings, named after the place they were found in the sea off southern Italy. The debate as to their original purpose and context, and the identity of the artist who made them goes on. But everyone agrees on the outstanding artistic quality of the two statues and their date of between 460 and 450 BC. They are now in the National Museum of Reggio Calabria.

As always, however, statuary witnessed the most important developments. The bronze Zeus (or Poseidon) found off Cape Artemisium, depicted in the act of hurling a thunderbolt or trident, marks the discovery of movement and the final abandonment of frontality in representing human figures. Even finer examples of this transitional process are the works of the unidentified sculptor of the pediments and metopes of the Temple of Zeus at Olympia. His imposing figures are sometimes static, sometimes in agitated movement. But his greatest achievement was surely the subtle but powerful way in which the figures' expressions convey their state of mind.

The Severe style reached its acme around the middle of the century with two exceptional sculptors. One was Myron, whose celebrated Discus Thrower – his body tense, ready to throw the discus – seems to epitomise the universal sense of direction that Heracleitus wrote about; the other was the brilliant Polyclitus. Polyclitus was the first sculptor to formulate a model of the ideal human shape, using mathematical rules based on the philosophy of Pythagorus. His famous Doryphorus (Spear Bearer) embodied this code – the so-called Canon – which was the first treatise on artistic theory. This period is also interesting for the increasingly close relationship between sculpture and painting: the achievements of one were swiftly reflected in the other.

From *Magna Graecia* comes rare evidence of the splendour of Greek wall painting. Around 480 BC, in Paestum, an anonymous artist painted a cycle of frescoes on the metopes of the so-called Tomb of the Diver.

138 The marvellous anatomical precision of Riace statue A, the younger of the two, is brought out in this three-quarter view, in which the co-ordination of the strong limbs and the powerful muscles seems almost perfect.

139 (opposite) In this frontal view the stylistic refinements and touches of realism given to the Riace Bronzes by the unknown artist can be better appreciated. The faces, framed by rich beards and thick hair, are brought even more to life by eyes made of ivory and glass paste, teeth of silver and lips and nipples of copper. The statues originally held weapons, also made of silver.

THE CLASSICAL PERIOD
(450–400 BC)

In the second half of the 5th century BC Athens established its definitive cultural leadership of the Greek world. Regional artistic expression was blended with innovative developments by Attic architects, sculptors, artists and vase-painters, and the Greek vision of the universe was made manifest in art. Major roles in this process were played by Pericles and an outstanding architect and artist, Phidias. Together in Athens they achieved 'the experiment in perfection'.

This was the beginning of the so-called Classical period, a term applied by the ancient Romans to literature of the 5th and 4th centuries BC and its

exceptional brilliance. However, the term 'classical' has long been used more broadly, and inaccurately, to create the myth of a 'golden age' of culture and art. The Humanism of the 15th century and the Renaissance of the 16th generated classicist movements inspired by the artistic and architectural legacy of Rome, heir to the civilization of ancient Greece. In the mid-1700s the rationalist spirit of the Enlightenment sparked off a new appreciation for Greek art, interpreted in more scientific terms; further contributions were made by the enthusiastism for archaeological finds and the fashion for travelling to the archaeological and artistic sites of

140 (opposite, left) The Doryphorus (Spear Bearer) by Polyclitus, is the work that is said to embody the true Canon devised by this great Peloponnesian artist in around 450 BC. It comes to us only through Roman copies, the most beautiful of which is found in the National Museum, Naples.

140 (opposite, right) Another Roman copy, this one found on Delos and now in Athens, illustrates the graceful gesture of the Diadoumenos, a young athlete shown tying the tainia, or fillet, of the victor around his brow. This is one of Polyclitus' most delightful works and dates to around 420 BC.

141 A calm, almost detached energy is released in the perfect movement captured in the Discobolus (Discus Thrower) by Myron (c. 450 BC), seen here in the most famous Roman copy. It is a superb example of the discovery of the possibility of representing the dynamic harmony of the human body in a single plane.

Italy, Greece and Asia Minor, and collecting antiques. Neoclassicism set out to counter the irrationality of 17th-century Baroque. Its image of classicism was conditioned by an 'evolutionary' view of art, which saw the art of antiquity as having followed a course from birth to maturity and 'death' (a theory already adopted by the Romans). Classicism was thus placed on a pedestal as the absolute model for western art and culture. The writings of the foremost exponent of artistic Neoclassicism, the Prussian J.J. Winckelmann, influenced artists already enthralled by the grandeur of the ancient world: G.B. Piranesi, for instance, as well as A.R. Mengs, Bertold Thorvaldsen and Antonio Canova. Winckelmann's ideas were held in high esteem and eventually

created an enduring myth which even today sometimes influences the critical sense and taste of art-lovers. Only in this last century has the art of antiquity gradually come to be viewed in its proper historical and critical light. Stripped of its hierarchical value, the term 'Classical' – like 'Archaic' and 'Severe' – can be used simply for its convenience, to describe the formal language of Greek art between the middle of the 5th and the last third of the 4th centuries BC.

Athens' leading role in all aspects of Greek culture meant that it was in this city that the process of artistic experimentation begun in earlier centuries came to fruition. Under Pericles and his successors, the city can be considered the cultural capital of 'Greekness' and great figures

converged on the city in search of recognition and success.

The spirit underlying the art of this period, more than any other, cannot be fully understood without taking into account the application of scientific enquiry to philosophical thought, by figures such as Anaxagoras of Clazomenae and Democritus of Abdera. Zeno of Elea, successor to Parmenides, kept alive the idea of the indivisible unity of Being – his vision still attracting attention in the 4th century BC. Lastly there were the Sophists, the first 'practitioners of knowledge', with persuasive and refined dialectic, they emphasized man's central role in the universe and his educatability. Their arguments were soon refuted by the controversial Socrates, himself –

142–143 Art of the Classical period revolves almost completely around the figure of Phidias: this sculpture from the west pediment of the Parthenon in Athens (c. 435 BC) depicts a reclining hero. Absolute Beauty, in its ideal form, is expressed in the spatial freedom and the naturalness of the pose.

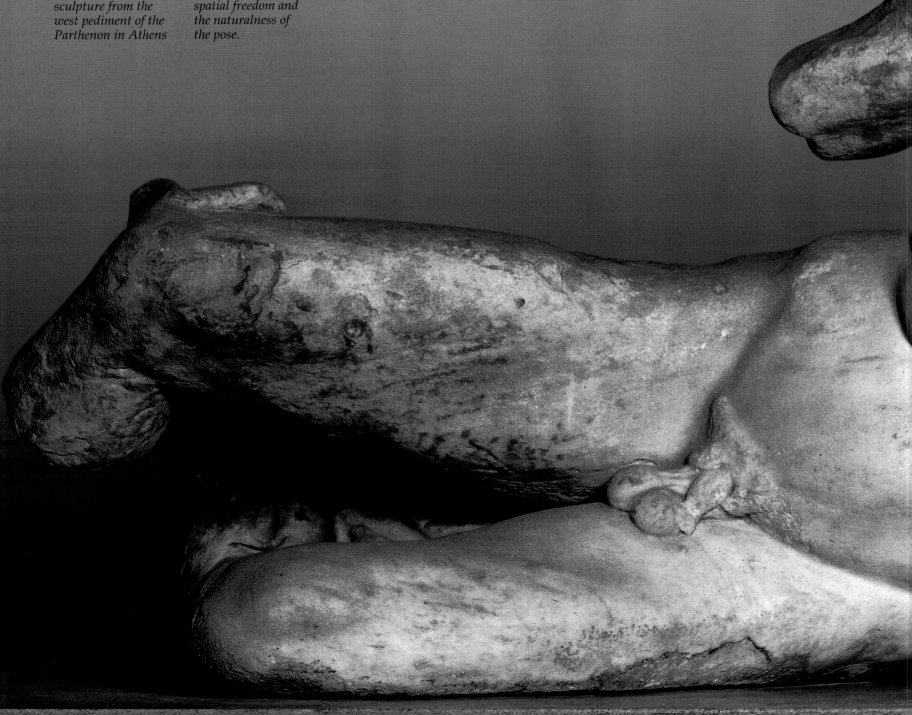

paradoxically – the greatest Sophist. And Socrates' ideas were taken up and enlarged on by his disciple Plato, with results of fundamental importance for the development of western thought.

The engine of Athens' vibrant cultural life was fuelled by the economic resources of the state and its citizens, whose political vision it embodied. As available funds grew, so did intellectual life, taste and an awareness of participating in an extraordinary period of history. In Athens the bourgeoisie thus became patrons of art on a vast scale.

The Persian sack of Athens in 480 BC had caused extensive damage to the Archaic city and the 'disarray' of the urban landscape was only partly improved under the Pisistratids.

Reconstruction progressed under Cimon and Pericles. Cimon began work on the reorganization of the Agora and laid plans for the construction of a huge temple dedicated to Athena Parthenos (Athena the Virgin) on the Acropolis, to replace the Archaic one restored somewhat haphazardly after the Persian Wars. Pericles, however, was the prime mover of the architectural embellishment of Athens. It was this man of outstanding culture and broad political views – Athens' 'first citizen' as Thucydides described him – who was instrumental in reorganizing the Acropolis and Athens as a whole, which took on a monumental aspect in the first large-scale urban improvement scheme in the western world. Pericles wanted the identity

and the political, ethical, religious and cultural values of the free Athenian people to be reflected in suitably grand architecture and art – an ensemble of buildings of unprecedented and unrivalled splendour that would be the envy of the world. Discounting the protests of a vociferous minority, his intentions seemingly echoed sentiments shared by all Athenians, whose ideas centred on society as a harmonious equilibrium between individual and community, public and private.

His scheme got underway in 449 BC, the year when a lasting peace was reached with the Persians. A series of major projects was undertaken in the Agora and in the city's residential districts, at Piraeus (to a plan of Hippodamus of Miletus), with

improvements to the general road system. But it was on the Acropolis that Pericles lavished most attention.

Athens was now a flourishing city, able to stand up to any enemy and underpinned by values both complex and profound. What it lacked was a monumental site that would be a symbol of its civic pride. Work was thus started on the construction of a series of buildings, under the personal supervision of Pericles and co-ordinated by an individual of exceptional technical and creative talent: Phidias. Working under him was a team of the finest architects and an energetic workshop of artists.

The hilltop was gradually encircled by elegant marble structures. The temple of Athena Parthenos, later known as the Parthenon, which had been left unfinished around 460 BC, was re-designed on an even grander scale by Ictinus and Callicrates. Using sophisticated mathematical calculations they based the whole complex on a harmony of proportions. Callicrates also designed the small Ionic temple of Athena Nike while the new Propylaea, an imposing gateway to the sacred precinct, was built by Mnesicles. Before long the Erechtheum – the original temple of Poseidon based on a scheme by Philocles – and a complex of small temples housing several cults were built. Construction of the monuments on the Acropolis proceeded at speed but not fast enough for Pericles to see their completion: by the time of his death, only the Parthenon and Propylaea had been finished.

The great Classical art of Attica sprang from the ambitious projects of Pericles, co-ordinated by Phidias, with contributions from a group of exceptionally talented sculptors, artists and masons. Their art encompassed complex ideas – it was an attempt to express the perfect unity and supreme beauty of the visible and invisible; to capture the dynamic and ever-changing equilibrium of reality, both seen and sensed; and to represent ideas using forms rich in meaning.

The Parthenon is the consummate example of creative genius fused with rational planning and execution, but its spatial and visual relationships with nearby buildings on the Acropolis also contribute to the overall impression of a studied and yet natural harmony. Elsewhere in Athens and in other parts of Attica, monumental building projects multiplied. Most notable were the Temple of Hephaestus in the Agora, the Temple of Poseidon at Cape Sounion and the Temple of Nemesis at Rhamnous, as well as embellishments to the sanctuary of Artemis at Brauron. The fame of the architects of the Acropolis quickly spread beyond regional boundaries. Ictinus, for example, after completing his project for the great sanctuary dedicated to the cult of the Mysteries at Eleusis, was called to the Peloponnese with

144 (left) Glimpses of the Phidian tradition can be seen in this work by Cephisodotus. It is a personification of Eirene and Ploutos – Peace and Wealth – as mother and son (374 BC). This version is a Roman copy, now in Munich.

144 (right) A Roman copy of the Wounded Amazon – could this be the sculpture by Polyclitus said to have been executed for a competition at Ephesus? It is certainly a beautiful rendering of a supple female figure, sensually draped.

Callicrates to modernize the Temple of Apollo at Bassae, in Arcadia. Phidias, once he had completed the huge ivory and gold statue of Athena Parthenos for the cella of the Parthenon, went on to make an equally enormous cult image of Zeus for the Temple of Zeus at Olympia.

Phidias dominated sculpture in these years. His work enhanced the rigorous system of proportions laid down by Polyclitus with a great variety of lines and rhythms. There were other artists contending with Phidias, such as Myron, Polyclitus and Cresilas. There was also a school of sculptors which developed around the construction of the Parthenon. Among its most prominent exponents were Alcamenes, Agoracritus and Callimachus, whose works took different directions in developing the Phidian model. The competition held at Ephesus around 440 BC is a valuable testimony to the stimulating artistic rivalry between the great sculptors of this period. Cresilas, Polyclitus and Phidias produced statues of the Wounded Amazon to contest the prize; these works are preserved in Roman copies. The lasting contribution of Phidias also emerges in the funerary stelai made in Attica between the mid-5th century and the end of the 4th century BC.

Close links between trends in sculpture and painting point to the unity of Greek artistic production. In Athens the reciprocal influence of sculpture and painting became more apparent in the second half of the 5th century BC, a sign of changing relationships between artists and a keener attention to the experiments of others in their respective fields. There were plenty of opportunities to keep pace with developments: sculptors, artists, potters, vase-painters, metalworkers, wood-carvers, goldsmiths and other craftsfmen often worked together on the same major projects. They also frequently came into contact while in the employ of ever more sophisticated and demanding patrons. The second half of the century was also marked by great achievements in painting, although the only surviving testimony is Attica's red-figure vases. The realistic portrayal of subjects was attributed increasing importance, as is evident from the fact that Anaxagoras and Democritus wrote treatises on perspective, eighteen centuries before Filippo Brunelleschi. Phidias himself was indebted to Anaxagoras. A successful painter as well as a sculptor, Phidias' approach to the Parthenon metopes reveals a pictorial vision of space enclosed in a frame. Apollodorus, Zeuxis and Parrhasius were instead influenced by Democritus.

Use of perspective, foreshortening and shading to give figures volume and dynamism is also apparent in a number of masterpieces signed by contemporary Attic vase-painters. Just as vase-painting acquired a greater sense of plasticity and perspective, so sculpture was enriched by pictorial elements. Line acquired importance as a decorative element. This is particularly evident in drapery – with veil-like folds of cloth seemingly detached from the structure of the figures – an element much favoured by Callimachus, but already introduced by Phidias and also adopted by Agoracritus. It is also evident in the grace of the 'Nike' by Paionios in the sanctuary of Olympia, dedicated by the Messenians and Naupactians as a permanent testimony to a victory over the Spartans at Sphacteria (425 BC).

145 Pliny tells the story of how the Ionian city of Ephesus held a competition for the best bronze statue of a wounded Amazon. Cresilas, Phidias, Polyclitus, Kydon and Phradmon entered works. Various Roman copies of such statues exist, and there is a lively debate over their attribution to the different artists. This may be a copy (perhaps not quite faithful) of Kresilas' version. It shows a beautiful woman with a traditional warrior aspect. Weakened by her wound, she raises her right arm with difficulty to her head, while her face betrays her suffering. The rich drapery and the pose of her splendid body indicate, according to some critics, the attempt to overcome the 'divine' balance of the work of Phidias. For the record, the competition is said to have been won by Polyclitus.

ART IN THE YEARS OF CONFLICT (400–338 BC)

The thirty years of the Peloponnesian War caused thousands of deaths, famine, epidemics, social disruption and economic crisis; it was also the historical backdrop for a change in the vision the Greeks had of themselves. People could no longer perceive the sense of unity of the universe, now overturned by violence and the absence of reason. In art, the 4th century BC can be described as the century of individualism and irrationality.

Pathos – the term frequently used to define the interior universe to which man is drawn, attracted by its complexities and contradictions – implies something more than simple emotions. It derives from the verb to suffer, and indicates a condition of passiveness, of man's inevitable subjection to the mystery of irrational feelings, whether positive or negative.

Confirmation of this flight towards the irrational, abstract, metaphysical and absolute can be seen in the evolution of philosophy. The success of Socratic dialectic coincided with the decline of the Sophists – their rhetoric, educational in intent, was infused with optimism but was also paternalistic – and it mirrored the mounting individualism of the Greek spirit. Plato perceived a rift between human and divine and postulated an absolute truth free from 'error'; he was critical of human imperfection and proposed – in political theory – an impossible model combining Spartan nationalism and 'communism', with Pythagorean mystical numerology and the disquieting figure of a 'demiurge' who, by revealing 'the way' and 'the truth' to the disorientated mass of humanity, imposes his guiding presence and nullifies free will. It was Aristotle who later offered models more feasible on ethical, political and scientific levels.

In religion, the gods no longer appeared as the reassuring, logical, superhuman projection of the perfection of Being. Instead, mirroring the fragility of all things when confronted with Destiny, they became the object of ritual homage and superstition, or disbelieving terror. In literature – and theatrical poetry in particular – Menander was the writer who most effectively represented this condition.

The 4th-century *polis* reflected the concerns of philosophers, politicians and urban planners with creating a city able to interact harmoniously with both the environment and the different economic, social and cultural needs of communities and individuals within it. Universally valid models based on 'scientific' theories were pursued: Hippocrates wrote about the importance of healthy surroundings, while Plato put forward arguments concerning what we would now call 'environmental impact'. Aristotle used his detailed knowledge of developments in various Greek cities to formulate his own theories. His ideal urban model combined the Hippodamean blueprint with the sensible, empirical approach of the Greek colonies – a model it would be worth following today. An interesting example of the evolving urban plan in this century is provided by Olynthus. The colonists who rebuilt the city adhered mostly to the Hippodamean grid but introduced variants, adapting the plan to the site and terrain. Kassope, in Epirus, initially an agglomeration of rural communities in a fast-growing region, also has some original and striking features in its urban layout and architectural solutions. Priene, in Ionia, situated in a spectacular position overlooking the valley of the Maeander River, was the first example

147 (below) Towards
360 BC, at the height
of his success,
Praxiteles created and
sold to the inhabitants
of Cnidos in Asia
Minor one of the most
admired, and
controversial, marble
statues of antiquity: a
bathing Aphrodite. By
depicting her
completely naked he
broke with the
convention of
displaying only male
figures in the nude
and he also created a
scandal for having
used his lover
Phryne as his
model.

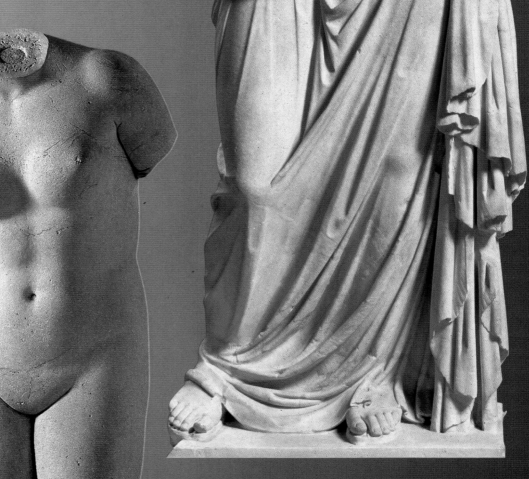

of 'scenic' urban planning, so popular in later centuries. In architecture there were also improvements and innovations: a 'standard' form was introduced for housing, based on rational and functional criteria which allowed houses to be built in blocks, or *insulae*. This change was not only intended to rationalize housing developments in line with new urban planning schemes, but it also reflected the shift towards to the new individualistic way of thinking. Theatre buildings still belonged in a public and collective domain. Increasingly built of stone, their design now followed a conventional form, of which Epidaurus is a splendid example. Theatres become a constant element of Greek cities, with examples in Dodona, Oiniadas, Priene and Pergamum – to name but a few. However, the works performed in them were now ones which the spectator could relate to more as an individual and less as part of a community. Architecturally, tendencies seen in the last three decades of the previous century continued: elegant design, graceful harmonies, intricate proportional relationships, stylistic mixes verging on eclecticism – all in pursuit of lightness– and a visual form which

moved in the opposite direction, to Platonic theories aimed at Beauty and what was vaguely defined as 'truth'.

Also interesting, in terms of the close relationship between structure and ornamental sculpture, are the *tholoi* at Epidaurus and Delphi, the Mausoleum of Halicarnassus and the Temple of Athena Alea in Tegea. The *tholos* of Delphi, in particular, has such grandiose characteristics that the celebration of the individual becomes practically a cult, echoing both renowned earlier Oriental structures and the most splendid temples of the Greek world.

Perhaps the most evident effects of existential disorientation can be seen in the sculpture and painting. In the early part of the following century Greek sculptors began to allow aspects of subjective experience to enter their work, with representations

of moods, sensations and emotions that stemmed from man's irrational inner being – testimony to the widening divide between human and divine. *Pathos* dominated the splendid creations of Cephisodotus, Praxiteles, Scopas, Timotheus and the craftsmen connected with them; the moving Attic funerary stelai are fine examples. Progressing from Phidean and Polyclitan traditions and more recent developments, these artists attempted to depict the volatile side of the human temperament. They set out to capture fleeting moments, symbolizing the ephemeral nature of things; they gave form to rapture and pain, tenderness and anger. Now far from Plato's scornful criticism of the art of his age as 'deceptive' and based on appearances, they surveyed reality and took stock of the void filled with illusions, lights, shadows and colours.

148 (opposite) The Dancing Maenad, seen here in a reduced-size Roman copy, is attributed to the genius of Scopas, and made originally around 335–330 BC. The devotee of Bacchus is depicted in the unbridled rapture of the orgy, in a feverish frenzy of winding and sensual motion. This copy is now in Dresden.

149 From the Temple of Athena Alea in Tegea (350 BC), Scopas' architectural and sculptural masterpiece, comes this beautiful head of the goddess Hygiea. Her expressive face is typical of the sentimentalism in art of the 4th century BC, and particularly of Scopas, perhaps the innovator of pathos in sculpture.

GREEK ART UNDER MACEDONIAN SUPREMACY (359–323 BC)

The central role of Macedonia in Greek history in the second half of the 4th century BC had major repercussions on the evolution of Greek art. Macedonia had already produced significant works of art from the 6th century BC on, when its contacts with central and southern Greece were still few. Closer links with the thriving city-states in the following century had a positive influence on the creative output of Macedonian artists. Aegae and Pella, the two capitals, welcomed men of letters of the calibre of Euripedes, the last in a series of eminent guests at the court of King Archelaus. It was here he wrote the *Bacchae*, first performed here too, and two other tragedies.

Greek contributions to Macedonian culture were most noticeable, however, from Philip II onwards. The king's admiration for the culture of the *poleis* of the 7th to 5th centuries BC prompted him to choose Aristotle, the greatest philosopher and disciple of Plato, as tutor for Alexander, heir to the throne. It is significant – and an indication of Macedonia's important contribution to Greek culture – that, on the basis of his experience, Aristotle laid the foundations for western philosophy and science over the next two thousand years. Human knowledge was based on 'scientific' insight into reality. And, looking beyond the abstractions and impossible theorems of Plato, Aristotle applied his thoughts on empirical science to every discipline.

The distinctive characteristics of Macedonian art stemmed from local interpretations of imported models, both from southern Greece and the Aegean, with occasional Oriental contributions, and from contacts – from the earliest times – with the southern Balkans and Thrace. Among

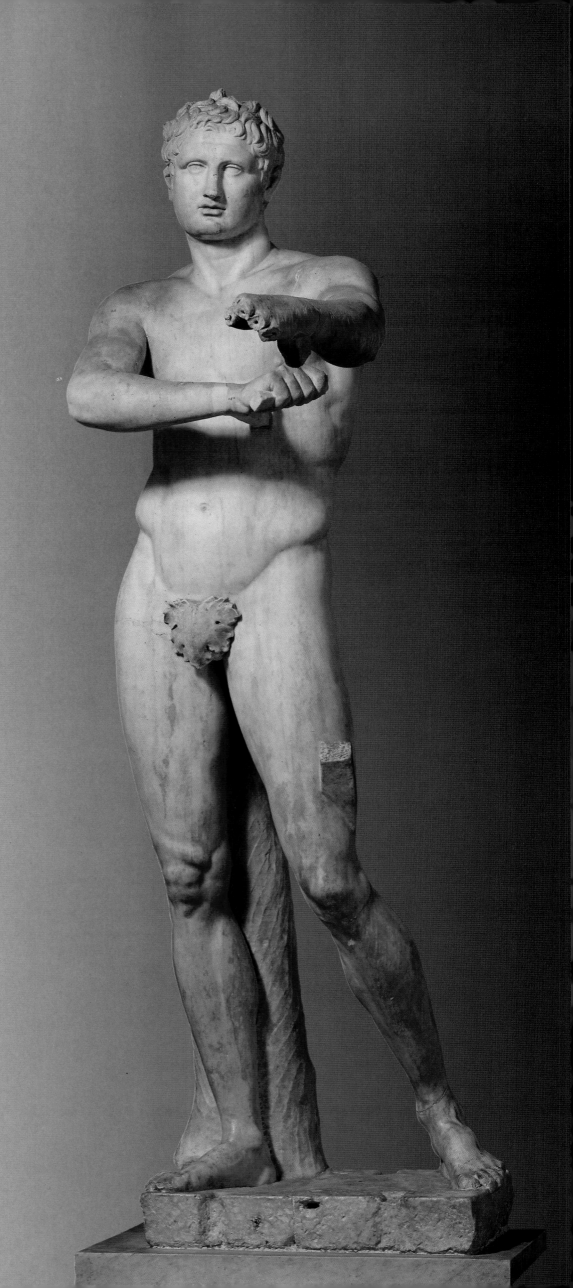

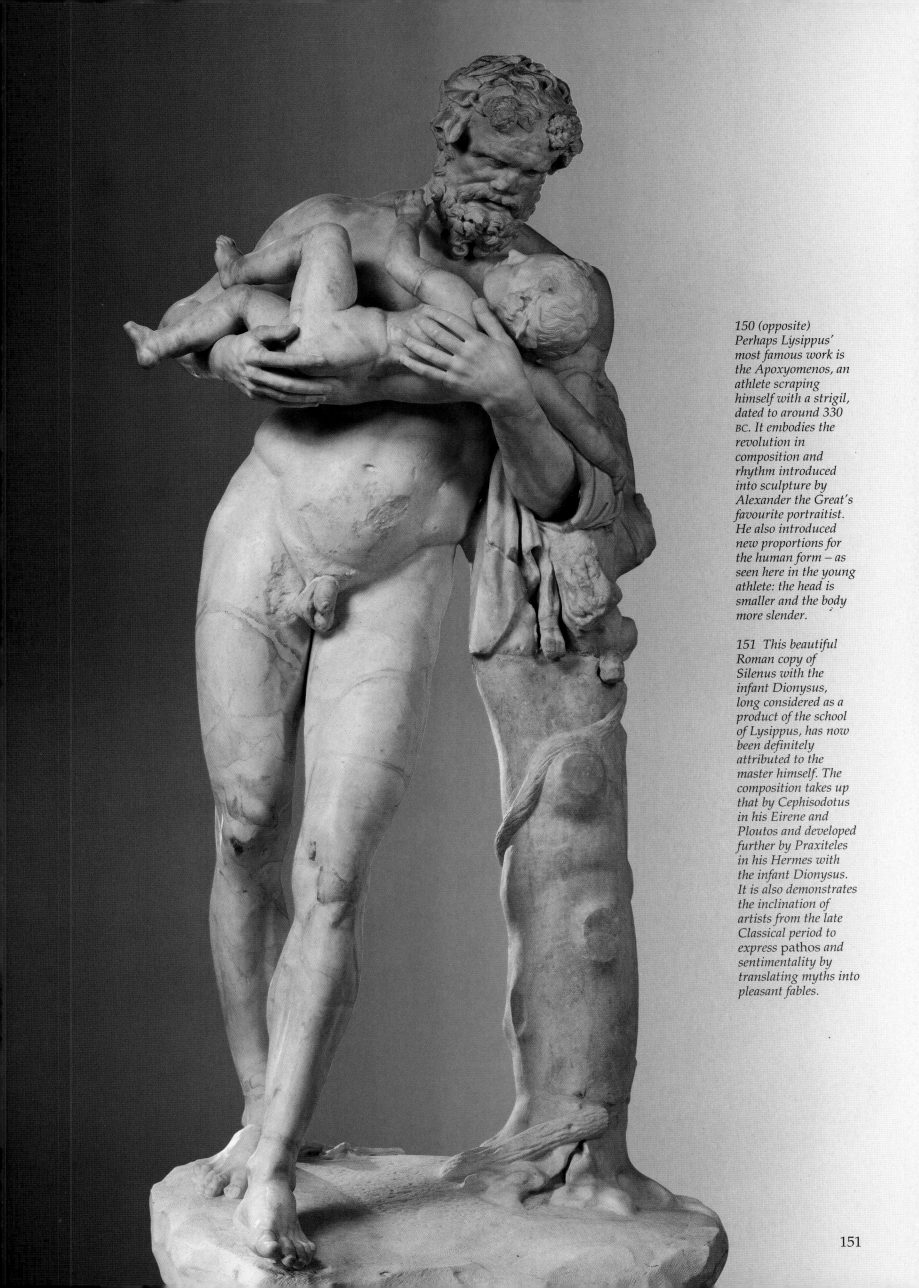

150 (opposite)
Perhaps Lysippus'
most famous work is
the Apoxyomenos, an
athlete scraping
himself with a strigil,
dated to around 330
BC. It embodies the
revolution in
composition and
rhythm introduced
into sculpture by
Alexander the Great's
favourite portraitist.
He also introduced
new proportions for
the human form – as
seen here in the young
athlete: the head is
smaller and the body
more slender.

151 This beautiful
Roman copy of
Silenus with the
infant Dionysus,
long considered as a
product of the school
of Lysippus, has now
been definitely
attributed to the
master himself. The
composition takes up
that by Cephisodotus
in his Eirene and
Ploutos and developed
further by Praxiteles
in his Hermes with
the infant Dionysus.
It is also demonstrates
the inclination of
artists from the late
Classical period to
express pathos and
sentimentality by
translating myths into
pleasant fables.

152 *Another celebrated bronze statue attributed to Lysippus, seen here in an excellent Roman copy, is Hermes at rest. The god, protector of merchants and thieves, is depicted in a very human pose – resting between adventures – not so different from a handsome young mortal if it were not for those winged shoes at his feet.*

the highlights of the 6th and 5th centuries BC is fine gold jewelry, the most typical local artistic product, from the cemeteries of Hagia Paraskevi and Sindos, near Salonika. Olynthus was the site of innovative urban planning, in which the Greek house acquired its standard configuration.

Under Philip II and Alexander the Great, Macedonia vied with the leading artistic centres of the south. City plans throughout the region reveal the application of Hippodamean principles. Local architects, encouraged by the reigning dynasty, contributed to a revival of the palace-settlement – the physical and ideological seat of monarchical power – an architectural model forgotten by the citizens of the *poleis*. The palace of Aegae displays the grandeur typically associated with power and prestige, but there are also signs of a rational and methodical scheme, which left its mark on public and private structures.

Recently unearthed near modern Vergina is the royal burial site of Aegae with the splendid tomb of Philip II, a consummate expression of a type of funerary architecture exemplified by around 70 similar tombs in the area of Edessa, Salonica and Katerini. Among the innovative architectural features of these single- or double-chamber tombs are barrel-vaulted ceilings and external wall

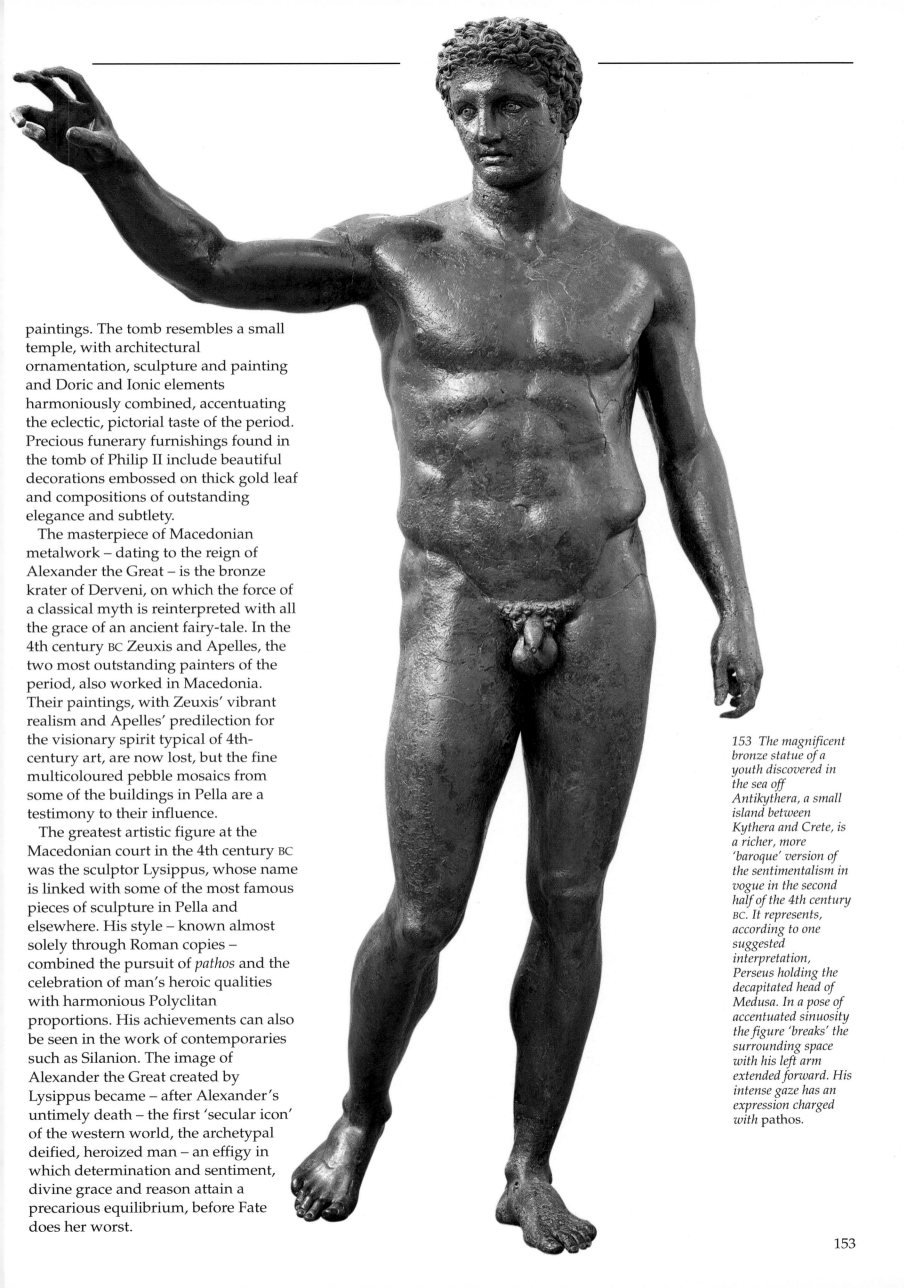

paintings. The tomb resembles a small temple, with architectural ornamentation, sculpture and painting and Doric and Ionic elements harmoniously combined, accentuating the eclectic, pictorial taste of the period. Precious funerary furnishings found in the tomb of Philip II include beautiful decorations embossed on thick gold leaf and compositions of outstanding elegance and subtlety.

The masterpiece of Macedonian metalwork – dating to the reign of Alexander the Great – is the bronze krater of Derveni, on which the force of a classical myth is reinterpreted with all the grace of an ancient fairy-tale. In the 4th century BC Zeuxis and Apelles, the two most outstanding painters of the period, also worked in Macedonia. Their paintings, with Zeuxis' vibrant realism and Apelles' predilection for the visionary spirit typical of 4th-century art, are now lost, but the fine multicoloured pebble mosaics from some of the buildings in Pella are a testimony to their influence.

The greatest artistic figure at the Macedonian court in the 4th century BC was the sculptor Lysippus, whose name is linked with some of the most famous pieces of sculpture in Pella and elsewhere. His style – known almost solely through Roman copies – combined the pursuit of *pathos* and the celebration of man's heroic qualities with harmonious Polyclitan proportions. His achievements can also be seen in the work of contemporaries such as Silanion. The image of Alexander the Great created by Lysippus became – after Alexander's untimely death – the first 'secular icon' of the western world, the archetypal deified, heroized man – an effigy in which determination and sentiment, divine grace and reason attain a precarious equilibrium, before Fate does her worst.

153 *The magnificent bronze statue of a youth discovered in the sea off Antikythera, a small island between Kythera and Crete, is a richer, more 'baroque' version of the sentimentalism in vogue in the second half of the 4th century BC. It represents, according to one suggested interpretation, Perseus holding the decapitated head of Medusa. In a pose of accentuated sinuosity the figure 'breaks' the surrounding space with his left arm extended forward. His intense gaze has an expression charged with* pathos.

153

HELLENISTIC ART

The term 'Hellenism' refers to the historical and cultural period between the death of Alexander the Great (323 BC) and the Roman conquest of Egypt (31 BC), the oldest of the kingdoms created from the dismembered Macedonian empire. It also sums up the forceful expansion of Greek influence by the son of Philip II in the vast territories he conquered in Africa and the Orient.

The term was first used in the 19th century by the German historian J.G. Droysen, who saw this as a period when Greek language, religion, political models, customs, culture and art spread to, and were assimilated by, the regions absorbed by Macedonian expansionism. In an art historical context, the term denotes the formal language of this period, which had a very long-lasting impact – at least until the 2nd century AD – due to of the enormous influence of Hellenistic culture on the art and architecture of ancient Rome.

After the death of Alexander, Greeks and non-Greeks were protagonists in the same historical processes and part of a universal culture which made Greekness its theoretical, logical and material focal point. A *koine dialektos* or 'common language' developed, bringing different traditions into contact, enhancing their respective contributions and fusing their cultural developments without destroying their original regional characteristics. In economic, social and political fields, too, the foundations of culture were no longer identified with assumptions related to ethnic origin, religion or political geography. Gone was the prejudiced belief that one model had to be superior to others or that

154 and 155 (right) Famous to the point of generating its own artistic myth, the Venus de Milo, now in the Louvre, was sculpted in the second half of the 2nd century BC by a great artist, probably a mainland Greek familiar with the style and composition of Lysippus' best works. It was found on the island of Melos, hence its modern name. Composed of six pieces of marble, each carved separately and then assembled, it today lacks its arms, which probably served to shield the beautiful naked torso. The head, miraculously well preserved, and the body reveal stylistic traits in the manner of Praxiteles and Lysippus, but the rhythm and movement are more complex – it is as if a quiver caused by the raising of the left foot had generated a ripple of restlessness through the whole figure, resulting in a suggestive natural asymmetry.

155 (opposite, below left) The beautiful Crouching Aphrodite from the Museum of Rhodes (c. 100 BC) takes up the pose of a famous model by Doidalsas, but adding the lively detail of the hands wringing the hair to help it dry, accentuating the play of light and shadow around the face.

diffusion of culture was necessarily a one-way process, with its misconceived distinction between winners and losers, dominating and dominated civilizations. This was gradually replaced by the idea of a universal dimension of mankind, with space for regional differences, generated by a culture both unitary – in keeping with Aristotelian doctrine

– and multiform. In city planning, once Hippodamean standards and their functional variants had been accepted, attention turned to monumental qualities and spectacle: expressions of the new political order which consisted of the monarchies that were the legacy of the Macedonian empire. Fully aware of the importance of popularity, these rulers exploited their demagogic bond with their subjects. Citizens on the receiving end of so much benevolent attention were impressed to the point of being dazzled by the largesse which transformed provincial cities into capitals of art and culture. Hellenistic cities are an immense and ostentatious show of architecture, often with oversized defensive walls and a profusion of public spaces. Its monumental and artistic structures became wonders of the world: the Pharos of Alexandria (site of the Universal Library), the bronze Colossus of Rhodes, the Great Altar of Zeus in Pergamum, the Nike of Samothrace. In private homes too, the plain approach typical of the houses of the *poleis*, was replaced by more appealing designs, with rooms to suit both spiritual and material

needs embellished by mosaic flooring – magic carpets of stone – wall paintings and furnishings, some elegant, others all too obviously mass-produced. Craftsmen were experimenting with the first factory processes while certain minor arts – above all, gold jewelry – reached new technical and stylistic levels. Houses built around a court, with or without a peristyle, became popular throughout the Hellenized world.

In sculpture and painting, the schools of the main centres of Alexander's old empire – Pella, Athens, Pergamum, Alexandria, Antioch and Seleucia, Rhodes – merged past experience with the varied tastes of new patrons. Technical virtuosity was accorded greater importance. All attention was focused on reality – frozen instants of the drama or tragicomedy of existence – or on the intangible realm of dreams – a magical smile, the swift flight of a goddess or dancer, goddess made mortal. This is the key to the trends in art of this period: the revival of the classicist myth and the development of a regal language in Macedonia; the unemotional composure of works produced in Athens; the entertaining 'penmanship' of the artists of Alexandria; the dramatic 'baroque' of the masters of Pergamum; the rousing sense of colour and movement typical of the school of Rhodes; the mastery of Tarentine goldsmiths; and the terracottas of a hundred cities. It is also the key to works as different as the 'Drunken old woman' and the Nike of Samothrace. And it helps us understand the artistic revolution in the non-Greek world in the 3rd and 2nd centuries BC: from the Romans to the Etruscans, from the Dauni to the Samnites and Lucanians, from the Iberians of Numantia to the banks of the river Indus.

156 This beautiful Roman copy is reconstructed from an original by Euboulides of the end of the 3rd century BC. It shows the Stoic philosopher Chrysippus seated engrossed in thought and clothed in a simple cape (in keeping with the austerity preached by the Stoics). The intense expression on his face, marked by time, the closed rhythm of the composition and the search for a calm naturalism are all typical of Attic Hellenistic sculpture of the 3rd century BC.

157 An artist of the late Hellenistic period from Rhodes seems to be the author of the imaginary portrait of Homer which has come down to us through Roman copies. The old blind poet, both a myth and a model of Greek culture, has been rendered according to formal stereotypes, producing a sort of icon emptied of interior tension.

An Archaeological Journey through Greece and Asia Minor

158–159 A close-up of the northwestern corner of the Parthenon. The pediment depicted the mythical struggle between Athena and Poseidon for the patronage of Athens.

The goddess of wisdom offered the olive tree, symbol of peace and prosperity, while the god of the sea gave a horse, or a salt spring. This pediment was executed by the great

Phidias between 438 and 432 BC, the period when most of the monuments on the Acropolis of Athens were commissioned by the democratic government of Pericles.

AMONG ANCIENT STONES, IN THE BLUE OF THE SKY AND THE SEA

160 (below left) The covered gallery of the Mycenaean palace of Tiryns (13th century BC) is an example of the megalithic technique of the 'false arch'. It allowed rapid movement around the city in the event of a siege.

160–161 This view of the north entrance of the Minoan palace of Knossos shows clearly the rather picturesque restoration. The immense complex was built on different levels, adapting the architecture to the lie of the land.

161 (opposite, above left) The palace of Phaistos, towards the south coast of Crete, was contemporary with that at Knossos. A monumental staircase formed the entrance to the southwestern part of the palace.

161 (opposite, above right) A view of the flight of steps between the houses and the palace of Mycenae, discovered by Heinrich Schliemann. Today the site is a popular tourist attraction.

The time has come to journey to some of the finest archaeological sites of ancient Greece. Others have not been included in our itinerary because they are less accessible and also because of lack of space. Neglect by passing generations and time has made them sad testimonies of history and culture, almost abandoned ruins awaiting restoration. We urge readers to seek out these sites, with their romantic charm, as they cross the evocative scenes of this ancient world. There is much more for visitors to Attica, the ancient heart of Greece, to see than the splendours of Athens: they can explore the ruins of the sanctuary of the Mysteries at Eleusis, or walk in the mountains, including the famous Hymettus and Pentelicus, whose quarries supplied marble for great masterpieces, and whose meadows, humming with bees, inspired writers of antiquity. There are paths and grottoes associated with deities and Muses, and there are the spectacular remains of the Temple of Poseidon at Cape Sounion. There are also the sanctuaries of Brauron,

Rhamnous, Oropos. The interested traveller can listen for sounds of battle carried on the wind across the plain of Marathon, or climb to the impregnable fortresses of Eleutherai and Phyle. On the way to Corinth a few moments must be spent gazing at the bay of Perachora, with the barely visible remains of two sanctuaries of Hera.

On the other side of the Corinth canal, close to the Aegean, is the sanctuary of Poseidon at Isthmia, site of the biennial Isthmian Games, second only to the Olympiad. Here we follow the route of the *diolkos*, the paved road along which huge carts carried boats from the Aegean to the Ionian. Corinth itself does not disappoint, especially Acrocorinth, high up on the acropolis, overlooking the gulf. The lower town is also rich in evidence of antiquity, with the imposing remains of the Doric Temple of Apollo and the agora which became a *forum* in Roman times. Close by, water still flows from the Fountain of Peirene, with its vast courtyard and elegant façade. Further south, at Nemea, are the ruins of the great Panhellenic sanctuary of Zeus, where other biennial games were held. Beyond Nemea a scenic mountain road leads to the lush-green depression of the mythical Stymphalean Lake, ringed by wooded peaks and high, grassy slopes. From here our route descends towards the coast, until we reach Sicyon, with its terraces, Hellenistic agora and well-preserved theatre. In the barren landscape of the Argolid we find Mycenae and Epidaurus as well as a multitude of tiny acropolis settlements of the early Greeks – Lerna, Assine, Midea – and the palace of Tiryns, with its massive walls. In the sanctuary of Argive Hera we listen as Herodotus narrates the legend of Cleobis and Biton.

The chaos of present-day Argos forms an unimpressive backdrop to the

162–163 (above) The Sacred Way at Delphi, viewed from near the Ionic Stoa of the Athenians (478 BC), seen on the right. In the background is the Treasury of the Athenians, a small, graceful Doric-style temple, once decorated with metopes which are now kept in the museum on the site.

162 (right) The small theatre (322 BC) of Oropos, in Attica, near the coast facing Euboea, was part of the sanctuary complex of Amphiaraos, a deified hero, and was probably the setting for festivals and performances in his honour, similar to the Festival of Dionysus in Athens.

city's imposing theatre: a fan-shaped auditorium with tiers of seating hewn from the rock of the steep hillside. In mountainous Arcadia, where Dionysus led the frolicking processions of Bacchantes, we find Orchomenos, with a theatre and important ruins in its circuit of towered walls; Mantinea, famous for its defensive walls; Tegea, where the great Scopas carved memorable sculptures in the now-ruined temple of Athena Alea; Megalopolis, proud rival of Sparta and birthplace of the historian Polybius, a grandiose city in every respect – from its theatre with seating for 20,000 and a mobile stage, to the 'Thersilion', precursor of parliament buildings.

Isolated by high mountain chains, Laconia centres on Sparta, the humble city of Menelaus, Lycurgus and Leonidas, devoid of ornamentation due to the Spartans' indifference to art. On and around the acropolis only a few barely visible ruins have survived destruction in antiquity and at the hands of modern developers. Messenia offers many beautiful landscapes. One site not be missed, after Messene itself, is the 'Palace of Nestor' at Pylos. In Elis, expanses of fertile plain alternate with gently rolling hills, except in the south where there are high mountains and narrow valleys. The low sandy shores fringing the Ionian Sea have wide bays interspersed with lagoons and marshes as far as the mouth of the Nedas. Here we find the sparse ruins of Elis, which gave the region its name, and along the coast, near Hagios Andreas, the submerged remains of Pheia; further south is the grotto of Kaiaphas, with the sulphur-rich waters in which Nessus the Centaur bathed his mortal wounds. Leaving Olympia behind, we journey to the mountains of Andhritsena to admire the spectacular Temple of Apollo at Bassae, built by the

same architects as the Parthenon. We turn northwards to Achaea with its low rocky cliffs and white pebble beaches, rugged mountains and deep valleys, where coniferous forests and fragrant vegetation grow next to citrus groves, oleander and eucalyptus. Leaving Patras with its Roman *odeum*, we cross the strait to Acarnania-Aetolia. Here, close to the meandering course of the mythical Achelous River, the traveller may chance on the picturesque theatre of Oiniadai, a port circled by long walls. Amid vast fields of tobacco are scattered ruins of the temple of Zeus and the imposing fortifications of Stratus, ancient capital of the region; at the foot of Mount Arakynthos patient searching discovers sites of Pleuron and Nea Pleuron. Along the road to Delphi is the splendid acropolis of Calydon, where

163 (right, top) The best architects and artists of the second half of the 5th century BC worked at the sanctuary of Nemesis at Rhamnous, in Attica. In addition to the temple dedicated to the goddess of vengeance, there was also the much-smaller Temple of Themis.

163 (right, centre) The sanctuary of Asclepius on Kos grew on a series of terraces between the 4th and 2nd centuries BC.

163 (right, below) At the sanctuary of Artemis at Brauron is the Portico of the Bears, as the priestesses of the goddess were called.

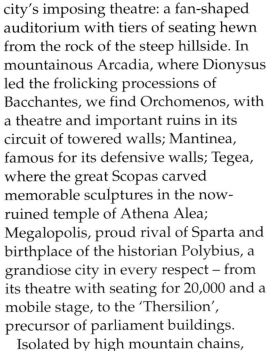

164 (opposite, top left) The remains of the imposing Archaic temple of Apollo at Corinth (550–540 BC) stand out against the low hill that dominates city. It was reconstructed in the Roman period.

164 (opposite, top right) The Terrace of Lions on Delos is one of the most striking sights on the island. On a series of pedestals stand the disquieting forms of the lions carved in the 7th century BC in the Oriental style.

visitors can search for traces of the legends of Meleager. In the heart of Aetolia is the Archaic temple of Thermum. Boeotia, noble land of the myths of Dionysus and the Muses, is a place of sun-filled plains and low hills. The ancient capital, Thebes, briefly dominant among Greek city-states, is a town with almost nothing to show of its ancient past.

More interesting sites await us: the 'Ptoion', sanctuary of Apollo; the huge Mycenaean fortress of Gla, scenically located on a former island of Lake Kopais; Thespies; Orchomenos with its magnificent *tholos* tomb; Chaeronea where the independence of the Greek city-states came to an end. After the tribute at Thermopylae to the 300 Spartans led by Leonidas, we arrive in Thessaly, with its broad plains stretching from the Aegean to the Pindos range. The sites of the fortified Neolithic settlements of Sesklo and Dhimini and the many-towered walls of Alos prepare us for our visit to Volos, ancient Iolcos. Not far distant are the ruins of Demetrias. The verdant Tempe Valley brings us to Macedonia, at the very foot of Mount Olympus, fabled abode of the gods, permanently wreathed in cloud. Continuously changing landscapes provide the backdrop for an exceptional archaeological heritage. As well as Pella and Vergina-Aegae, there are

164–165 Standing on ground consecrated in times long gone by are the remains of the sanctuary dedicated to Poseidon on Cape Sounion. After its destruction by the Persians in 490 BC, the temple was rebuilt in 444 BC, probably the work of the same architect who built the Theseum in Athens and the Temple of Nemesis at Rhamnous. It is no exaggeration to state that some of the most beautiful sunsets in the world can be seen from this most striking spot.

165 (top) A fragment of a Severe style Attic votive stele depicts a naked youth, perhaps an athlete, crowning himself with the victor's wreath. It dates to around 470 BC and comes from Cape Sounion.

165 (centre) Another beautiful view of the light and slender columns of the Temple of Poseidon at Cape Sounion. Such careful attention to the effects of light and shadow shows the probable Ionian origin of its architect.

166 (bottom) On the
ancient acropolis of
Assos in Phrygia
(Turkey) stands the
well-restored Doric
temple of Apollo. One
of the most important
philosophical schools
created by Aristotle
was born here.

166–167 In this
reconstruction we see
Assos at the height of
its prosperity, between
the 4th and 1st
centuries BC. Its vast
agora, flanked by
stoas with double
rows of columns,
ended with the
bouleuterion, the

'parliament'. Baths,
temples and luxurious
residences were
situated around it.
Magnificent walls,
still well preserved,
encircled the entire
centre and connected
it to the acropolis, the
seat of the cult of the
city god.

many memorable sites: the ruins of
Dion and of Leukadia, surrounded by
luxuriant vineyards which reveal
splendid royal burial chambers.

Other notable archaeological sites are
found in northern Greece – Edessa,
Olynthus, Philippi, Thasos, Abdera –
all of interest. The archaeological
riches of Epirus are not limited to
Dodona. One fascinating site is the
'Nekromanteion', below which
Phlegethon, Cocytus and Acheron,
mythical rivers of the underworld,
converge. At this ancient oracle
pilgrims obtained replies from the
souls of the dead.

A little further south we come to
Kassope, a fine example of the
application of Hippodamus' theories
in a limited space, on uneven terrain
and with an early taste for proto-
Hellenistic scenic architecture. It
would take a never-ending cruise to
visit all the archaeological treasures of
the Greek islands of the Ionian and
Aegean. The main Ionian islands –
Corfu, Paxi, Leucas, Kalamos,
Meganissi, Ithaca, Cephallonia,
Zakynthos – are strung out, from the
heights of ancient Bouthroton, in
Albania, as far south as Elis. In every
corner of these islands – along coasts
formed of craggy white cliffs, broken
now and then by tiny pebble beaches
fringed with olive groves; in the

countryside dotted with tranquil
villages and wooded ravines – we
discover traces of the remote past,
from the Mycenaean Bronze Age to the
flourishing Archaic period, and the
later thriving Roman age.

In Corfu, among the archaeological
museum's exhibits is the famous
Archaic pediment from the temple of
Artemis. On Leucas is the spectacular
white limestone cliff from which –
according to legend – the poet Sappho
threw herself into the sea. Hidden in
the beautiful landscape of Cephallonia
are several sites of archaeological
interest: the fine Mycenaean necropolis
of Mazarakata is in an isolated rural
location, while the massive walls that
encircled Krane are high up a steep
hillside. In Ithaca, homeland of
Homer's Odysseus, excavations have
unearthed evidence of the island's
importance in the Mycenaean and
Geometric periods.

Scattered across the Aegean are
hundreds of islands. Some are
described in this book but many others
deserve mention: Euboea, with the
important excavations of Eretria;
Chios, with site of Emborio;
Samothrace, where the celebrated Nike
was unearthed and its base still stands
in a splendid sanctuary; Syros,
stupendous island of the Aegeans;
Melos, with the site of Phylakopi. In
the eastern Aegean the island of Kos
has close associations with Asclepius,
god of medicine. There is not space
here to describe the fascinating
remains of its Roman city, among the
very finest in Greece, or the Hellenistic
structures jostling, in the harbour area,
with Roman/Early Christian remains.
The island's most remarkable site is
the sanctuary of Asclepius, built
between the 4th and 2nd centuries BC.
After an ascent through Roman baths,
Hellenistic porticoes, stairways, altars,

fountains, temples and a Corinthian
temple of Roman origin, the visitor at
last reaches the summit of the hill and
the ruins of the great Asclepeion, a
temple set in splendid isolation on
four terraces levelled from the hillside.

And beyond the Greece of today is
the Greece of yesterday – of Asia, of
Smyrna and Miletus, Didyma and
Ephesus, and a hundred more cities:
scattered heirs of Greek civilization,
from Agamemnon to Alexander.

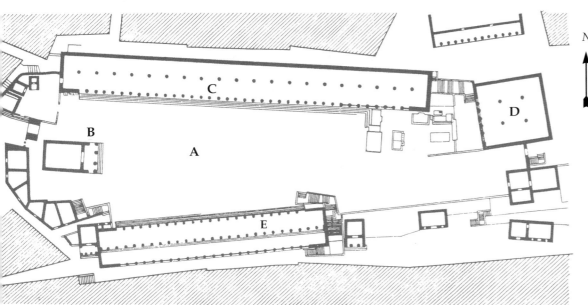

A Agora
B Temple of Dionysus
C Great Stoa
D Bouleuterion
E Baths

N

168–169 (above)
The symmetry and
harmonious
proportions of the
Parthenon are evident
in this view of the
Acropolis of Athens,
from the nearby hill
of Philoppapos.

168 (right) Phidias'
gods and heroes seem
to appear everywhere
among the ruins of
Athens' Acropolis.

ATHENS, THE CITY OF THE GODDESS

A Dipylon
B Sacred Gate
C Temple of Hephaestus
D Agora
E Stoa of Attalus
F Areopagus
G Pnyx
H Acropolis
I Theatre of Dionysus
J Monument of Lysicrates

Travellers drawn to Athens by an interest in the history of the ancient world's cultural capital have many choices to make. The Acropolis is certainly the focal point of any visit and every archaeological tour inevitably starts with the Parthenon, the temple that symbolizes Greek architecture and represents the very essence of Greek civilization.

Built in 448–438 BC, to a design by Phidias, Ictinus and Callicrates, the temple is a classic example of the Doric order, with a colonnade of eight columns at each end. Its structural and decorative elements were based on complex mathematical calculations, successfully expressing in architecture the harmony of proportions already experimented with and codified by Polyclitus in his sculpture. The underlying principles are probably to be found in the philosophical debates of the Pythagoreans and Anaxagoras regarding universal harmony. The peristyle, comprised of 8 x 17 columns and still virtually intact, stands on an imposing stylobate approximately 70 m (230 ft) long and 31 m (102 ft) wide. Inside, the *pronaos* and *opisthodomos* seem to have been reduced to a minimum, to the advantage of the *cella*, on the east side, and the smaller 'Chamber of the Virgins' – the Parthenon proper – on the west. In the *cella*, a double row of Doric columns framed the cult statue of Athena Parthenos on three sides. This colossal chryselephantine masterpiece by Phidias stood around 12 m (40 ft) high. In the other chamber, where the ancient wooden cult statue of the goddess was kept, were four Ionic columns. This was the first example of a combination of Doric and Ionic orders in a single building, frequently repeated later. A unit of measurement of 10 Attic dactyls (19.24 cm or 7½ in), was repeated throughout in infinite multiples in both plan and elevation.

The colonnade is unusually close to the walls of the *cella* (and its columns are also closer to one another), and the same ratios recur in different elements of the temple. Ictinus introduced a series of architectural refinements to ensure that the harmonious perfection of the Parthenon was instantly evident to anyone entering from the Propylaea. The effects of perspective, the play of light and shadow, dimensions, the relationship between solids and voids and so on, tend to produce a slightly deformed picture of reality to the human eye. And so Ictinus made some astounding 'optical corrections'. For instance, an upward curvature – by as much as 6 cm (just over 2 in) – of the stylobate, and the almost imperceptible

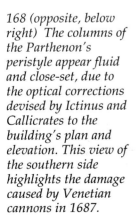

168 (opposite, below right) The columns of the Parthenon's peristyle appear fluid and close-set, due to the optical corrections devised by Ictinus and Callicrates to the building's plan and elevation. This view of the southern side highlights the damage caused by Venetian cannons in 1687.

169 (right) The so-called Mourning Athena – a votive relief showing the goddess in a reflective pose, perhaps reading a list of Athenian dead. The relief dates to around 460 BC and is a good example of the 'Severe' style.

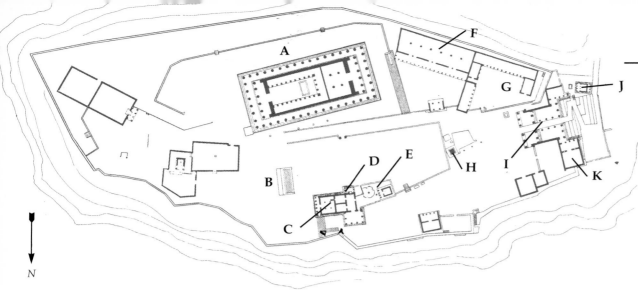

A Parthenon
B Altar of Athena Polias
C Erechtheum
D Porch of the Caryatids
E Precinct of Athena's olive tree
F Khalkotheke
   (depository for weapons)
G Sanctuary of Artemis Brauronia
H Statue of Athena Promachos
I Propylaea
J Temple of Athena Nike
K Pinakotheke

170–171 This view of the Parthenon is from the northeastern side of Athens. The goddess' temple had been designed and work had already partly begun around 460 BC under Callicrates' lead, but was halted for a long time due to the chaotic domestic political situation during the period between the Persian Wars and the Peace of Callias. Pericles then initiated a new project, the outcome of which we see today. It was the result of a valuable co-operation between the architects Ictinus and Callicrates and Phidias, the great genius who co-ordinated all the operations on the Athenian Acropolis.

172–173 (overleaf)
In this reconstruction
of the Acropolis in
the late 5th century
BC we can gain some
impression of the
visual impact on
ancient visitors
created by the upward
sequence leading from
the Panathenaic Way

through the
wonderful Propylaea
of Mnesicles to the
crowning perspective
of the temple of the
goddess. The
Acropolis also housed
other architectural
monuments designed
by Phidias and his
followers.

convexity (*entasis*) of the columns which – especially at the corners – were also very slightly bowed towards the *cella*. So for today's visitors, too, the traditional heaviness of the Doric order is transformed by the austere elegance and harmony of forms and proportions, while the white Pentelic marble enhances the interplay of light and shadow on the temple's lofty structures.

The decorative features of the Parthenon, completed in 432 BC, abound in political, civic and religious significance. The sculptures were entirely designed and perhaps in the main also executed by Phidias, assisted by some of Attica's finest emerging artistic talents. Works that survived the fury of Christian fundamentalists after the Edict of Theodosius I (of AD 395), Muslim iconoclasm after the Turkish conquest of 1456 and Venetian cannon-fire in 1687 can be seen still *in situ*, in the Acropolis Museum nearby, in the British Museum in London and in the Louvre in Paris.

The pedimental groups (over 4 m (13 ft) high) showed, on the east, the birth of Athena from the head of Zeus, in the presence of all the gods of Olympus; and on the west, the mythical contest between Athena and Poseidon for the patronage of Attica, watched by Cecrops. The 92 metopes of the Doric frieze – on which only the very faintest traces of the once-vibrant colours now remain – represented a sequence of four versions of the struggle between good and evil, justice and injustice, civilization and barbarism, using mythological and epic imagery. On the east was the battle between the gods and giants (gigantomachy), on the south between Greeks and centaurs (centauromachy), on the west between Greeks and

Amazons (Amazonomachy) and on the north between Greeks and Trojans – an evident reference to the recent victory over the Persians. On the Ionic frieze along the wall of the *cella* were reliefs showing sporting events and the important four-yearly Panathenaic procession in honour of the goddess, part of the festivities symbolizing the Athenians' faith and their devotion to their patron. For the first time, therefore, contemporary events and symbols joined myths and legend to create images with a religious, ethical and political message. Depicted alongside gods and heroes were humans and their city, glorified as a mortal manifestation of the values of eternal deities and immortal heroes, bringing to mind the Homeric adjective *isotheos*, meaning god-like.

170 (opposite, below) The Doric frieze of the Parthenon was probably the first decoration begun by Phidias. Some think that the master only provided his pupils with guidelines, while others note a strong consistency in its sober expression, characteristic of Phidias.

171 This rather heavy, much-reduced Roman version is the only evidence we have of the sumptuous appearance of the gold and ivory cult image of Athena made by Phidias for the cella of the Parthenon's cella. Known as the Athena Varvakeion it dates to the reign of Hadrian (2nd century AD).

174 (above) A section
of the Ionic frieze
which decorated the
Parthenon's cella
shows young
Athenians carrying
water jars – hydriai –
in a procession during
the four-yearly
celebrations in honour
of Athena. This
masterpiece of Greek
art undoubtedly
reveals the hand of
Phidias, with his
unique narrative skills
and stylistic traits.

174 (below) Another
section of the
Parthenon's Ionic
frieze shows a
cavalcade of horsemen.
Here Phidias' skill is
evident in the
composition, which
evokes the confusion
involved in the event
with great mastery.
Naturalism reaches
its peak in the bodies
and faces of the
participants.

174

175 The terror of the cattle destined to be sacrificed to the goddess, led by young priests, is one of the best demonstrations of Phidias' superb naturalism. There is a particularly strong contrast between the restless motion of the animals and the quiet repose of the youths wearing cloaks.

In 437 BC the architect Mnesicles began his project for the Propylaea, the monumental new gateway to the sanctuary of the Acropolis, on the site of a much more modest one built under Pisistratus. After five years' work, almost certainly by the same craftsmen who had only recently completed the Parthenon, the Propylaea became the point of arrival for the last, winding ramps of the Sacred Way. It was a fitting entrance to the marble 'treasure-chest' that the hill dedicated to Athena was fast becoming. Providing the immense Parthenon with an entrance of appropriate proportions, elegance and dignity was no easy task. The space available was asymmetrical and limited, the terrain was uneven, and existing monuments and sacred precincts had to be taken into account. Mnesicles cleverly designed a marble structure which, at the top of steeply rising steps, sat astride a rocky ridge, well adapted to and concealing the rugged terrain. The proportions and dimensions of each element of the building were carefully worked out, to take full advantage of the building's spectacular position and its function. A Doric *pronaos* with six columns at the front, formed the imposing entrance to the entire sanctuary of Athena. The vestibule was divided into three naves by two rows of three slender Ionic columns. In the surrounding walls were five doors, at the top of a flight of five steps interrupted in the centre by a passage for chariots and animals. The steps follow the slope of the hill, an ingenious solution to the problem of the gradient. Beyond the doors another Doric *pronaos*, identical to the

first, overlooked the sacred enclosure and provided a splendid frame for Phidias' huge bronze statue of Athena Promachos and a view of the Parthenon. At the sides of the Propylaea were two colonnaded wings. The northern one comprised a rectangular chamber, the Pinakotheke, eventually used to house famous paintings. The Ionic temple of Athena Nike stood at the side of the Propylaea on the southwest bastion, which had been faced in Pentelic marble in previous decades. It was built between 430 and 410 BC, with frequent interruptions caused by war, to a plan of thirty years earlier by Callicrates and then used for a temple of Demeter and Kore on the banks of the Ilissus river (of which only a few 18th-century sketches remain). Beautifully harmonious in its proportions and built of Pentelic marble, the temple was enhanced by slender Ionic columns only at the front and rear, surmounted by a running frieze with scenes of the war between Greeks and Trojans. An elegant marble balustrade, decorated with very low-relief sculptures portraying a procession of figures personifying Victory, ran around the temple, to protect worshippers on the terrace perched high on the slopes of the Acropolis. The quality of execution bears clear evidence of Phidias' influence. But it shows an even greater ability to convey the subtle play of light and shadow on the drapery and in the dynamic poses of the figures, and the name of Callimachus – one of Phidias' most talented pupils – has been suggested. One interesting aspect is the change in the building's political message:

176 (right) The elegant small temple of Athena Nike (Victory), rather optimistically built at the end of one successful phase of the Peloponnesian War, stands on the southwestern bastion of the Propylaea, completely faced with white Greek marble.

176–177 (above)
The Propylaea, by
Mnesicles (437–433
BC), forms the
architectural threshold
between the city and its
sanctuary, and provides
a glorious entrance to
the Acropolis. The
structure was
combined with the
famous Picture Gallery,
where paintings by the
greatest masters of the
time were kept.

177 (right) This
view shows the
eastern part of the
Propylaea, on the
inner side of the
sanctuary. It is well
preserved and reveals
how the Doric style is
developing towards
more elegant forms,
although its typical
and traditional
features – simplicity
and severity – are
still evident.

178 (right) On the eastern side of the Erechtheum was a high and airy Ionic pronaos, with six-columns, leading to the cella where the ancient wooden cult statue of Athena Polias, the protector of the city was preserved and worshipped. The same solemn airiness is also to be found in the northern arcade, where the mark left by Poseidon's trident during the dispute with Athena for Attica was preserved.

178–179 (below)
The Erechtheum –
seen here from the
southwest – was the
last building erected
on the Acropolis
before the end of the
5th century BC. It
replaced an ancient

temple of Athena
Polias, which was
destroyed during the
Persian Wars. It was
built between 421 and
405 BC, based on a
project by Philocles or
Callicrates, and has a
very unusual plan.

179 (above) The
famous porch with the
Caryatids marked the
legendary tomb of
Cecrops. The six
beautiful statues of
young women
wearing Ionic
costumes are perhaps
the work of one of the
best disciples of
Phidias, Alcamenes.

179 (below) The plan
of the Erechtheum is
certainly unusual as it
had to accommodate
various ancient cults,
including that of
Poseidon Erechtheus.
Also visible in this
view is a descendant of
the legendary sacred
olive tree, the gift of
Athena.

designed in 460–450 BC to celebrate Athenian victory over the Persians, the temple was actually built much later, during the Peloponnesian War, and so it became essentially a tribute to Athenian successes over their new enemy – the Spartans.

The last addition to the Acropolis before the end of the 5th century BC was the new temple of Athena Polias, known throughout history as the Erechtheum, after the Attic name for Poseidon. It was built north of the Parthenon, between 421 and 405 BC, to a plan by Philocles or – according to some – Callicrates or Mnesicles. Its undeniably unusual plan stemmed from the need to respect ritual tradition and the sanctity of the site, and house several different, age-old cults under one roof. The Ionic portico with six columns on the east gives access to the *cella*, where the ancient wooden cult icon of Athena Polias was zealously kept; on the west side, on different levels, were spaces for the cults of Poseidon Erechtheum, Hephaestus, the hero Bute and the serpent-boy Erichthonius, particularly dear to Athena. Outside the building on the west side grew the sacred olive tree, traditionally believed to be the gift of Athena in her dispute with Poseidon. On the north side a high Ionic portico protected the mark left by the trident thrown by Poseidon to make a sea-water spring gush from the rock. The only decorative feature of the entire temple was a long frieze in Eleusinian black stone on which relief figures in Pentelic marble were mounted, portraying scenes of Attic ceremonies and episodes involving Erichthonius. As the architect clearly intended, the viewer's gaze is

immediately drawn to the south side and the porch which protected the tomb of the mythical king Cecrops. Supporting the porch in the place of columns are the celebrated Caryatids, six statues of young women in Ionian dress, an architectural device that succeeds in combining the refined elegance of Ionic with the formal perfection of Phidian artistic expression. It seems likely that the designer of the Caryatids – whose forced immobility cannot restrain their intrinsic vitality – was Alcamenes, another pupil of Phidias. However, the main interest of the ensemble lies in the configuration of its buildings, built on different levels to follow the rising, rocky terrain of

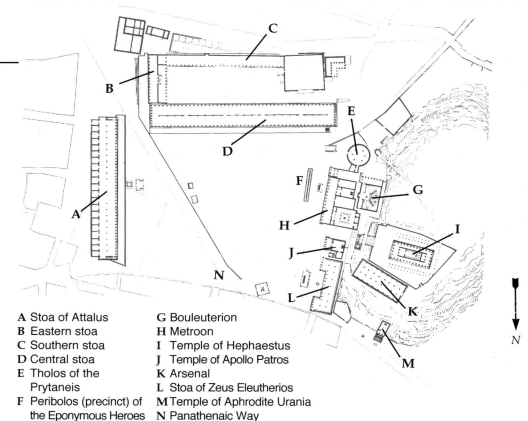

A Stoa of Attalus
B Eastern stoa
C Southern stoa
D Central stoa
E Tholos of the Prytaneis
F Peribolos (precinct) of the Eponymous Heroes
G Bouleuterion
H Metroon
I Temple of Hephaestus
J Temple of Apollo Patros
K Arsenal
L Stoa of Zeus Eleutherios
M Temple of Aphrodite Urania
N Panathenaic Way

the Acropolis. There is also evidence of great precision in the way that the buildings respect several ancient sacred sites. Near the north wall are the poorly preserved remains of the 'House of the Arrephoroi' (5th century BC), with an enclosure for the leisure activities of the young women who wove the *peplos* for Athena's statue.

The famous Theatre of Dionysus stands on the southern slope of the Acropolis, in the precinct of the god who protected the dramatic contests held during the festival of the Great Dionysia. The visible structures date to 330 BC, with Roman additions.

Around it are remains of a Hellenistic portico used as a promenade and the *odeum* of Pericles (445 BC), a large auditorium rebuilt in Roman times.

The agora, with the nearby hill of the Areopagus, is Athens' other main area of archaeological interest. Its most prominent structures today are the modern reconstruction of the Stoa built by Attalus II of Pergamum in the 2nd century BC, now housing the Agora Museum, and the Doric Temple of Hephaestus, still miraculously intact. The temple stands on a small hill west of the agora, once crowded with metal workshops. Built in Pentelic marble in the same period as the Parthenon, the temple is still an important landmark in the lower part of Athens. It is about 32 m (105 ft) long and 14 m (46 ft) wide, with six columns at the ends and 13 at the sides. Its plan appears conventional

Doric, but its *cella* resembles the larger one in the Parthenon. Indeed, the structural elements of the temple, especially its proportions, were clearly inspired by the Parthenon, whereas the decoration fluctuates between pre-Phidian models and innovations seen on the Acropolis. A few fragments of the pediments and acroteria bear a resemblance to the work of Alcamenes. The metopes with relief decoration – only 18 in number – are rather Archaic in style, while the Ionic frieze instead reveals the definite influence of the Parthenon.

What is interesting about the building is its cult connection with an area of the city where metallurgical activities had long been concentrated. It is not clear whether it was actually built under the patronage of metalworkers, though there are many cases of donations from guilds and private individuals keen to contribute to the embellishment of Athens and to benefit from the resulting prestige. It is certain that the whole area, not previously linked with any cult, was laid out as a garden, perhaps with the intention of transforming an old 'industrial' area – hardly the most pleasant of places – into a space to be enjoyed by the public, visually linked with the Acropolis and its shining marble.

Also of interest are the nearby Cerameicus quarter, with the Dipylon cemetery and remains of potters' workshops. Finally, a visit to the National Archaeological Museum provides an overview of ancient Athens.

180 (opposite, left)
The Temple of
Hephaestus, known
also as the Theseum,
with its elegant
proportions derived
from the Parthenon,
stands near the Agora
of Athens.

181 (left) The present
appearance of the
Theatre of Dionysus,
where dramatic
festivals took place, is a
result of restorations in
the Roman period.

180–181 (below) This
view of the Athenian
Agora reconstructs its
probable appearance
during the Hellenistic
period. It highlights
how constraints
enforced by the
topography of the
northern slopes of the
Acropolis and pre-
existing buildings
limited a more
rational development,
in spite of several
attempts at
improvement.

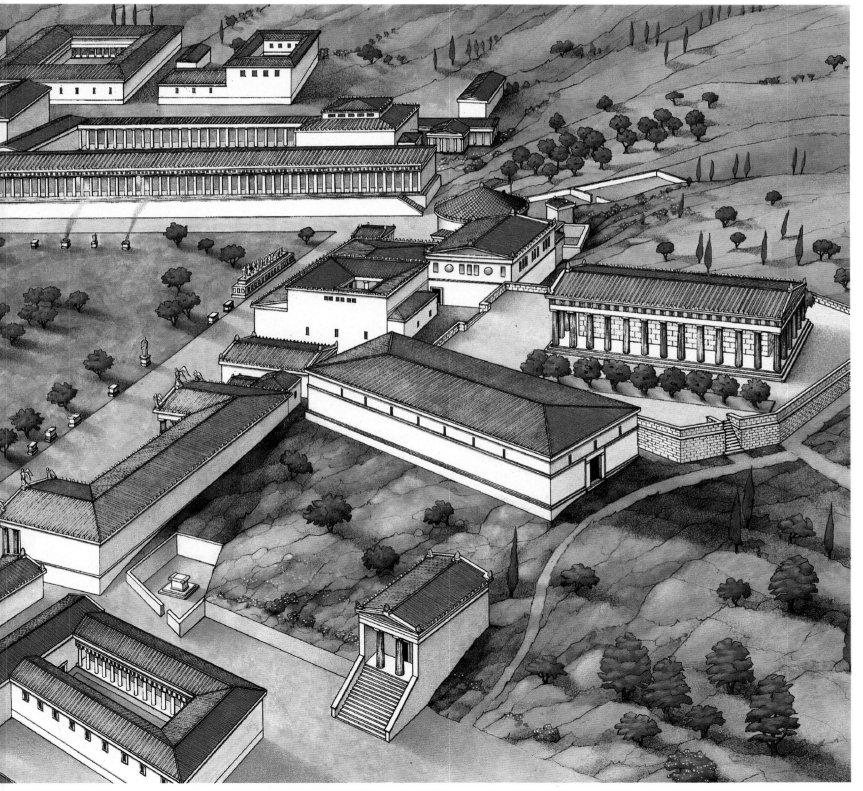

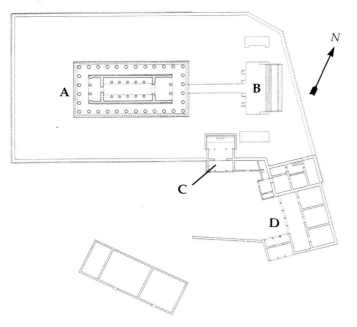

AEGINA, THE ISLAND TEMPLE

A Temple
   of Aphaia
B Altar
C Propylaea
D Houses
   of the priests

In the Archaic period Aegina, in the Saronic Gulf, challenged the commercial supremacy of its rivals, Athens and Corinth. Around 500 BC it celebrated its power and prestige by building a magnificent temple in honour of Aphaia, a goddess linked with Athena. This Doric building, with six columns at each end, is still in an excellent state of preservation. In terms of structure and proportions, it represents the first strong move towards the balance characteristic of Classical architecture. The temple's slender columns convey a wholly new sense of airiness and lightness, while another original feature is the layout of the *cella*, which was built on two storeys and divided by two rows of Doric columns, supporting a ridged roof topped with acroteria and other architectural decoration in marble.

However, the temple owes its important place in the history of Greek art to its pediments – now in the Glyptothek in Munich – which mark the transition from Archaic art to the so-called Severe style. Carved in late Archaic style by an unknown sculptor, the life-size figures portrayed the miraculous appearance of Athena in the midst of a battle between Greeks and Trojans – a reference to the war between Greeks and Persians. The pediments were damaged in an earthquake that rocked the island early in the 5th century BC: the west pediment survived virtually intact; while the east one, left in pieces by the tremors, was recarved with the same theme around 490 BC or not long after, but by another sculptor. During that short time artists had begun to break away from Archaic conventions. On both pediments the goddess is shown dressed and armed with lance, shield and breastplate decorated with a terrifying Gorgon's head with serpent hair; she stands prominent among groups of warriors depicted taking aim before shooting an arrow, or grappling in a duel or lying on the ground, mortally wounded. As well as coloured elements – somewhat over-restored by the Danish sculptor Bertel Thorvaldsen in the early 19th century – many details (arms, ornaments) were added in gilt bronze, as is shown by holes for attachment visible on the statues.

The stylistic developments differentiating the two pediments emerge both on a general level and in many details. Not only does the composition set the later, east pediment apart from the west one: the artistic language used points clearly to the advent of the new 'Severe' style. If we look, for instance, at Athena: on the late Archaic west pediment her face still has a solid look and essentially

frontal features, fixed in the smile that masks the detachment of men and gods. The east pediment Athena has no smile; her face bears a serene expression conveying the goddess' superiority over events involving the mortals around her. Delicate relief work gives credible form to the face of Zeus' wise daughter, reflecting the search for a new artistic language, more receptive to the spirit, in which rationality and the subconscious are merged.

182 (opposite) Two views of the Doric temple of Athena Aphaia on Aegina highlight the balance of the colonnade and the innovative cult cella with two storeys of columns, which supported a ridged roof.

182–183 (above) and 183 (left) Two views of the Temple of Athena Aphaia, on Aegina, with its finely balanced proportions. The solid-looking columns, some of which were carved from a single piece of stone, give the appearance of great strength.

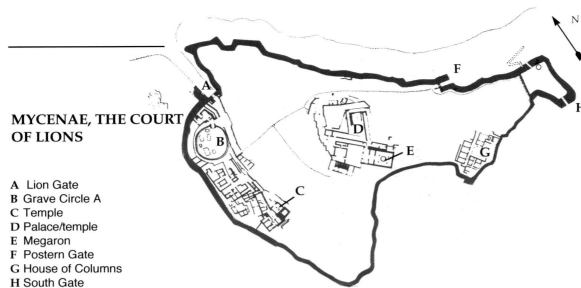

MYCENAE, THE COURT OF LIONS

A Lion Gate
B Grave Circle A
C Temple
D Palace/temple
E Megaron
F Postern Gate
G House of Columns
H South Gate

184 (left, above) Grave Circle A at Mycenae was enclosed within the second circuit walls.

184 (left, below) The ramp approaching the Lion Gate, the main entrance to Mycenae.

184 (centre) The northern postern, a secret gate concealed among the huge blocks of Mycenae's walls, is an excellent example of the 'false arch' technique using megalithic, irregular-shaped blocks.

In the northeast of the Peloponnese is the Argolid. An endless series of hills and mountains, smoothed by erosion and made barren by millennia of overgrazing and deforestation, extends as far as the coast, with its countless sheltered inlets and bays. Water is in short supply but wherever the terrain permits, the land produces citrus and other fruits, olives and grapes, as well as cereals. The region also has abundant archaeological treasures: the first proof of the presence of human groups in the peninsula was found here, in the Franchthi Cave, dating to the Upper Palaeolithic, as well as evidence of extensive human settlement from the Neolithic through to the end of the

Bronze Age, and early signs of recovery after the Dark Ages.

Mycenae is the region's most famous site, its name linked with some of the most memorable myths of Greek epic poetry and tragedy. Its rapid decline and abandonment at the end of the 2nd millennium BC have preserved its fundamental and most distinctive features. Of particular significance is its location – on a steep hill within sight of the fertile plain of Argos and the gulf of Nauplion, protected at the rear by two mountains and deep valleys. This is a typical choice for the settlement site of a warfaring community. Encircling the acropolis are two rings of walls, the first built in the 14th century BC, using the cyclopean technique of large, irregular blocks. The second, larger, ring of walls of the 13th century, was built of more regular blocks. In the later circuit – which incorporated Grave Circle A of the celebrated shaft-graves unearthed by Heinrich Schliemann in 1876 – there were only two entry points: the first was the Lion Gate (in fact they are probably two lionesses);

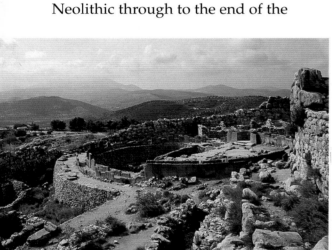

185 (right) The two
lions (in fact probably
lionesses) decorating
the famous gate to
which they give their
name, rest their paws
on two altars topped
by a column similar to
those of the Cretan
palaces.

184–185 (below)
An aerial view of
Mycenae's ruins
reveals the
dominating position of
the royal palace over
the other structures in
the city, and
highlights the absence
of any town-planning.

186–187 (overleaf)
At the period of its
greatest prosperity
(14th–13th centuries
BC) Mycenae may well
have looked something
like this. Mycenaean
architecture shared
some aspects with
Cretan palaces, but
there were also
fundamental
differences, including
the use of cyclopean
masonry – large,
irregular blocks.

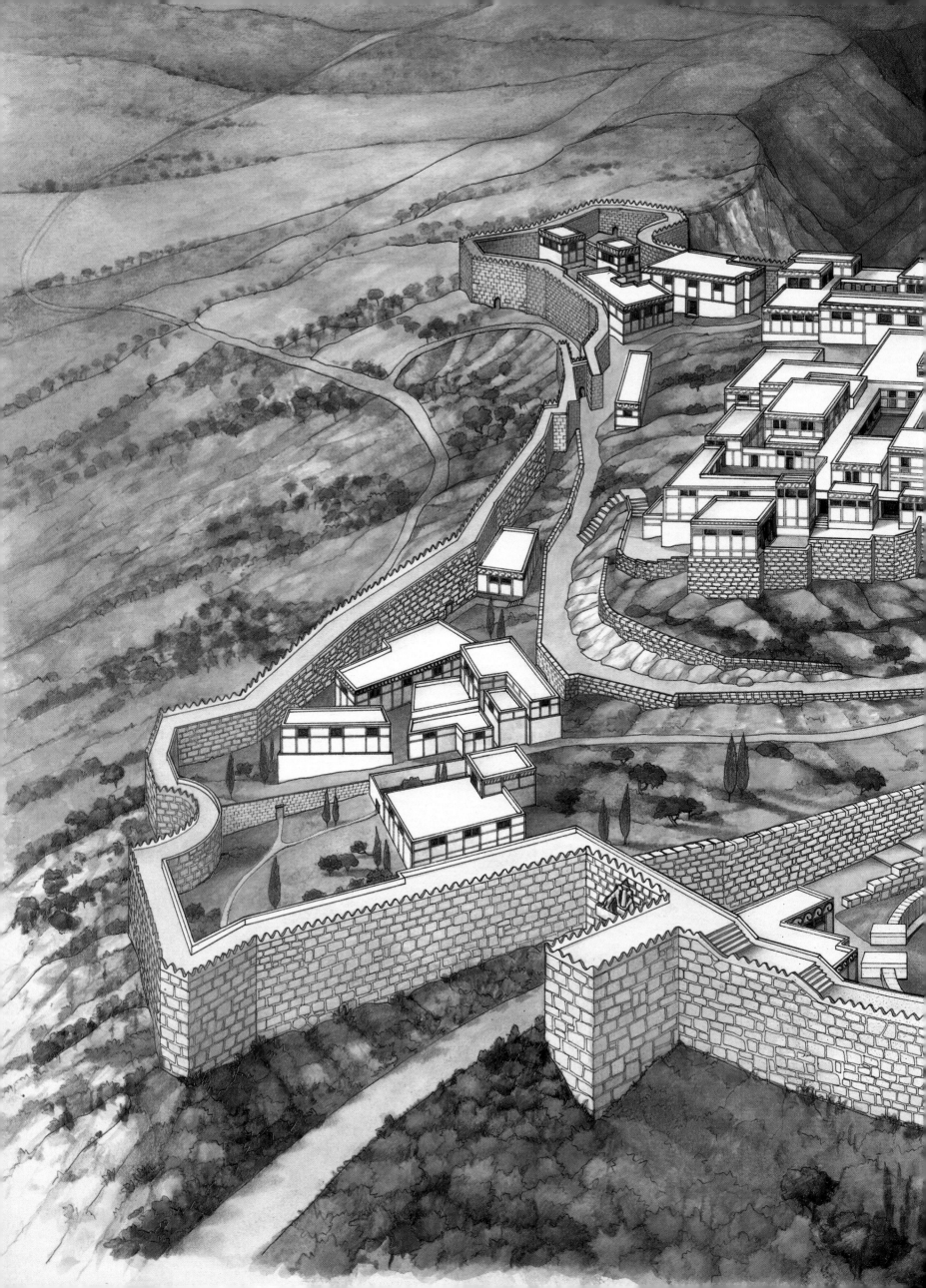

the second was the Postern Gate. This postern provided access along the northeast stretch of the walls, towards the mountain; it was clearly visible to the inhabitants but practically imperceptible to anyone approaching from outside. Not far from the north postern is Mycenae's most amazing feat of engineering: a gallery, over 90 m (295 ft) long, with steps hewn from the rock, descends to a huge subterranean cistern that guaranteed a constant water supply, with safe access in the event of a siege.

Visitors to the site climb a ramp leading across the cemetery where huge mounds conceal *tholos* tombs (many of them still accessible) which have been attributed – with great leaps of the imagination – to figures from Homer's epic tale: Atreus, Clytemnestra and Aegisthus. At the top of the ramp is the stunning sight of the Lion Gate and its adjoining bastions. The relief decoration above the huge monolithic lintel has clear

parallels with Near Eastern art and exemplifies the symbolic force of the art of this warrior society.

The Lion Gate is now virtually a symbol of this land and its past and is one of many examples of the skills of Mycenaean architects. It was built with two colossal door jambs supporting a massive lintel, slightly convex at the centre. Instead of their entire weight resting on the lintel, the huge blocks above are positioned in successively projecting courses, so that the weight is discharged on the ends of the lintel, and hence on to the uprights. The resulting 'relieving triangle' is filled with the famous relief. The gate also attests to the notable figurative skills of Mycenaean sculptors. In the Mycenaean concept of naturalism, the vibrant colours and soft chiaroscuro effects of the Cretans are replaced by an expression more profoundly influenced by symbolic and ideological values.

Inside the circuit of the city walls is Grave Circle A, within its own imposing enclosure wall formed of cleverly interlocking upright stone slabs. The wall surrounded the fabulously rich royal shaft graves brought to light by Heinrich Schliemann. Also within the city is the palace, of which the entire central section and at least two floors have been identified and the 'House of Columns', a fine example of an aristocratic dwelling.

The so-called 'Treasury of Atreus' is a typical, imposing Mycenaean *tholos* tomb. Its approach is a *dromos*, 36 m (118 ft) long and 6 m (20 ft) wide, open to the sky and flanked by sloping walls of enormous blocks of stone arranged in regular rows. The

entrance, opening in a lofty façade, is over 5 m (16 ft) high and almost 3 m (10 ft) wide. Its probable original decorative facing, showing evidence of Minoan influence, was carved from red and green marble. Surmounting the lintel of the doorway is a relieving triangle. Inside, the large circular chamber towers to a height of over 13 m (43 ft), with a diameter of 14.5 m (48 ft). The concentric courses of slightly projecting blocks, carefully shaped to make the curve of the corbelled dome perfectly smooth, rise gently and regularly to the top slab which seals the structure. The huge pieces of stone are wedge-shaped and the entire curving structure was covered by the mound of earth, helping to discharge the weight. A small side burial chamber is hewn out of the rock: only its dome – covered with earth which also slopes down at the sides of the *dromos* – is visible from the exterior. In the so-called Tomb of Aegisthus the access passageway is hewn from the rock as part of the circular chamber, instead of being built from huge blocks.

From a technical and ideological point of view, the *tholos* tombs are one of the most interesting Mycenaean architectural developments. Stylistically, they can perhaps be seen as standing at an intersection between the long tradition of European (and Indo-European) megalithic structures and the tectonic gigantism of Near Eastern and Egyptian architecture. *Tholos* tombs were first experimented with in Crete in the 16th century BC in a distinctive local form; they reached the Peloponnese in the period following Mycenaean conquest of the island of Minos.

188 (above) The impressive body of the most famous Mycenaean tholos tomb, the so-called Treasury of Atreus, stands at the end of its long access dromos, also built of well carved blocks.

188 (below) The interior of the Treasury of Atreus is built of beautifully regular courses of blocks, each projecting slightly beyond the one below to form the corbelled vault.

189 Two of the gold funeral masks found in the rich tombs of Mycenae. While probably not true portraits in the modern sense, they do give us a haunting impression of the great rulers of Mycenae. The masks were placed of the face of dead person – a ritual practice exclusive it seems to the Mycenaean kings between the 16th and the 15th century BC.

EPIDAURUS, IN HONOUR OF ASCLEPIUS

Another famous site in the Argolid is Epidaurus, home of the ancient sanctuary of Asclepius, which flourished from the late 5th century BC until the end of the Roman era. The town's magnificent theatre, still almost intact, stands in a wooded hollow of a hill not far from the Archaeological Museum. Beyond are the vast ruins of a hotel with no fewer than 160 rooms on two floors, built in the 4th century BC to accommodate visitors to the sanctuary. Its four courts with peristyles and fountains can still be seen. The nearby gymnasium and baths date to the Hellenistic era. They were linked with the stadium which was set in a natural dip in the terrain where the ground had been levelled in order to create long tiers of seating. The remains of the north Propylaea also belong to the Hellenistic era.

A Incubation Stoa
B Temple of Asclepius
C Tholos
D Temple of Artemis
E Propylaea
F Stadium
G Hotel
H Theatre

The most interesting area is within the *temenos* of the god, in the sacred wood where birth and death were strictly forbidden. Here a sloping ramp leads to the Temple of Asclepius. Attributed to Theodotus (380 BC), the structure is a fairly conventional Doric temple. Its pediments and acroteria were carved by Timotheus (a few surviving fragments are now in Athens). A wide range of the finest-quality materials – Pentelic marble, ivory, gold, exotic timbers, coloured stones – was used in the building. It replaced an earlier temple, converted into *enkoimeterion*: the portico where patients slept hoping for divine cures – some were successful, as witnessed by numerous votive plaques.

To the south are the remains of the Temple of Artemis (330 BC). But the architectural masterpiece of Epidaurus is the 'Tholos', a small, circular temple by Polyclitus the Younger (who also built the earlier sanctuary of Athena Pronaia at Delphi).

The Tholos at Epidaurus stands at one of the most important transitional phases in Greek art in the 4th century BC, with a move towards rich decoration and graceful structures, designed to create a luminous kind of beauty, as fleeting as the 'pictorial' effects of carved surfaces. It is as if, through art, solid forms were to be deprived of material substance and turned into shadows of a truth which, in that century of anguish, seemed more and more elusive.

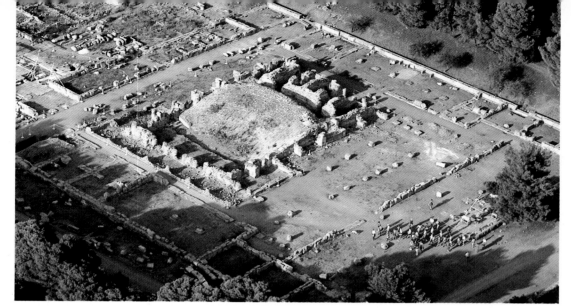

190–191 (below)
This aerial view of the sanctuary of Asclepius places it in its spectacular setting in a region of soft hills covered with pinewoods. It is not far from the Aegean coasts of Argolis and was on ancient Mycenaean routes (a well-preserved Mycenaean bridge is not far away). Epidaurus is today visited by huge numbers of tourists, who are especially attracted by its theatre where classical works are still performed.

MESSENE, A FORTIFIED CITY

A Theatre
B Temple of Asclepius
C Heroon
D Arcadian Gate
E Acropolis

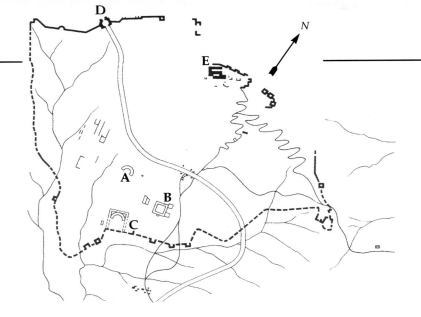

The coastline of Messenia is indented and the hills are rugged; only the plain of Pamisos, in the south, briefly interrupts the succession of spurs and ridges rising up to the sharp peaks of the legendary Taygetus range, on the border with Laconia. In the heart of the region is the city of Messene, on the slopes of Mount Ithome, close to the modern village of Mavromati. Messene was built in 370 BC by Epaminondas, mastermind of the short-lived hegemony of Thebes, for centuries the luckless rival of Sparta. The city flourished until AD 395 when it was destroyed by the Goths.

Its circuit of colossal walls is a truly impressive sight, built of huge blocks and forming a ring 9 km (6 miles) long

and 4.5 m (15 ft) high. Much of its north side – with the Arcadian Gate – can be walked along. This gate is the finest example of a fortified gateway in Greek architecture. Flanked by two towers over 6 m (20 ft) wide, its portals open on to a circular courtyard almost 20 m (66 ft) across. At regular intervals around the circuit are semicircular and square towers, and walkways once topped the walls. In several parts of the huge urban area – where excavations are still in progress – are stretches of ancient paved roads, with the ruts made by chariot wheels. Close to the agora is the sanctuary of Asclepius, with its courtyard opening on to numerous votive treasure-houses of the late Classical, Hellenistic and Roman periods. There is also the delightful *odeum* and – in a prominent position – the temple of the god of healing and other deities associated with him, with a huge open-air sacrificial altar in front of it. Remains of other temples are found on the summit of Ithome, while the ruins of the theatre and stadium are closer to the Temple of Asclepius.

192–193 Messene, on the slopes of Mount Ithome, is a surprise for many visitors to Greece as it has the most impressive surviving circuit of walls from ancient times. The great Arcadian Gate (above) has a 'pincer-shaped' structure between internal and external towers. Visitors to the site can still walk along a section of the 4th-century BC walls, bristling with towers (opposite). Research in the area of the sanctuary of Asclepius has uncovered a large temple in the middle of a monumental site including a small covered theatre (top left). There are also the flowing springs of Arsinoe (bottom left).

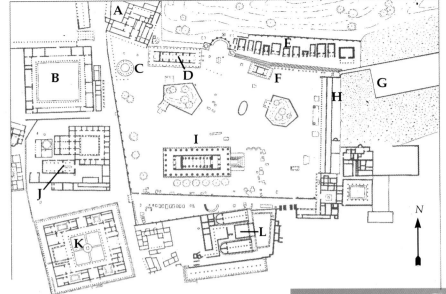

Legend:
- A Prytanaeum
- B Palaestra
- C Philippeum
- D Temple of Hera
- E Treasuries
- F Metroon
- G Stadium
- H Echo stoa
- I Temple of Zeus
- J Workshop of Phidias
- K Leonidaeum
- L Bouleuterion

N

OLYMPIA, ANCIENT CAPITAL OF PEACE AND SPORTS

194 (below) Seen from the air, the ruins of the sanctuary of Olympia emerge from among the remnants of the ancient precinct, the wooded Altis.

194 (right) An unusual image of the starting line of the stadium in Olympia, where the Olympic Games held in honour of Zeus took place from 776 BC to 395 BC. According to legend, the games were established by Heracles, on his return from the northernmost limits of the world.

195 (opposite) A spectacular view of the sacred site of Olympia highlights the symmetrical plan of the Leonidaeum (foreground), a hotel with a broad inner court with fountains for athletes and distinguished guests (4th century BC). This stood within an area on the boundary of the temenos *and was also served by facilities for training – a gymnasium, sports ground – and relaxation – hot baths with sophisticated sanitation, considering the early date.*

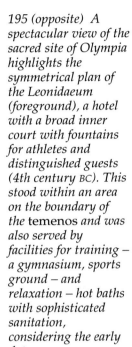

In the heart of Elis, in a peaceful and luxuriant valley at the confluence of the rivers Alpheus and Cladeus, the vast archaeological site of Olympia stretches over the lower slopes of a hill covered with pines that fill the air with fragrance on hot summer days. The ancient sanctuary of Zeus was the place where all ancient Greeks abandoned the political rivalries of their city-states and were united in worship of the gods as they celebrated their common ethnic and cultural roots. Every four years Greeks from all over the Greek world gathered in this sanctuary to participate in the Olympiad. A sacred truce was kept during the period of the games and attempts were made to settle wars and conflicts between the *poleis* based on reasoning inspired by Zeus.

Olympia's origins as a cult centre date back to the end of the 2nd millennium BC, although there is evidence that the hill of Cronos and the Altis – the sacred grove which was the earliest cult precinct – have been permanently populated since 2800 BC. Because of its remote origins, Olympia, like many sanctuaries, is a place of convergence of cults and myths centring on the figure of Zeus but also involving other deities and heroes. It was reportedly Heracles who brought the sacred olive tree here from the Hyperborean region and founded the Olympic Games to honour Zeus and commemorate Pelops. The part played by the river-god Alpheus, renowned for his love of the nymph Arethusa in Syracuse, testifies to the link with the Western Greeks. And the fact that the hero Pelops came from the east emphasized the sanctuary's equally important bonds with lands colonized by Greeks even before the coasts of Italy and Sicily. Pelops' defeat of the cruel king Oenomaus in the legendary chariot race is commemorated on one of the temple's pediments. The entire region, the Peloponnese, is named after him. Lastly there was Hera, wife of Zeus, to whom a temple was dedicated when, following an ancient custom, the lord of Olympus was worshipped in the Altis, on an open-air altar of which no trace remains.

The site – with its sacred buildings and complex of structures and facilities for athletes, and also for visitors, pilgrims and groups who came to the sanctuary at other times – had none of the scenic splendour of the sanctuary of Apollo at Delphi. Olympia's prestige stemmed instead from its vast dimensions, its monumental buildings and its works of art. From the 7th century BC to the 4th century AD – when the emperor Theodosius I brought about the demise of Olympia with his ban on pagan cults and the suspension of the games – countless votive treasuries and other structures were built all over the area. Some impression of

196 An almost complete view of the Temple of Zeus shows its colossal body. The ruins of the wide ramp for access to the pronaos *and those of the* cella *are clearly visible – it was in the* cella *that the famous, huge gold and ivory statue of the god, perhaps the last masterpiece by the great Phidias, was kept.*

196 (below) This aerial view of Olympia highlights the bouleuterion. This arrangement consists of two apsidal buildings, perhaps preserving an ancient tradition, with a third structure between, perhaps a courtyard, where the altar of Zeus Horchios once stood, on which athletes took their oath before the games began.

their grandeur can be gained from the scale relief models exhibited in the Archaeological Museum. Near this are the ruins of the gymnasium, a huge rectangle enclosed by four porticoed wings where, as in the *palaestra* (wrestling school), competitors trained for the games.

A visit to Olympia is, above all, an opportunity to enjoy an exceptional chronological review of art and architecture. The site's treasures range from the Orientalizing phase of Archaism, through the Classical age – with magnificent works by Libon, architect of the Temple of Zeus, Phidias, sculptor of the colossal statue of Zeus which stood in the *cella* of the temple, Praxiteles and Paionios, pre-eminent sculptors – to Olympia's period under Hellenistic kings and, eventually, Roman rulers. To the visitor today, as in ancient times, the most striking feature of the entire complex is the Temple of Zeus, in spite of its now ruined state. The Doric temple, with a peristyle and two rows of columns in the *cella*, was built between 470 and 460 BC in stuccoed limestone. Decorating it were the two famous pediments, masterpieces of Greek sculpture of the transitional phase from Severe to Classical, and metopes depicting the twelve labours of Heracles, all carved by the great anonymous Olympia Master.

Through the centuries since the sanctuary was abandoned, numerous earthquakes have rocked the region and flooding by the two rivers has also had devastating effects. The entablature and sturdy columns have collapsed and their drums and capitals lie in pieces at the foot of the high steps of the stylobate.

The pediment sculptures, now in the main room of the museum, are unmatched by any other temple of the Greek world for the intensity of their ethical and religious content and richness of meaning, heightened by vibrant colours. On the east pediment, the legend of Pelops is portrayed at a moment of great tension, when all the figures sense the approaching destiny,

now in the hands of Zeus who presides over the scene. Pelops defeats Oenomaus, king of Elis, weds his daughter Hippodameia and ends the cruel reign of the king. Only the arrogant Oenomaus is unaware of the drama unfolding. The poses of all the other figures are only apparently static, they in fact betray an almost tangible sense of disquiet – for example the old soothsayer who twists his beard, already 'seeing' the outcome, a presentiment inspired by the god, and Hippodameia in a ritual stance typical of the marriage ceremony, or the young stableboy

playing with his thumb. A feeling of dynamism pervades the scene on the west pediment, where a fierce battle is being fought by Lapiths and Centaurs, watched by Apollo. It is an imposing representation of the eternal conflict between good and evil, justice and injustice, reason and base instincts.

North of the Temple of Zeus is the Doric Temple of Hera, with six columns at the ends and a double row of columns in the *cella*, built to a somewhat elongated plan in the mid-7th century BC, and richly decorated with painted terracotta sculptures. It was initially used to house votive offerings but, after the inauguration of the larger temple, became a kind of museum of sacred art within the sanctuary, itself one huge and ever-richer 'open-air museum'. More and more statuary was installed on the site, as attested by numerous remains of stone bases from different periods – heroes, victorious athletes, deities and political personages dotted the site in self-portrayals characterized by mutual glorification, somewhere between exhibitionism and veneration. Among the statues found here – now in the museum – is the famous group of Hermes with the

196–197 An artist's reconstruction of the sanctuary of Zeus at Olympia during the Hellenistic period. It was surrounded by a high precinct wall, enclosing religious buildings and hundreds of works of art dedicated to the god over the centuries – a real open-air museum. The entire ensemble was dominated by the huge mass of the Temple of Zeus, with elegant arcades, and the Terrace of the Treasuries in the background. Olympia is one of the sites that should not be missed in any visit to Greece. As well as its remarkable and romantic ruins, redolent of the site's sanctity, the Archaeological Museum contains a number of important works of art – above all the pediments of the Temple of Zeus and the Hermes with infant Dionysus, attributed to Praxiteles.

infant Dionysus, attributed by some to Praxiteles but certainly a masterpiece of the late Classical period.

Other outstanding buildings in the Altis, still in line on a terrace at the base of the Hill of Cronos, are the state treasuries built by cities including Sicyon, Sybaris, Cyrene, Selinus, Megara, Gela, Metapontum, Syracuse, Byzantium, Epidamnus and others. Here, over the centuries, cities stored votive offerings to the deity as lasting evidence of their gratitude and power. The 'Zanes', at the foot of the terrace, are a somewhat intriguing feature: this row of 16 statues of Zeus – paid for by the heavy fines exacted by Olympia's judges from athletes guilty of attempts (successful or otherwise) at bribery – served as an unequivocal warning since they flanked the tunnel through which competitors and spectators reached the stadium. The stadium itself had seating space for 45,000 people on the low slopes.

Another interesting monument is the Philippeum, a small, elegant, circular temple built by Philip II after the Battle of Chaeronea (338 BC) and completed by Alexander the Great. Its exterior has an Ionic peristyle, inside are Corinthian columns. The building once housed five gold-and-ivory statues of the Macedonian conqueror with his parents and ancestors – a lost masterpiece by Leochares. A faint idea of this outstanding work of art can perhaps be obtained from five miniature ivory heads found in Philip II's tomb at Vergina. Other buildings of Olympia worth mentioning are the 'Leonidaeum', a kind of luxury hostel at the heart of the sanctuary, with gardens and fountains; numerous sports structures including a wrestling school, baths and a gymnasium; and the spacious studio used by Phidias while working at Olympia.

PELLA, SPLENDID COURT OF MACEDONIAN RULERS

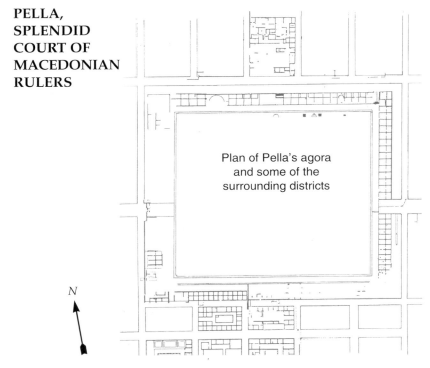

Plan of Pella's agora and some of the surrounding districts

N

200–201 One of the marvellous mosaics made of river pebbles found at Pella (late 4th century BC). It portrays Alexander and Hephaestion, a Macedonian officer and friend of the king, in the drama of a lion hunt – an event which we are told of by Alexander's official historians. The two men, naked like Homer's heroes, stand out against a neutral and unspecific black background. Trapped between the two, the lion, with its gaping jaws, seems unsure which of the men to attack.

Pella, the capital of the Macedonian kingdom from 410–400 BC on, is a required visit for anyone interested in the archaeology of the region where the first universal empire – that of Alexander the Great – originated.

Little is known about the city before it became the capital and its palace, where Euripides' tragedy *The Bacchae* was first performed, was built. After the Roman conquest (168 BC) and Pella's relegation to chief town of a district, its role was taken over by Thessaloniki.

Pella offers a fine example of a grid-based urban plan, with a sophisticated water-supply and drainage system. It had blocks of well-appointed peristyle houses, some probably on two floors, with mosaic-paved rooms on the

ground floor. The finest building was the palace, with its pebble mosaics of black-and-white geometric patterns and coloured figurative designs (around 300 BC), a few of which bear the artist's name. Among the best are those depicting Alexander and Hephaestion hunting a lion, a deer hunt, the battle of the Amazons and Dionysus riding a panther.

Also in this region are the royal tombs of Vergina and the palace of Palatitsa-Aigai (Aegae) where the Macedonian monarchy oversaw a renaissance of monumental palace architecture. The remains of the palace – of a truly impressive size, about 105 x 89 m (345 x 292 ft) – stand on the edge of a low hill overlooking a broad river valley. A huge, square arcaded court with 16 Doric columns on each side was surrounded by structures protected externally by high walls; the wide gateway was probably the only point of entry. The building was divided into spacious rooms with various features and functions. The façade was a worthy complement to the building's status; it was also the first example in Macedonia of the spectacular approach seen in the urban plan of Kassope and Priene, and which later became typical of Hellenistic Greek architecture. The high-quality materials used in the palace – from the polychrome stone pavings, to fine multicoloured pebble mosaics, true 'stone carpets', and the hardwoods – demonstrate a taste for luxury, as well as for spaciousness,

201 (below) Many wealthy Pella houses were decorated with mosaics, often translations in stone of celebrated works by the greatest painters of the time. These 'carpets in stone' therefore preserve their work, which would otherwise be lost to us.

202–203 (overleaf) The head of Hephaestion is vividly and realistically delineated in this detail of the river-pebble mosaic of the lion hunt shown on this page.

colour and light. It has been noted that the plan of the palace of Aegae is a monumental version of the central peristyle house, with its rational use of space. From the 4th century on, this layout was found in both luxury and standard private houses of planned cities, as well as in large public complexes.

204–205 (above) This view of the theatre encapsulates the beauty of the site of Dodona and its landscape setting. The inaccessible mountains of Epirus stand out around the green plateau which hosted the very ancient sanctuary of Zeus. Today the theatre is still used for performances of classical plays.

204 (right) The imposing external walls of theatre at Dodona seem almost to belong to a fortress. This effect is produced by the rustic work, which creates a pleasing contrast with the regularity of the courses of the blocks, laid using a technique typical of the time.

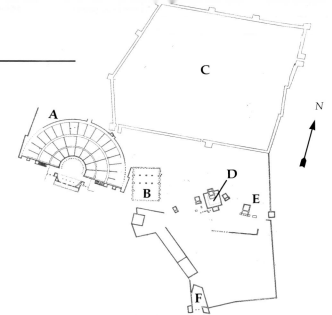

A Theatre
B Bouleuterion (council house)
C Acropolis
D Temenos (precinct) of Zeus
E Temple
F Propylaea

DODONA, WHERE OAKS WHISPERED TO MORTALS

Epirus has a varied landscape – from the peaks of the Pindos range to the rolling hills that slope down to the sun-lit shores of the Ionian Sea. In places the scenery is clad in lush green vegetation; elsewhere the land is stony and barren, its scant grass overgrazed by sheep for thousands of years and its trees largely felled.

The logical starting point for a journey through Epirus is the hill at Dodona, with its fascinating ruins of the Oracle of Zeus. This sanctuary, of extremely ancient origin, flourished especially in the 4th and 3rd centuries BC and was for a long time the most important religious centre in this remote region of Greece. Zeus' oracle spoke through the rustling leaves of the age-old sacred oak tree which grew in the sanctuary precinct. The priests who interpreted the sounds came from a small group of families of ancient origin, who observed ancestral rites such as sleeping on the bare ground and never washing their feet. Responses to questions put to the oracle were also based on the cooing and flight of sacred doves, the bubbling of a spring, throwing dice and the ringing of a bronze gong.

Between the 7th century BC and the Roman age the temple was destroyed many times and reconstructed with the same form, size and orientation. Built of large stone blocks laid in regular rows, the structure of 219 BC is still clearly visible. Access to the *temenos* is via an Ionic gateway, opposite which is a small temple on a podium-like structure, flanked by an Ionic colonnade.

Dodona also has a splendid theatre. It was built in its present monumental form by King Pyrrhus early in the 3rd century BC and enhanced by Philip V towards the end of the same century. Its enormous semicircular *cavea*, hewn

from the hillside just below the city's fortifications, is larger than that at Epidaurus. Divided horizontally by three corridors and vertically by ten stairways, it could seat 18,000 spectators. The massive retaining walls, also made from local limestone, still stand over 20 m (66 ft) high. Beyond the scant remains of the stone-built *proscenium* are the ruins of the stadium, partly adjoining the west side of the theatre and surrounded by 20 tiers of seats – further testimony to the religious significance of sporting contests in the ancient world. On the opposite side are the ruins of the *bouleuterion*, the 'parliament' of the Epirots, comprised of a large hypostyle hall with Ionic columns and a Doric portico in front.

205 (top) The sacred precinct of Zeus' sanctuary at Dodona contained the oak, whose rustling branches were used to prophesy the god's will.

205 (above) The stage of the theatre at Dodona is a typical Hellenistic architectural arrangement. We do not know whether this theatre – like that at Megalopolis in Arcadia – had a system of equipment to change sets.

206 (right) A view of Apollo's temple at Delphi, built in 373 BC, with tall Doric columns made up of thick cylindrical sections stacked on top of one another. In its adyton, *the god's oracle spoke through the Pythian priestess.*

206–207 A jewel of the first half of 380 BC, the famous Tholos of Delphi is a work by Theodorus of Phocaea in Athena Pronaia's sanctuary. Its elegance is made even richer by its fine proportions, by the deliberate choice of balanced colour contrasts between the materials used, and by the architectural decoration, some traces of which still survive on part of the peristyle – a good example of variations on the theme of the Doric frieze.

DELPHI, THE NAVEL OF THE WORLD

A Stadium
B Hieron (sacred precinct)
C Sacred Way
D Theatre
E Temple of Apollo
F Castalian spring
G Gymnasium
H Marmaria
I Tholos

Delphi stands high on the slopes of Mount Parnassus, in the heart of Phocis, at the crossroads of important routes of the ancient world. Seemingly suspended midway between the 'glittering' cliffs and massed olive groves that make the valley below gleam like silver, the site has great fascination and charm. The celebrated sanctuary of Pythian Apollo was built in the Geometric period (10th–9th century BC), while the smaller temple of Athena Pronaia was added later, on an artificial terrace below.

The site had been used by the Mycenaeans for their chthonic cult practices. Here, as in many other pre-Hellenic religious centres, the new choice of a cult of an Olympian god rather than earlier deities is a sign of the last migration of Indo-Europeans to Greece. But the legend of Apollo's victory over Python, serpent-son of Ge (the Great Mother Earth), who stood guard over a rock chasm – the vapours from which inebriated men and enabled them to make prophetic utterances – had deeper significance than others. Apollo's triumph had stemmed from a 'necessary act of violence' over the primitive ferocity symbolized by Python. Implicit in this deed was the determination to do away with the barbarities of the 'dark ages', instead enforcing civilized behaviour and law and order, and establishing reason, equilibrium, knowledge and creative skills as the god's gifts. According to the legend, Apollo was the appointed protector of the mysterious, primordial natural force emitted by the chasm; likewise, he was endowed with its powers. Disclosure of the oracular prophecies was delegated to the Pythian priestess, whose utterances were interpreted by attendant priests. It is therefore not difficult to see why

Delphi had such a prominent role in religious and political matters, especially in the 7th and 6th centuries BC. Here, at the 'navel of the world', all initiatives of the Greeks – from founding colonies to wars between city-states – were condoned or vetoed by word of the deity, through the prophecies and answers of the oracle.

Proof of the importance of Delphi comes from the impressive ruins of the sanctuaries of Apollo and Athena, with their imposing buildings (stadium, theatre, gymnasium, hotels) for the celebration of the Pythian Festival, with contests in arts and sport held in honour of the god.

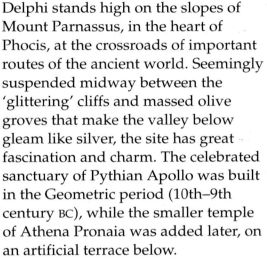

207 (right) Delphi, according to an ancient myth, was at the centre of the earth. This 5th-century BC copy of the famous omphalos, an 'umbilicus' wrapped in the sacred net, is a reminder of that myth. The stone was also the funeral symbol of god Python, the son of Ge, the Earth, murdered by Apollo who inherited his precious oracle.

207 (above) An unusual view of the Treasury of the Athenians at Delphi reveals the marked slope of the site of the sanctuary, which was built on a pre-existing settlement of the Mycenaean period. Delphi is in a spectacular situation and contains fascinating ruins of many different ages. The famous Byzantine monastery of Osios Loukas is close by.

208 (below) Still a destination for visitors to the site today, the romantic rocky setting of the Castalian spring is between Athena's and Apollo's sanctuaries.

208–209 (right) The well-preserved auditorium of the theatre at Delphi stands on top of the sanctuary's hill, not far from the stadium, as in other Greek sanctuaries.

209 (opposite, above left) On a terrace east of Athena Pronaia's sanctuary was the gymnasium. This was where the athletes trained before taking part in the Pythian Games in Apollo's honour.

209 (opposite, above right) The stadium for the Pythian Games seen from the starting posts appears as a grand structure bordered by high tiers of seats.

Delphi is full of works of art, ornamental structures, altars and 'treasures', in particular the treasuries built here by many cities of the Greek world – from Asian Ionia to the Cyclades, from the colonies to Attica and the Peloponnese – as temples to house offerings and as a show of propaganda, opulence and prestige. From the 6th to the 4th century BC, governments, tyrannies or, later, monarchs and magistrates, commissioned hundreds of building projects in the huge *temenos* of Delphi, on either side of the Sacred Way which zigzags up the hill. There is no evidence of any planning scheme: buildings of different – and sometimes chronologically far distant – periods occupy adjoining areas, with no regard for existing orientations. Nor is there any trace of changes to the urban fabric: in Delphi, as in other sanctuaries, new structures were added but none were demolished, while those damaged by natural disasters or the ravages of time were repaired or faithfully rebuilt.

Built in the 6th and 5th centuries BC with huge stone blocks, the Sacred Precinct has nine gateways, the largest on the southeast side, where there is a Roman agora, flanked by porticoes

with shops selling votive offerings and souvenirs. The Sacred Way begins here. All around are bases of statues erected by Greek cities in the 5th and 4th centuries BC as memorials to important events in their history. Today we can get only a faint idea of the once fabulous collection of offerings, often in bronze, that embellished the precinct from the first ramp beyond the entrance. This spectacular sight did not stem from co-ordinated efforts of architects and urban planners, as in the Hellenistic world: it was simply the outcome of chance affinities or – perhaps – contrasts between monuments designed to glorify one Greek *polis* or another.

Further along the path is the first of the series of treasuries built in honour of Apollo by the city-states of the Greek world: Sicyon, Thebes, Megara, Syracuse, Cnidos, Corinth and many others whose identity we are unsure of. Of these only scant traces now remain, with fragments of sculpture and architectural ornamentation. The Siphnian Treasury and the Treasury of the Athenians are two exceptional testimonials of Archaic and Severe style architecture and sculpture. Only the foundations of the Siphnian Treasury are still visible – all remains of the building are now in the Archaeological Museum on the site. It was an Ionic temple, with two elegant caryatids as original replacements for the columns between the side walls of the *pronaos*. Built in 530–525 BC, it is one of the most eloquent examples of late Archaic art; especially notable are the north and east sides of its frieze, on which a battle between the gods and giants and the council of the gods on Olympus are portrayed with outstanding vibrancy, plasticity and bold use of space.

210 *Agias, an almost intact statue dedicated by the Thessalian Daochos II to the champion boxer and his fellow-citizen and attributed to Lysippus (337–336 BC). The athlete stands on his long legs, one taut the other relaxed, in a pose typical of the artist. His gaze is lost in a far-away point and the beautiful face is free of marks of blows – the athlete as an ancient mythical hero.*

211 *(opposite, left) A dramatic moment in the clash between gods and giants – a detail from the late Archaic Ionic frieze of Treasury of the Siphnians at Delphi. This stood at the side of the Sacred Way travelled by pilgrims seeking a response from the god of wisdom and the arts.*

211 *(opposite, right) A much admired work in the Archaeological Museum of Delphi is this statue group from the top of a votive white Greek marble column, over 13 m (43 ft) high, offered by the Athenians in 335–325 BC. It represents three dancing* korai *on top of a wide capital decorated with acanthus leaves and is one of the best expressions of late 4th-century BC art from Athens.*

The Treasury of the Athenians was built after the battle of Marathon (490 BC) to display some of the spoils taken from the Persians. Now beautifully restored, it stands almost intact in its original position. This temple is similar in plan and just slightly larger than the Siphnian Treasury below it, but constructed in the Doric order. Its most significant features are the simple harmony of its proportions and a frieze with alternating triglyphs and metopes depicting the battle between Greeks and Amazons, the adventures of Theseus and the labours of Heracles, in a Severe style still with late Archaic elements.

The overall visual impact of the area occupied by the Treasuries can now only be restored on paper. These buildings once conveyed powerful political messages: for example, after its crushing victory over the Athenians in the Peloponnesian War, Syracuse built its Delphi treasury directly opposite the Athenian one, which had become the symbol of Greek independence.

The most important building in the main sanctuary was, of course, the Temple of Apollo. The remains visible today are the sixth construction phase, which follows the dimensions of the previous Archaic temple. It is a classic Doric hexastyle, peripteral structure built of limestone and tufa with stuccoed tufa columns; resting on its artificial base was a stylobate with three steps. Throughout the temple were works of art and objects of cult and historical significance. As was frequently the case with important Greek sanctuaries, the temple and its surroundings had a secondary role as a sacred art museum. The imposing forms of the temple must have dwarfed surrounding buildings, and was situated significantly about halfway between the two springs and the chasm traditionally associated with the Pythian Oracle and its rituals.

High above the temple terrace is the theatre, in an excellent state of preservation. Following Greek custom, it was built on the mountain

slope and completes the panorama of structures of the sanctuary complex. It was reached by an elegant semicircle of frescoed porticoes, decorated with sculptures and offerings in gleaming bronze. That of the tyrant Polyzalus of Gela, dated 475 BC, was particularly famous. It showed a chariot group, of which the splendid 'Charioteer' has survived.

Outside the *temenos* was the stadium where the athletic events and horse races of the Pythian Games took place, watched by as many as 70,000 spectators. Partly cut from the hillside, it was about 180 m (590 ft) long and surrounded by tiered seating on a high podium. In a picturesque setting along the road leading to the sanctuary of Athena Pronaia are the remains of the sacred Castalian spring, in which priests and pilgrims purified themselves before their encounter with Apollo. Although smaller, the lower sanctuary incorporates the ruins of the two Archaic temples of Athena: the first of the two – very significant for the evolution of the Doric capital – still bears evidence of a disastrous landslide which destroyed much of the building. A short way further on is the splendid moulding on a high foundation plinth of the Treasury of the Massalians (530 BC), which had rare Aeolic capitals (now in the Museum).

The most fascinating building in the precinct is the Tholos (380–370 BC), a masterpiece by the architect Theodorus of Phocaea: the origins of this rather rare rotunda-like form may well be found in prehistoric traditions.

212 Among the most famous Archaic Greek statues are undoubtedly the twins Cleobis and Biton, of around 580 BC and dedicated to the two youths who devoutly sacrificed themselves in the Delphi sanctuary to help their mother, a priestess of Hera. The heavy forms and the sharp features are typical of the Archaic style.

212 Some idea of the appearance of chryselephantine (gold and ivory) statues in ancient art is provided by this superb gold-plated ivory head dating to the 6th century BC. It was found, together with many other equally important and valuable pieces, in a sort of warehouse concealed in front of the Stoa of the Athenians, along the Sacred Way, just below the Temple of Apollo.

An Attic influence is seen in the building's elements – its proportions, mathematical ratios and style – as is amply demonstrated by the external *peribolos* of 20 Doric pillars which follow the standard set by Ictinus, architect of the Parthenon. But there are also new features: an innovative configuration of the limited internal space and application of the Corinthian order to the ten columns of the *cella* which – touching the wall but not joined to it – rise from a high base of dark limestone, in striking contrast to the white Pentelic marble they are carved from. The Doric frieze (repeated on the outer wall of the *cella*), the peristyle ceiling, still with its original coffering and the rainspouts show a modified approach to decoration, one that goes beyond usual frames of reference to introduce the common language and forms of architectural and artistic eclecticism subsequently absorbed by Hellenism.

The works in the Archaeological Museum at Delphi bear witness to almost three thousand years of history, brought to light by French archaeologists who began excavations in 1892. The very earliest traces of man's presence in the region are to be found here, together with pottery from various periods, grave goods, votive offerings and domestic objects. Some of the rooms contain finds of outstanding interest. In one room are several splendid bronze tripods, votive offerings to Apollo, richly decorated in Geometric or Orientalizing style. Another room is dominated by two huge *kouroi* of Cleobis and Biton (590–580 BC); around its walls are the remains of the beautifully carved Archaic frieze (560 BC) from the Sicyonian Treasury. All the surviving decorations from the Siphnian Treasury are to be found together, along with the Archaic Sphinx dedicated to Apollo by the Naxians (570–560 BC), once at the top of a high pillar. The 24 metopes from the Athenian Treasury are also displayed, as are the statues from the Late Archaic pediment of the Temple of Apollo (510 BC), attributed to Antenor and undoubtedly among the great Athenian sculptor's finest works. In solitary splendour is the famous 'Charioteer', an undisputed masterpiece of the Severe style. It depicts a young man in the tunic typically worn for chariot races, his eyes – of ivory and glass paste – still glow with success. Further on is the last artistic masterpiece of Delphi: the statues comprising the offering of Daochos II, probably contemporary copies of bronze originals by Lysippus (*c*. 360 BC), formerly in a prominent place northwest of the temple.

213 This disquieting Sphinx was dedicated at Delphi by the citizens of Naxos to Apollo around 570–560 BC and is marked by the typical iconographic and stylistic features of early Archaic art. It originally stood on top of a votive column over 12 m (39 ft) high and faced the god's temple. The Sphinx was seated on the abacus of a huge Ionic capital. Naxos was an important sculptural centre during the 7th and 6th centuries BC, and works by artists from this island are found all around the Cyclades, thus demonstrating the political and economic influence held by this small island over the central Aegean in this period.

Plan of the temple
of Apollo

N

214 (below) Near Apollonas, a picturesque village jutting out into the sea, is an unfinished kouros, 10 m (33 ft) high, of the second half of the 6th century BC. It still lies, as abandoned, in a marble quarry exploited in ancient times.

214–215 (right) The marble doorway of the cella of Apollo's Ionic temple, an unfinished work of the 6th century BC, is perhaps the symbol of ancient Naxos. It stands on a small rocky island facing the harbour of the modern village of Naxos, the island's main centre.

A great many of the hundreds of islands that dot the Aegean were inhabited in ancient times and preserve traces – sometimes of great significance – of the civilizations which came and went, from prehistory to the end of antiquity. Some islands are of such archaeological importance as to make them essential on the itinerary of every cultural tourist. Only a few, however, can be included in our imaginary journey across Homer's 'wine-dark sea', whose purple reflections enhance Greece's vivid dawns and splendid sunsets and do full justice to the poets' descriptions.

Other islands must regrettably be left out: Euboea, with Eretria; Chios; Thassos; Samothrace, once the home of the Nike now in the Louvre (its base still stands in the sanctuary); Syros, stupendous island of the Aegeans; Melos, with ancient Phylakopi; and Thera, with the Minoan town of Akrotiri, some of whose splendid wall paintings are illustrated in this book.

At the heart of the Cyclades is Naxos, the largest island of the archipelago, place of exile of Ariadne who, abandoned by Theseus, was consoled by Dionysus. It was the birthplace of enlightened tyrants, such as Lygdamis, and of talented sculptors who displayed their own brand of insular-Ionic Archaic art, their work doubtless aided by the fine-quality local marble.

The ancient city is not far from the modern town of Naxos. A number of eloquent examples of Classical statuary discovered here are now exhibited in the Archaeological Museum, which also has excellent collections of Cycladic 'idols' and Mycenaean pottery. On the islet of Strongyli – site of a Cycladic settlement in the 3rd and 2nd millennia BC and linked to Naxos by a narrow causeway – was the island's most important monumental structure: the unfinished Archaic Ionic Temple of Apollo (540–530 BC), one of the oldest of this architectural order. Among its characterizing features is a *cella* divided into three by two rows of four columns, with *pronaos* and *opisthodomos* with two columns and a chamber on the west side. The huge marble portal is still standing intact, its frame decorated with typical insular-Ionic motifs. Beyond it are the deep-blue waters of the Aegean, stretching as far as the eye can see.

At Apollonas it is possible to visit the abandoned marble quarries: lying in one of them is a colossal (10 m, or 33 ft, high) unfinished *kouros* statue, dating to the second half of the 6th century BC.

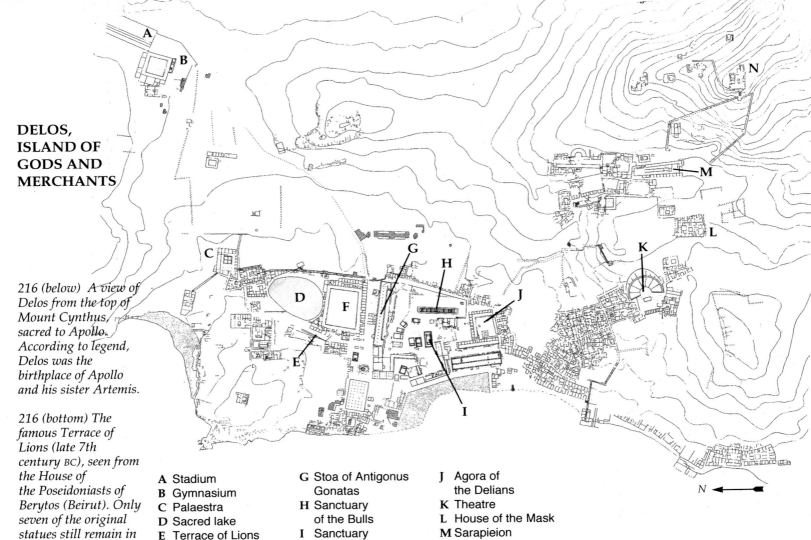

DELOS, ISLAND OF GODS AND MERCHANTS

216 (below) A view of Delos from the top of Mount Cynthus, sacred to Apollo. According to legend, Delos was the birthplace of Apollo and his sister Artemis.

216 (bottom) The famous Terrace of Lions (late 7th century BC), seen from the House of the Poseidoniasts of Berytos (Beirut). Only seven of the original statues still remain in place.

A Stadium
B Gymnasium
C Palaestra
D Sacred lake
E Terrace of Lions
F Agora of the Italians
G Stoa of Antigonus Gonatas
H Sanctuary of the Bulls
I Sanctuary of Apollo
J Agora of the Delians
K Theatre
L House of the Mask
M Sarapeion
N Mount Cynthus

216 (right) Two huge phalluses – symbols of Dionysus – stand at the sides of the god's Hellenistic votive chapel. Dionysian themes are also found on the sides of the tall bases of the phalluses.

217 (opposite) A detail of the Terrace of Lions. The animals all face the place where Apollo was born, the Sacred Lake, now drained for environmental and safety reasons.

Delos was the religious heart of the Cyclades and one of the greatest sanctuaries in Greece. This tiny island is the legendary birthplace of Apollo, who was worshipped here for centuries, even in Roman times. The archaeological site is divided into four distinct areas: sanctuary; city, with residential and commercial quarters; a terrace occupied by temples of the foreign gods; and the sports centre – gymnasium, *palaestra* and stadium).

Behind the ancient port and a late Hellenistic/Roman agora, used by guilds of merchants, begins the Sacred Way. Nearby are the remains of the stoa built by the Attalids around the mid-3rd century BC and those of the portico which Philip V of Macedon had constructed in 210 BC and which was 'duplicated' on the seaward side a few years later. In front of them are numerous bases of monumental statues. Another agora – the so-called 'Agora of the Delians' – attests to the organization of non-religious activities on the island sacred to Apollo. In the sacred precinct, behind the grandiose Propylaea (2nd century BC), was the unfinished temple of the god, a Doric hexastyle, peripteral structure (the only one on Delos), of the early 5th century BC with finishings added, rather badly, in the 4th.

218–219 (overleaf) A spectacular aerial view of the barren expanse of Apollo's island and its uneven coasts shows the unplanned layout of the town built around the god's ancient sanctuary. Here, where no man was allowed to be born or die, were based the Delian League (478–456 BC) and – also under Athens' lead – the Ionic Amphyctyony.

220–221 An artist's reconstruction of Delos during the period of its greatest prosperity, between the 3rd and the 1st century BC, when the Macedonians and later the Romans brought about its economic fortune.

222 (top) One of the most beautiful Hellenistic houses on Delos is this peristyle mansion, the House of the Trident, in the elegant Theatre Quarter, inhabited by rich merchants whose shops are still visible.

222 (centre) The House of Hermes in Delos, with its double row of columns around the peristyle, was probably the residence of a merchant guild operating on Delos between the 3rd and the 1st centuries BC.

222 (above) In the House of the Trident was a peristyle supported by slender Doric columns. The Romans derived their domestic architecture from such Hellenistic houses on Delos and elsewhere.

222 (right) A famous Hellenistic mosaic representing a Siren once decorated a room of a beautiful house, overlooking a picturesque bay on Delos, not far from the area of the Sacred Lake.

223 (opposite) A general view of the archaeological core of Delos reveals the charm of the island of Apollo.

Around the temple are foundations of numerous treasuries and several Archaic and Classical temples, all of modest size. Among them is the celebrated House of the Naxians, a rare example of an Archaic temple (7th century BC) with two-part *cella* and *pronaos* with four columns. Near the portico close by are fragments of a gigantic *kouros*, probably portraying Apollo, a votive dedication of the Naxians of the 6th century BC, and the Archaic '*Porinos Naos*' in which the cult statue of the god was housed.

Beyond the minor sanctuaries of Artemis and Dionysus are the remains of the huge 'stoa' –124 m (407 ft) long, with 48 Doric columns – built by Antigonus Gonatas of Macedon in the 3rd century BC, an eloquent example of the predilection for monumental architecture in the Hellenistic period. Amid these remains are some curious stone phalluses dedicated to Dionysus and the even more intriguing 'Sanctuary of the Bulls' – originally a colossal structure, supported by bulls, which housed a warship, a votive offering by a Hellenistic king.

Along the shores, north of the sanctuary of Apollo, is another series of monumental structures of the Hellenistic age. Prominent among them is the vast exchange chamber, once supported by a forest of Doric and Ionic columns. East of the sanctuary of Poseidon is the celebrated Agora of the Italians (2nd century BC), a grandiose precursor of modern trade centres. Here we are close to the oval Sacred Lake, drained in 1924, where swans and geese sacred to Apollo once swam. To the west of the lake is one of the best known spots on the island: the Terrace of Lions, named after its marble lions – survivors of the original nine – a superb example of Orientalizing

statuary (7th century BC). Further on is the Hellenistic residential quarter, with the remains of sumptuously appointed homes with central courts surrounded by columns, mosaic-paved floors and painted walls. Also here are prestigious houses such as the House of the Poseidoniasts, built in the 2nd century BC by Syrian merchants from Beirut. It was they who commissioned the famous marble group found here of Aphrodite chasing away Pan with her raised sandal. South of the sanctuary of Apollo is the residential area known as the Theatre Quarter, because of its proximity to the theatre, still well preserved and which seated 5500 spectators. In the 2nd and 1st centuries BC more houses with central courts were built here on a grid plan. Lastly, there is the steep path to the summit of the legendary Mount Cynthus, with a fine view of various religious buildings, culminating in the reconstructed proto-Hellenistic sanctuary of Zeus and Athena.

224 (below) The Temple of Isis, partially restored, stands at the foot of Mount Cynthus, in an area sacred to several eastern deities. It was rebuilt in 135 BC by the Athenians. A statue of the goddess is visible in the background.

224–225 (below, right) The theatre on Delos was built around the late 4th century BC in a picturesque hollow close to the harbour. The stage building had columns on four sides – the only ancient example of this kind.

225 (opposite, above left) Near the modern landing stage is the wide Agora of the Compitaliasts of Delos, a group of Roman merchants operating on the island who had their own business headquarters and religious centre.

225 (opposite, above right) A view of the prosperous Theatre Quarter on Delos includes the statues of the Athenian couple Cleopatra and Dioscurides, the owners of this fine Hellenistic mansion.

226–227 (above) A reconstruction of the Sanctuary of Athena Lindia. It stood in the most spectacular site on the island of Rhodes, on a sort of natural acropolis from which one of the best views in Greece may be enjoyed. The complex, built in its monumental form between the 3rd and the 2nd centuries BC, is a good example of the theatrical architecture of the Hellenistic age in Ionia and the Dodecanese.

226 (right) The high rocky cliffs of Lindos, still surrounded by Byzantine walls that were enlarged in the 15th century, give a good impression picturesque site chosen for Athena's temple.

LINDOS, THE SANCTUARY OF ATHENA

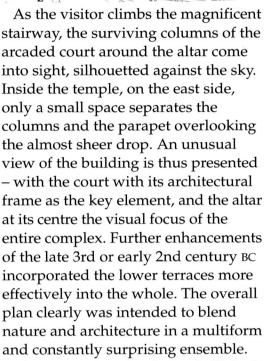

A Sanctuary
  of Athena Lindia
B Great stoa
C Propylaea
D Ionic stoa
E 'Ship of
  Hagesandros'

227 (right) Some of the columns of the pronaos *and porticos of Athena's temple on Rhodes still survive. They were restored at the beginning of this century and stand in a charming spot, near the island's wonderful beaches.*

Rhodes, the largest island of the Dodecanese, has many areas of great interest – among them, the ancient cities of Rodhos, Ialyssos and Kameiros. But the island's greatest attraction is Lindos. Spectacularly situated on the ancient acropolis, high above one of the loveliest beaches in Greece and almost encircled by the ruins of fortifications and a castle built over Byzantine structures, is the proto-Hellenistic sanctuary of Athena Lindia. The cult site is of truly ancient origin and in the first half of the 6th century BC a Doric temple was built on the very edge of a precipice, above a grotto where the first cult rites were celebrated. Between the second half of the 4th and the early 2nd century BC, after buildings on the acropolis had been destroyed by fire, the entire area was re-planned and re-built. The scheme was based on theatrical combinations of stairways and colonnades, typical of Hellenistic architecture, in Asia in particular.

The terraces of the acropolis were designed to direct visitors towards the temple, remains of which are still visible. This Doric building is positioned eccentrically with respect to the axis on which a series of spectacular structures were arranged. In ascending order these were the immense façade of a large stoa, a magnificent stairway leading up to the Propylaea and an arcaded court with an altar. Visitors to the Propylaea today are still struck by the simple combination of five doorways, each lining up with a pair of the ten columns of the façade, already visible from the terrace below, where the long portico adds to the overall grandeur of the structures. At the sides of the Propylaea is a reference to Mnesicles' design for the Athenian Acropolis – a pair of rooms with a columnar porch.

As the visitor climbs the magnificent stairway, the surviving columns of the arcaded court around the altar come into sight, silhouetted against the sky. Inside the temple, on the east side, only a small space separates the columns and the parapet overlooking the almost sheer drop. An unusual view of the building is thus presented – with the court with its architectural frame as the key element, and the altar at its centre the visual focus of the entire complex. Further enhancements of the late 3rd or early 2nd century BC incorporated the lower terraces more effectively into the whole. The overall plan clearly was intended to blend nature and architecture in a multiform and constantly surprising ensemble.

The sanctuary was also embellished with many works of art. There were votive offerings to Athena between colonnades, in the open spaces and along the steep Sacred Way. Still visible is a sculpture in the form of ship carved from the rock to form the base for the statue of Hagesandros, a follower of the cult of Poseidon.

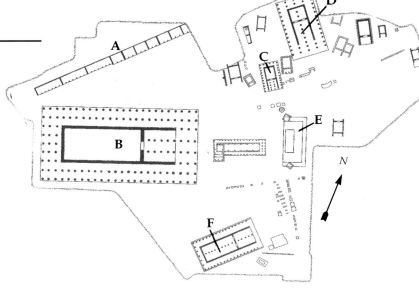

SAMOS, HERA'S CRADLE

A North stoa
B Great temple of Hera
C Temple of Hermes
D Temple of Apollo
and Artemis
E Altar
F Temples of Hermes
and Aphrodite

228 (above) A general view of Hera's sanctuary in Samos; the temple of the goddess was reconstructed repeatedly between the 7th and the 4th centuries BC. Here and in the Temple of Artemis at Ephesus, important developments of the Ionic style took place.

228 (below) Copies of a few statues of the famous votive offering made by Geneleos of Samos (c. 560 BC) are still visible on the site where they were placed to decorate Hera's sanctuary. The originals are now kept in the Vathy Museum on Samos.

228–229 (below) Another view of Geneleos' votive offering highlights its location along the Sacred Way that led to Hera's sanctuary, where architectural monuments alternated with works of art.

229 (opposite, above left) The only surviving column of Hera's temple is a part of the reconstruction of the grand temple by Rhoikos and Theodoros after a fire had destroyed it in 525 BC. The work was never completed.

The island of Hera – for legend has it that the goddess was born and married Zeus here – is a lush splash of green, emerging from the Aegean close to the coast of Asia Minor. Samos has a very ancient history: the first settlements, dating to the 3rd millennium BC, soon prospered. In the Dark Ages, Samos – like all the islands and coasts of Asia Minor – was occupied by the Ionians and an important *polis* was founded here. After an aristocratic oligarchy, the tyrant Polycrates (540–522 BC) led the thriving island, famous for its wine and pottery, to exceptional wealth and success.

The main archaeological site of Samos is the famous Heraion, built in the 9th and 8th centuries BC on the banks of a small river. Initially it consisted of an altar, shrines and a temple, about 40 m (130 ft) long – a *hecatompedon* (100 Greek feet). Its entrance faced east and its long *cella* was divided into two sections. Nearby was a sacred pool, used for ritually bathing the ancient wooden cult image of the goddess. The temple building was enhanced in the mid-8th and mid-7th century BC. But it was around 560 BC that it experienced its finest hour. Two local architects, Rhoikos and Theodoros, were commissioned to build a colossal new Heraion, with a different orientation to bring it on the same axis as an equally imposing altar. The complex included colonnades and was embellished with prestigious works of art, including the celebrated Hera of Samos, now in the Louvre. Here the Ionic order was experimented with and its some of its key features were defined.

The huge temple was surrounded by a double peristyle of 104 columns approximately 18 m (60 ft) tall. In front of the vast *cella* was a deep *pronaos* divided into three sections; the large pillars, with no fluting, created the effect of a true 'forest of stone'. The mathematical precision of their arrangement allowed refinement of proportions and balanced the overall perspective.

The remains of this building now merge with those of the incomplete reconstruction, begun during the tyranny of Polycrates after a terrible fire had destroyed Rhoikos' and Theodoros' masterpiece within only a few years of its inauguration. One column still stands amid the ruins of the temple, but the many capitals and bases give an impression of what the pillars looked like in the Archaic age, before volutes were used to decorate the mouldings of the *echinus*.

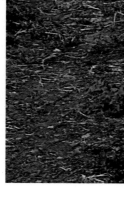

229 (left) A detail of one of the Archaic capitals of Hera's Ionic temple shows how different these elements looked around the mid-6th century BC.

230 (right) A wonderful view of the Acropolis of Pergamum shows the varied and impressive monuments built there between the age of the Attalids and the Roman empire. In the background, the white colonnade belongs to Trajan's Temple.

PERGAMUM, THE ACROPOLIS OF THE WINDS

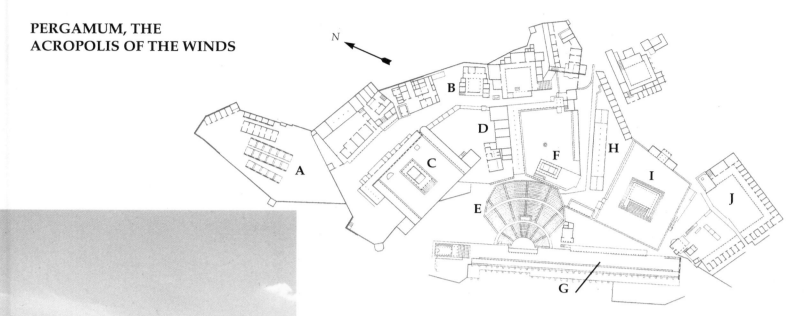

N

A Arsenal
B Palace
C Temple of Trajan
D Library
E Theatre
F Temple of Athena
G Great terrace
H Stoa
I Great Altar of Zeus
J Upper agora

Many ancient Greek cities are located in what is now Turkey. Listing and describing them would be a hard task; it would be harder still to include all those – from Sardis to Halicarnassus – which, although of predominantly Asian culture, assimilated aspects of Greek civilization. We therefore here describe just two of the most important ancient cities in Asia Minor: Pergamum and Priene. However, the reader should not overlook the outstanding assets of many others – Miletus, Smyrna, Assos, Phocaea, Teos, Cnidos, Didyma, Ephesus, Cyme, Clazomenae, Colophon, Claros – almost all of them on or close to the shores of the Aegean.

Pergamum – the impressive capital of the prosperous Hellenistic kingdom of the Attalids – is the perfect starting point for a journey back in time to the very roots of Greekness in Asia Minor. Its entire urban scenario stems from the vast monumental programme instigated by the ruling dynasty, and it provides the most typical example of a Hellenistic city. Its architectural shape is defined entirely by the division into acropolis, lower city and sanctuary of Asclepius – an approach designed to create a spectacular and awe-inspiring ensemble, in keeping with the flowery sentimentalism expressed also in figurative art and known, unsurprisingly, as 'Pergamene baroque'.

The upper city, encircled by substantial multi-towered walls from different periods, comprises royal palaces – large-scale versions of the sumptuous houses with peristyles,

230–231 (left) This wide-angle view from the Acropolis of Pergamum shows the auditorium of the theatre, perched high on the hill and in a spectacular situation.

231 (above) An unusual image of the capacious cistern that supplied water to the royal palaces of the Attalids. A huge system of waterworks provided the whole town with water.

232 (opposite) A detail of the battle of the Giants on the Great Altar of Zeus from Pergamum reveals the expressive power of Pergamene art. Its vigorous and deep sentimentalism has earned it the label 'baroque'.

233 (below) An entire hall in the Berlin Museum contains the reconstructed frieze of the Great Altar of Zeus. Here the ancient theme of the battle between gods and giants received perhaps its finest expression.

234–235 (overleaf) A reconstruction of the probable appearance of the Acropolis of Pergamum in Roman times, after centuries of improvements, apparently in a constant quest for greater theatrical and dramatic effects.

built in the aristocratic tradition – and temples dedicated to the cult of heroized deceased kings.

The system used to supply water to the acropolis from surrounding higher areas is based on amazingly advanced engineering works, perfected in Roman times. Several cylindrical cisterns and long stretches of pipes have survived. Still visible on the acropolis are the splendid and picturesque ruins of the sanctuary of Asclepius, with its 'miraculous' springs, covered walkways, porticoes to accommodate patients, theatres and hotels, all extensively altered in Roman times. Today, however, the most prominent feature seen from the

plain below is Trajan's magnificent marble temple, currently undergoing restoration.

Most important in terms of the history of Greek architecture and urban planning are the modest remnants of the once-imposing late Classical sanctuary of Athena. Built on a terrace above the dizzily steep slope from which the huge theatre was carved, the sanctuary complex had a trapezoidal shape. There were three stoas with a double row of columns, Doric and Ionic. One served as a *propylaeum*, framing the open space on which the temple, a classic Doric hexastyle peripteral building, stood. At the foot of the theatre, the great

ensemble was completed by a spectacular series of colonnades: prominent on one side – and reached by means of unusually steep flights of steps – was the Ionic temple and sanctuary of Dionysus.

All that is left of the Great Altar of Zeus, erected on a terrace over 70 m (230 ft) long and decorated with friezes depicting the battle of the giants and the legend of Telephus, are the sad remains of the *crepidoma*. The rest forms one of the main attractions of the State Museum in Berlin. Still visible nearby are remains of the agora of the acropolis while, on a lower level are the imposing ruins of the sanctuary of Demeter.

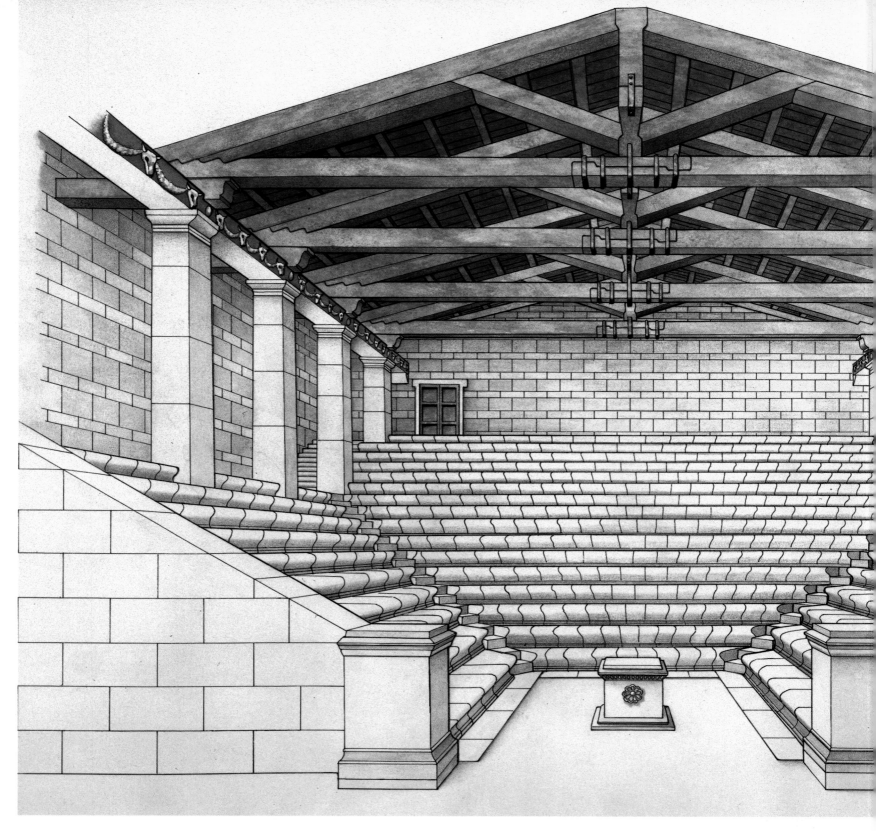

A Temple
   of Demeter
B Theatre
C Temple of Athena
D Upper gymnasium
E Stoa
F Agora
G Sanctuary
   of Zeus
H Gymnasium
I Stadium

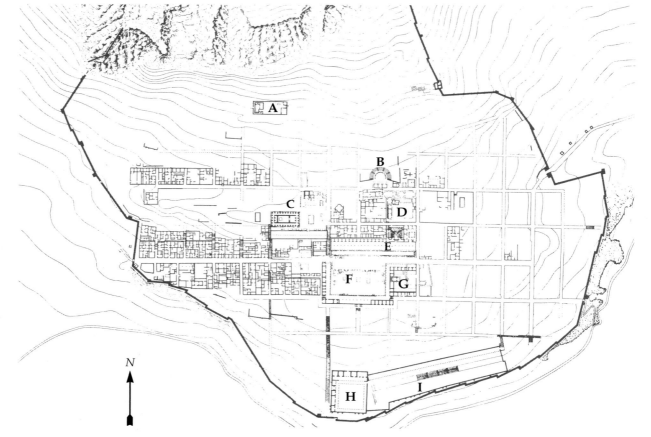

N

PRIENE, AN OUTSTANDING URBAN PLAN

The small, ancient *polis* of Priene, in Caria, was re-founded by its 5000 or so inhabitants in the mid-4th century BC, to escape the devastation caused by the Meander river in flood. Their chosen site was on the slopes of a hill.

Four parallel terraces were built in the narrow space between the cliffs above the river valley and the practically inaccessible ones closer to the acropolis. Excavations in the late 19th century revealed a rectilinear grid plan in the Hippodamean tradition. Set between the streets of varying widths are elongated rectangular *insulae*, with a harmonious proportional ratio of 3:4. As in Olynthus and Kassope, the residential quarters appear to encircle the city centre, with its agora flanked by colonnades, shops and the Temple of Zeus. The four terraces are linked by a series of north–south parallel paths, almost always stepped and therefore usable only on foot or with beasts of burden – unlike the east–west ones. The agora is connected physically to the Temple of Athena above it by a long, monumental stairway, which accentuates the temple's lofty position. Dominating the town is the theatre, one of the best-preserved of the Greek world, its tiers climbing up from the last terrace where the hillside becomes even steeper. The stadium and other sports facilities were intelligently sited on the edge of the first artificial terrace. Like the theatre, they are away from the centre of town, easing the movement of the thousands of spectators.

However, the most interesting aspect of the city is the spectacle of its entire urban ensemble, enhanced by an almost exclusive use of stone for its buildings. And Priene preceded the Hellenistic cities of Asia Minor, with their bold 'stacking' of quarters and monuments, by over half a century.

236–237 (above) One of the interesting buildings of Priene was the bouleuterion *or* ekklesiasterion, *reconstructed here. It was a wide meeting hall, with long rows of seats divided by access staircases on the diagonals. People waiting to speak sat by the altar. The roofing was probably supported by long and imposing wooden tie beams.*

237 (right, above) This is how the ekklesiasterion *of Priene looks today. Buildings with the same plan were found in other Greek towns of Asia Minor.*

237 (right, below) A few columns of the majestic Temple of Athena in Priene still survive, with their elegant Ionic capitals. The temple was built in the 4th century BC based on a project by the great architect Pytheos.

238–239 (overleaf) Priene probably looked like other Greek towns in Asia Minor that had been improved, rebuilt, or newly founded, with a regular layout of monumental blocks located in outstanding sites. The human, built environment blended with the natural setting – as shown by this reconstruction.

KNOSSOS, THE LABYRINTH
OF THE MINOTAUR

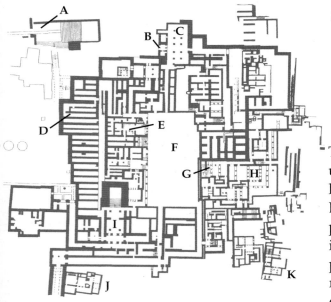

A Theatral Area
B North entrance
C Pillared hall
D Magazines /
    storerooms
E Throne Room

F Central Court
G Grand Staircase
H King's megaron
I South entrance
J South House
K South-East house

The gem of Cretan archaeology is undoubtedly Knossos, the island's largest and most important palace. During excavations at Knossos over a period of over thirty years, beginning in 1899, by Sir Arthur J. Evans, the palace was uncovered and partly restored. This restoration was based on sound, excavated evidence and today enables the visitor to recapture some of the colour and elegance of this great Cretan palace. Further evidence of Minoan architecture has been uncovered at Phaistos, with the detailed and meticulous excavations of the Italian School of Archaeology in Athens; and at Mallia by the French School. Archaeology has therefore determined the fundamental schemes and technical solutions adopted by the Cretan architects.

The surviving structures of the great palace of Knossos – for the most part rebuilt in the 17th century BC – point to outstanding skills in the design and organization of this huge complex. It comprised hundreds of rooms, often built two or three storeys high, cleverly adapting the structure to the lie of the land. The amenities included staircases, corridors, porticoes and ramps suitable for vehicles, arranged around a huge rectangular central court. One significant feature of all the Minoan palaces is the absence of fortifications. The materials used were a combination of wood and stone for load-bearing structures, which may have helped make them better able to withstand earthquakes. There is a logical distribution of facilities among the various wings of the palace, in spite of their apparent maze-like appearance. Particularly striking is the elegance of the architectural and pictorial decoration in the corridors and rooms, displaying a highly developed sense of colour.

240 (left, above and centre) The palace of Knossos in Crete is world famous. Thanks to its partial restoration, tourists can wander through its corridors and rooms (top), as well as climb its spectacular stone staircases (centre).

240 (left, below) Within the palace are rooms of great elegance and refinement, with plaster and painted walls and paved floors. Light wells allowed light and air to circulate through the elegant residential quarters of Knossos.

240 (above) A very characteristic element of Minoan architecture was the column which tapered from the top downwards. They were originally made of wood and painted in bright colours, here restored.

241 (opposite) The north entrance to the Knossos is one of the most interesting parts of the whole Minoan complex.

A splendidly paved royal road leads to the theatral area, identified by its well-preserved tiers of seating. A miniature fresco found in the palace shows crowds watching religious ceremonies, perhaps in just such an area. Another paved road leads to the west entrance and the so-called Corridor of the Procession, where copies of frescoes are displayed.

The main structures of the palace are all arranged around the central court. This is entered by passing through an impressive propylaea, supported by imposing pillars originally made of painted wood. From here the route ascends the grand staircase to the floor above. Luxurious royal apartments are organized on several levels and fitted with surprisingly sophisticated facilities and decorated with painted frescoes and geometric designs, once more in the bright colours so typical of Cretan art. Many rooms on the west side of the central court seem to be connected with cult, and also include the stupendous frescoed throne room where the alabaster throne is still intact, flanked by painted gryphons. In this area too we find some of the best evidence of the skills of the Minoan architects, who devised ways of bringing natural light and fresh air into rooms, chambers and corridors. Also on the west side of the palace are magazines, with huge *pithoi* (clay jars) in which foodstuffs were kept. On the opposite side are the workshops of potters and goldsmiths.

244 (top) Minoan architects made clever use of the so-called light well. This was open at the top and so allowed air and light to penetrate the lower levels of the palace.

244 (bottom) The Queen's apartment is decorated with the famous fresco showing dolphins darting among the waves. Other architectural features are painted with colourful flower patterns.

244–245 (below) The Throne Room of the palace of Knossos still contains the alabaster throne on which the king, or perhaps a high priestess, sat, between frescoes with images of gryphons and exotic flowers.

245 (opposite above) This view of the palace of the legendary Minos shows the different levels the palace was built on, linked with each other by stone staircases.

246–247 (overleaf) A reconstruction of the palace of Knossos in the Second Palace Period, after it was rebuilt following a destruction of around 1700 BC.

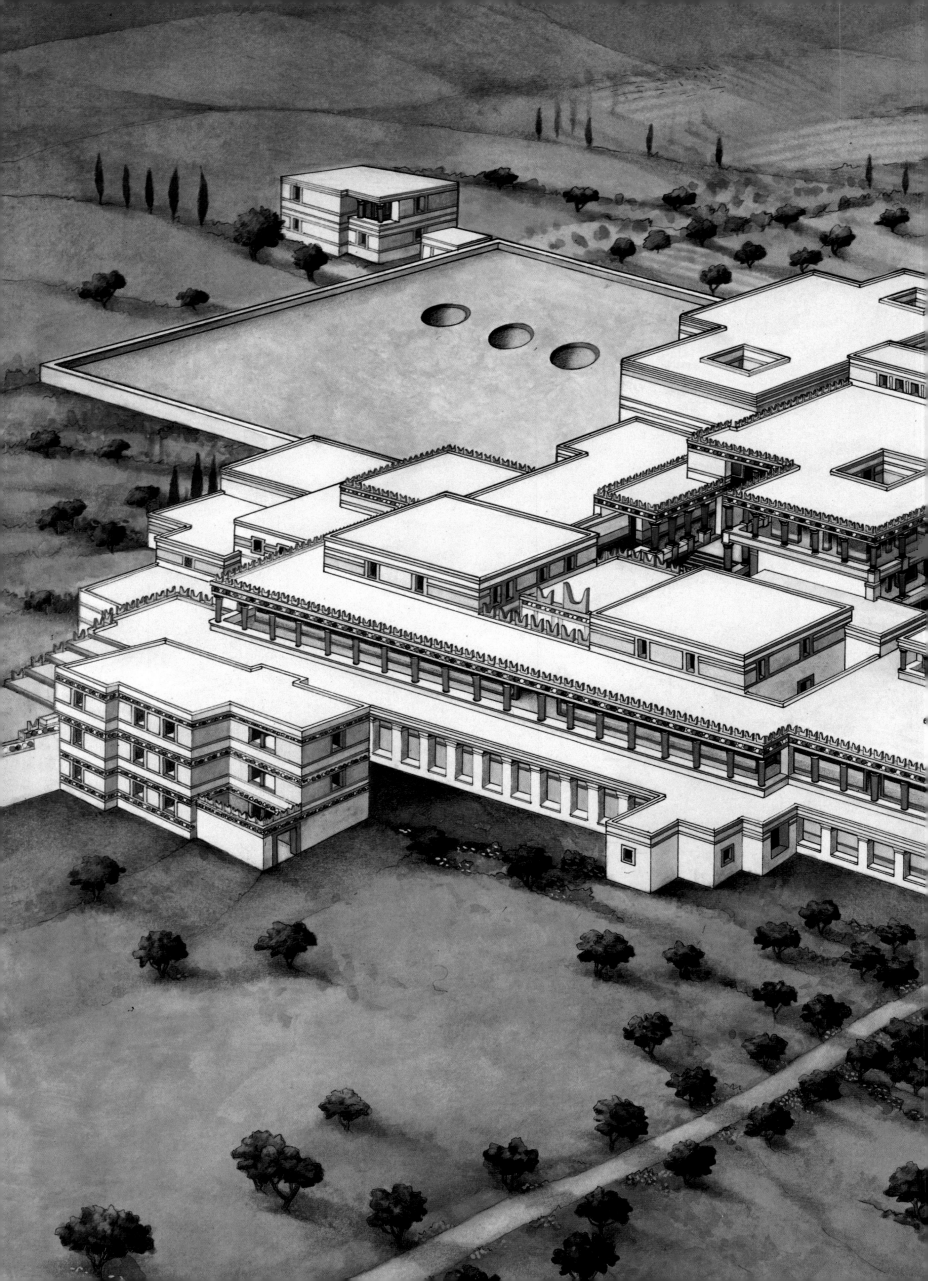

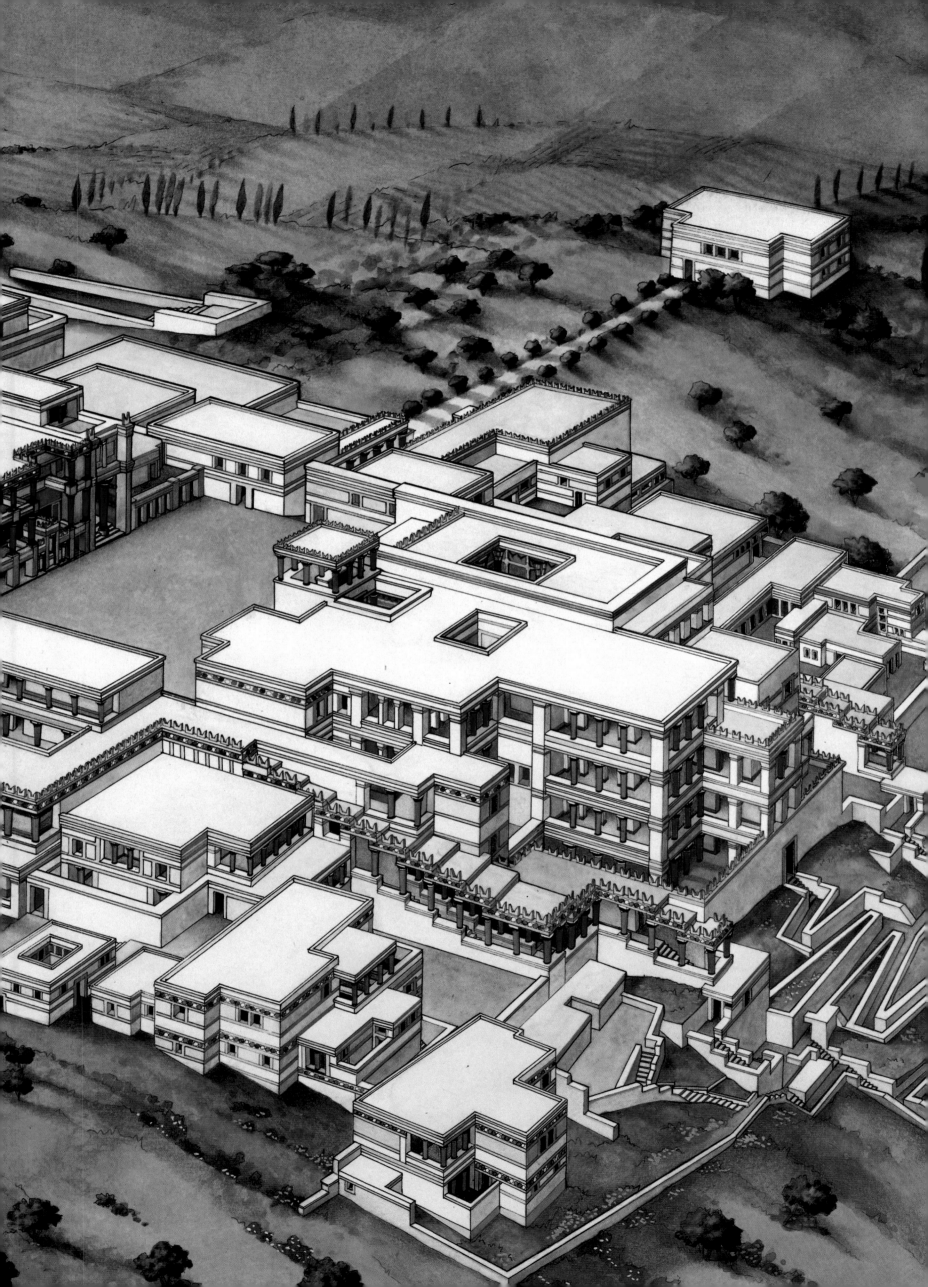

AN ARCHAEOLOGICAL JOURNEY THROUGH *MAGNA GRAECIA*

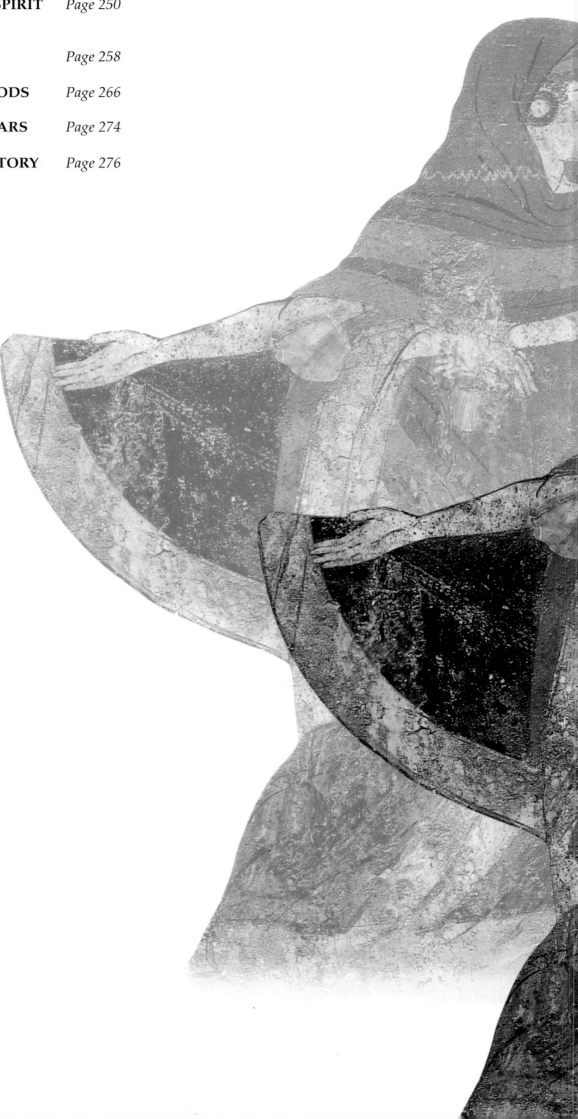

248–249 A fitting image with which to preface our tour of Western Greece, this is a detail from a famous painting in a tomb at Ruvo di Puglia, dating to the second half of the 5th century BC, now kept in the National Museum in Naples. It shows a choros of dancing women. Their expressive, natural faces are reproduced with confident and swift brush-strokes and can be compared with those portrayed on contemporary pottery of local origin or imported from Attica.

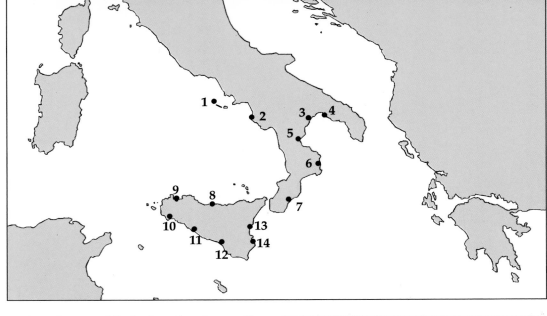

THE GREEKS IN ITALY: FOUNDATION OF A NEW WESTERN SPIRIT

There is no corner of southern Italy and Sicily – from Cumae to the Strait of Messina, from Selinus to Syracuse, from Metapontum to Tarentum – that does not bear direct or indirect traces of the ancient Greeks and their centuries-old civilization. From desolate, windy Daunia to the deep valleys of Lucania, from luxuriant Sila to the fertile lands of the Elymians – through trade, coloniziation and economic and political interaction – Greek culture was transplanted to the ancient heart of Italy, beating beneath the silent wooded peaks of the Appennines. Greeks once sailed the shores of the Adriatic from Leuca to the Po delta – a coastline with few safe anchorages and myriad rocks and unforeseen sandbanks – where Mycenaean merchants had already come laden with pottery and textiles, to the *emporia* of Adria, Spina, Mantua, among Etruscans, Venetics and Celts. Others journeyed across the Tyrrhenian Sea. Here their routes crossed with those of merchants and pirates, Phoenicians and Etruscans. They experienced risky encounters with Ligurians and traded with the Sardinians, buying and selling, selling and buying. They gave names to headlands and bays and founded Cyrene, Massilia (Marseille), Ampurias and the hundreds of *emporia* established in the far west of the Mediterranean, venturing further and further afield, sometimes never to return. Mythology and philosophy, fact and legend, abstract theory at its most sublime and practical efficiency at its most concrete: the west – and Italy in particular – owes everything to the Greeks.

To the nymph Arethusa and to Alpheus, for instance, we owe a tale of invincible love beneath the sea near Syracuse; to Pythagoras, a

250 The surviving columns of a possible temple of Hera at Metapontum of the late 6th century BC, known as the Palatine Tables, stand out against the bright blue sky of Lucania.

1 Pithekoussai	8 Himera
2 Paestum	9 Segesta
3 Metapontum	10 Selinus
4 Tarentum	11 Agrigentum
5 Sybaris	12 Gela
6 Croton	13 Syracuse
7 Locri	14 Megara Hyblaea

250–251 The fifteen columns known as the Palatine Tables at Metapontum still stand, despite being twenty-five centuries old. The entasis – a slight swelling in their profile – and the shape of their capitals are typical elements of Archaic Doric architecture. It should be noted that the colonies of **Magna Graecia** *were a crucible for experiments in architecture and town-planning,* sometimes far in advance of those carried out in the towns of Greece proper. Metapontum was a flourishing agricultural colony and trade centre on the Lucanian coast of the Ionian sea.

251 (right) The so-called Temple of Neptune, actually dedicated to Hera, the goddess of marriage and wife of Zeus, stands almost intact at Poseidonia, better known as Paestum. This wonderful archaeological site is in Campania. The typical local limestone used for the building has now taken on a warm golden colour, enhancing the elegant features of Doric architecture and the well-balanced relationships between the full and empty spaces of the colonnade.

252–253 (above) One of the most fascinating archaeological sites in Syracuse, and indeed in all Sicily, is the Castle of Euryalus. This complex system of fortifications was established for the protection of the town in the 4th century BC, under the tyrant Agathocles. His military engineers succeeded in creating a complex that was both virtually impregnable, and also adaptable to the different requirements of defence and counter-attack.

252 (left) A view of one of the galleries of the Castle of Euryalus, Syracuse, which allowed the defenders to move without being seen by the enemy. It also demonstrates the variety of solutions adopted by the builders.

mathematician who made Italy his home, the pleasure of numbers and the harmony of a temple or a musical score; to Parmenides and Zeno of the Eleatic school, the certainty that Being is one and unique, a delight in paradox as a means of guarding against excessive wisdom, hatred of tyrants, even on pain of death; to the tyrants of Sicily, deliverance from orientalization (as deplorable as westernization of the Orient); to the Greeks at large, an alphabet, countless words, dreams, projects, technologies and markets, the desire to read, the courage to risk and write, and always to face up to stormy seas – whether those of the mind and its eternal darkness, or those that alternate with calm, blue waters – the certainty of doubt and the willpower to be bold and change things. This is what our itinerary in *Magna Graecia* – however brief – is concerned with. But before setting out to explore the temples and houses of Paestum, Segesta, Syracuse, Selinus and Agrigentum, we must pay tribute to other outstanding sites of the multi-faceted archaeological heritage of *Magna Graecia*: Pithekoussai, on the island of Ischia; the acropolis of Cumae; Pozzuoli – once called Dikearchia – which is near Naples, with its wonderful National Museum; Velia (Elea), home of philosophers Parmenides and Zeno, and its splendid 'Pink Gate'; the colonies of Calabria and Basilicata – Metapontum and Locri Epizephyrioi; Reggio find-spot of the Riace bronzes; Sybaris renowned for its affluent lifestyle; the spectacular and solitary sanctuaries of coasts and inland regions; Greekness mingled with Italic roots in Puglia, from Salento to Gargano. And lastly Sicily with colonies forgotten and rediscovered: Gela, dominated by powerful tyrants and impressive fortifications; Megara Hyblaea and Thapsos, Leontini and Catania, Himera and the hellenized towns of the interior. Underlying this immense archaeological heritage are the very roots of western culture, which we must never lose touch with. For to do so would mean losing our last opportunity to rediscover ourselves.

253 (top) Temple E in Selinus, dating to the first half of the 5th century BC, is generally believed to be a Heraion, a temple dedicated to the cult of the goddess Hera, who was widely worshipped in the cities of Magna Graecia. *An unusual feature of this temple is that the floor of the* adyton *is higher than that of the* cella.

253 (centre) Performances still take place in the theatre of Syracuse during a festival of Classical tragedies and comedies. The auditorium is much less steep compared to others in the Greek world, and was carved from the white limestone of Syracuse, a resource much exploited in the past.

253 (bottom) The impressive form of Temple E at Selinus is an unforgettable sight for those who visit the Greek colony in western Sicily for the first time.

254 (left) One of a number of votive plaques found in excavations at Locri – a good example of **Magna Graecia's** pottery production. Made in the early 5th century BC, it is still bound to late Archaic forms in the depiction of Hades and Kore seated on a throne. This archaizing may be due to customer demand or ritual tradition.

254 (above) **Magna Graecia** produced works of art and craft in abundance. This clay antefix with the terrible face of Medusa highlights the development of pottery in some towns, such as Tarentum, which is where this comes from (dating approximately to the late 6th century BC). Such pieces were made using moulds, and often reveal close links between the colonies and the places of origin of their population. In this case, all the expressive power and toughness of the Doric style is preserved. This powerful Spartan colony was founded in 702 BC on the Ionian Sea and soon turned into a prosperous centre for the diffusion of Greek culture.

255 (right) This clay lion's head is evidence of the practice of attaching gargoyles along the edges of roofs to allow rainwater to run off, and at the same time producing startling visual effects.

255 (below) A clay statue representing one of the Dioscuri riding a horse, supported by a Sphinx with rather human traits, was an **acroterium** of around 470–450 BC from a temple at Locri.

256 (right) Italic pottery often took its inspiration from Attic pottery and even surpassed it in quality from the 4th century BC. *Production in Puglia, Campania, Lucania, as well as in a few centres in Greek Sicily attained an excellent level, as shown by this beautiful Apulian* lekythos *with red figures and overpainted colours with a Dionysian theme.*

256 (below left) The myths and legends of Dionysus and his cult are often included in the decoration of vases in Magna Graecia, as shown by this richly painted krater with volute handles (350–325 BC).

256 (above) This lekythos *dated to around 340* BC *is painted in the typical style of the Apulian town of Gnathia. It probably contained ointments, as indicated by the female subject in a sensual pose.*

257 This beautiful 1st-century BC head comes from Tarentum and is probably a copy taken from a classical, or classical-style, original of the Hellenistic age. It is made from the fine white marble of the island of Paros.

POSEIDONIA (PAESTUM), SACRED TO POSEIDON

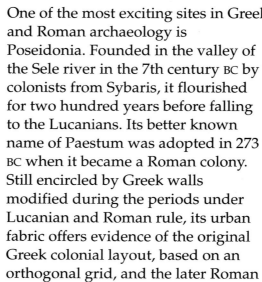

A Wall
B Temple of Hera I ('Basilica')
C Temple of Hera II ('Temple of Neptune')
D Heroon
E Temple of Athena ('Temple of Ceres')

258 (below) This small clay statue of a female deity probably dates to the second half of the 6th century BC. It was found in the southern sacred area and is now in the Paestum National Museum.

258–259 (right) An aerial view of the archaeological site of Paestum highlights the sacred area with Hera's temples I (the 'Basilica') and II (of 'Neptune'), still in excellent condition.

259 (opposite, above left) The two Doric temples of Hera, known as the 'Basilica' (left) and the 'Temple of Neptune' (right) have different plans and structures. The former, with nine columns, dates to around 550 BC; the latter is a century later.

259 (opposite, above right) In the northern sacred area is the Temple of Athena, known as the 'Temple of Ceres', built around 510 BC.

One of the most exciting sites in Greek and Roman archaeology is Poseidonia. Founded in the valley of the Sele river in the 7th century BC by colonists from Sybaris, it flourished for two hundred years before falling to the Lucanians. Its better known name of Paestum was adopted in 273 BC when it became a Roman colony. Still encircled by Greek walls modified during the periods under Lucanian and Roman rule, its urban fabric offers evidence of the original Greek colonial layout, based on an orthogonal grid, and the later Roman plan, based on a *cardo* and *decumanus*.

The ancient city was dedicated to Poseidon but had important shrines to Hera and Athena too. Built with the invariable east–west orientation, and a short distance apart, are the two temples of Hera, commonly known as the 'Basilica' and the 'Temple of Neptune'. Both were originally part of a single sanctuary precinct and are extremely well preserved. The Basilica is the oldest cult building in Paestum (*c.* 550 BC). Built of brownish local limestone, once stuccoed, it rises from an ample stylobate with a peristyle of 9 x 18 columns, unusual in a Doric temple, and an entablature of metopes and triglyphs. Traditional Archaic elements such as the division of the *cella* into two naves, the massive profile of the loadbearing elements and the heaviness of the ensemble are mixed with an unexpected taste for monumental forms of Ionian / Asian derivation. The so-called Temple of Neptune is the largest and best-preserved sacred building in Paestum, built around 540 BC in local limestone which, with the passage of time, has taken on a golden hue. Its proportions have similarities with the Temple of Artemis of Kerkyra (Corfu) and contemporary temples in Syracuse.

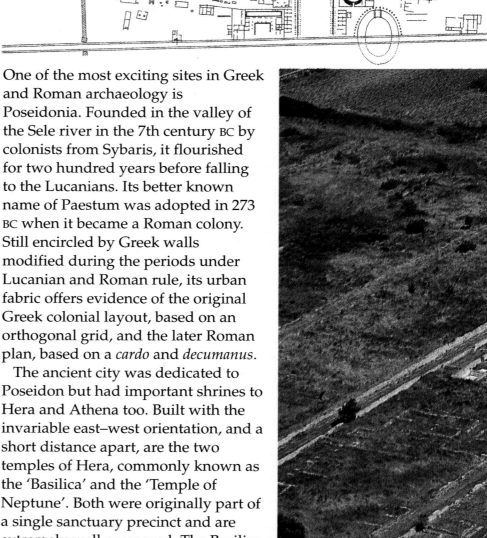

260–261 (above)
Another view of the
Temple of Hera II, of
around 450 BC,
highlights the overall
harmony of its
limestone structure,
originally plastered
and painted.

Slightly larger than the 'Basilica', it is a classic hexastyle, peripteral structure of the Doric order. The play of light and shadow produced by its peristyle softens the sharp edges of the fluting and the traditional bulkiness of the column shafts, which seem to defy gravity. The canonical decoration of the entablature and classical layout of the *cella* make the temple an eloquent testimony of the autonomy of interpretation and elaboration typical of the colonies. Taking the ancient Sacred Way and continuing past the Roman Forum and the remains of republican and imperial Paestum, the visitor comes to the Temple of 'Ceres' (in fact dedicated to Athena). It was built around 500 BC with classic Archaic measurements but already influenced by the Doric order (peristyle) mixed with the Ionic order (*pronaos*).

Paestum's Archaeological Museum contains one of the finest and richest collections in Italy. It includes the series of carved metopes from the temple of the sanctuary of Hera beside the Sele river, which are of fundamental importance for an understanding of Archaic art in the western colonies. There are also votive and ornamental clay objects, statuary, imported pottery and several beautifully crafted bronze vases. But the highlight of the museum is the famous group of painted limestone slabs found in numerous 5th- and 4th-century BC tombs – rare and precious testimony of Greek wall paintings, for the most part now lost.

The most important piece is undoubtedly the painting discovered in the south cemetery at Paestum in 1968, in the so-called Tomb of the Diver. This was a traditional tomb of the 'stone coffin' type: its limestone walls and 'ceiling' slab were decorated with extremely well-preserved paintings. Grave goods make it possible to date the tomb to around 480 BC, a reliable chronological framework for the stylistic analysis of the paintings. Painted on plaster on which the artist had first incised sketches, the frescoes portrayed a festive, aristocratic symposium on the wall slabs, while the 'ceiling' slab has an unusual theme: a naked youth diving into a pool of water. On the long sides, taking part in the symposium, are ten semi-naked male figures, wearing laurel wreathes and reclining on *klinai* – as was the custom – beside garlanded low tables. On the short sides are a young cup-bearer pouring wine from a krater and a female flute-player leading two men.

260 (opposite, below left) The Temple of Hera II, known as the 'Temple of Neptune' is perhaps the best preserved of all Greek temples. There is a pleasing harmony in the fluid rhythm of the columns and their capitals.

260 (opposite, below right) The cella of the so-called 'Temple of Neptune' is divided into three by two rows of slender Doric columns, like the Temple of Athena Aphaia on Aegina.

261 Another reference to the cella of the Temple of Athena Aphaia on Aegina made by the anonymous architect of the Temple of Hera II at Paestum is the double row columns in the cella.

Depicted on the north slab two men are reclining on a couch in an affectionate pose: their intense looks, tender movements and seemingly whispered words are conveyed with simplicity and elegance. Another pair of men are in the centre – one looks at the two lovers and seems to be saying something to them; in his hand is a *kylix*, identical to one his companion is using to throw wine towards another held by a single figure on the left-hand

262 (below) On one of the two short sides of the Tomb of the Diver is a scene recalling Etrurian models. Two guests, preceded by a female flute-player, are setting out to the symposium or perhaps are leaving it – thus symbolically hinting at a farewell to life by the man who was placed in this tomb in 480 BC.

262 (below left) On the other short side a slave pours wine from a huge krater standing on a table decorated with garlands.

262 and 263 (below) The two drawings show the original layout of the scenes in the Tomb of the Diver. On the long sides the paintings show five men lying on klinai and facing low tables. *Some are playing an instrument, others seem to be listening to the performances of the guests, others still are raising their wine* kylikes *in a toast.*

262–263 (above) Music has just stopped during the symposium: the instrument set aside and the plectrum still in his hand, the young bearded man wearing a laurel wreath seems to be turning towards the two men on his left, holding wide flaring wine cups, the *kylikes.*

263 (above) The interpretation of this diving scene is still a fascinating enigma. A young naked man dives from a sort of spring-board into a pool of water, in a natural setting reproduced with great simplicity. Is this a purifying dive into the next world and reincarnation, or a more straightforward reference to a sporting event?

kline (the game is *kottabos*, played at aristocratic banquets). With freshness and realism, the anonymous artist has captured a moment of the last toast at a banquet which – in this funerary context – does not just celebrate the symposium, a drinking party at which the friendship between guests was ritualized in festive style with wine, a refined and costly product. It is clearly a metaphor for life, a melancholy elegy dedicated to pleasure and *joie de vivre*, inexorably swallowed up by death. Interpretation of the scene on the 'ceiling' slab is important for a full understanding of the profound philosophical message contained in these paintings and the sophisticated cultural level of their audience. The diver is caught in flight between diving-board and water, in a natural setting defined by two stylized trees. The suggestion that the figure is a deceased athlete has been rejected. It is almost certain that the dive symbolizes the soul's journey to the next world: a dive into the unknown, which relates to Pythagoras' teachings and his doctrine of the eternal reincarnation of souls.

264–265 The impressive west façade of the so-called Temple of Neptune highlights the harmonious proportions of this building. It has a number of features which date its construction to the period of the Severe style, such as the 24 grooves on the columns instead of 20, which soon after became the canonical number, and the 14 columns on the temple's long sides, instead of 13 or 12.

265 These exquisite bronze hydriae and the celebrated black-figured Attica amphora depicting the Apotheosis of Heracles were discovered in the Heroon, an underground sanctuary in the agora of the ancient Greek colony at Paestum where they had been placed in 510–500 BC as part of a votive offering. One of the amphora's feet had broken off and been re-attached with bronze pins in antiquity.

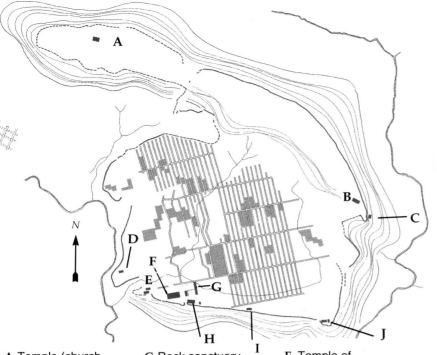

A Temple (church of Santa Maria dei Greci)
B Temple of Demeter (church of San Biagio)
C Rock sanctuary of Demeter
D Temple of Hephaestus
E Sanctuary of the Chthonic Gods
F Temple of Olympian Zeus
G Agora
H Temple of Heracles
I Temple of Concord
J Temple of Hera

AGRIGENTO, THE VALLEY OF THE GODS

Agrigento was described by Pindar as the 'eye of Sicily' and the 'world's finest city'. It was founded in 581–580 BC by colonists from Gela (itself founded from Rhodes and Crete) in a broad valley sloping gently down to the sea, between the rivers Hypsas and Acragas (after which the city was named). To the north it was protected by the Rock of Athena on which the acropolis was built, to the south by a ridge which eventually became the site of one of the most magnificent sacred areas of antiquity: the Valley of the Temples. Inside the city walls, part of its defences, Acragas was organized on a grid plan incorporating rationally distributed piazzas and streets. The city had an essentially agricultural economy, based on parcels of farmland and an efficient use of every cultivable area – to the extent that the gods were confined to temples on less fertile, stonier hills. Within decades, the wealth and political prestige acquired under the tyrant Phalaris made it one of the leading powers of Greek Sicily. In the dramatic upheavals in the region towards the end of the 5th century BC, the city was destroyed by the Carthaginians. It was re-settled twice, in the late Classical and Hellenistic periods, and enjoyed a period of prosperity under Roman rule before its decline in late antiquity.

The Archaeological Route to the Valley of the Temples and the remains of the ancient city is dotted with outstanding architectural monuments, and the Regional Archaeological Museum contains many treasures.

The city's archaic and mysterious past is evoked by the rock sanctuary of Demeter and Persephone-Kore. A vestibule leads to a double chamber

266 (left) On a high rock projecting over the valley are the imposing ruins of the so-called Temple of Hera, in classic Doric style (450–430 BC) and based on the proportional unit of the Parthenon. In front of the entrance are the ruins of a huge altar.

266 (above) A typical product of the small bronze workshops of Greek Sicily: a mirror handle in the form of a kouros.

267 (opposite) An architectural masterpiece of Magna Graecia, the so-called Temple of Concord (450–430 BC), probably dedicated to the Dioscuri. Its perfect proportions have become the symbol of Agrigento.

268 (right) The surviving corner of the peristyle of the so-called Temple of Castor and Pollux, built in the late 5th century BC, has elegant classical Doric forms which were modified during the Roman age.

268–269 Another spectacular view of the Temple of Concord, the most magnificent building in the superb Valley of the Temples which justifies its title of the Parthenon of Magna Graecia.

269 (above) A huge capital of Temple of Olympian Zeus (480 BC), the largest of all Doric temples, but unfinished. Its magnificent forms proclaim the largesse of Agrigento tyrants.

269 (below) The only surviving male figure that once graced the exterior of the Temple of Olympian Zeus. They were shown with their arms above their heads, as if supporting the temple.

hewn from the rock. Surrounded by fountains, its visual impact is heightened by the terracing of the ground. Close by are the remnants of a defensive bastion with outworks and a reinforcing tower near Gate I.

The best-preserved quarter of the ancient city is that built in the Hellenistic/Roman age, with a more rational arrangement of urban space and different building types of Greek and Italic origin. Beyond this quarter is the so-called Oratory of Phalaris, a sacred structure of the Hellenistic period over the remains of a kind of rock-cut theatre. The first structure encountered in the Valley of the Temples is the colossal Temple of Olympian Zeus (112 x 56 m or 367 x 184 ft), one of the largest ever built by Greek architects. Begun around 480 BC it has been completely destroyed by earthquakes which rocked the island on several occasions. It was a Doric temple with half-columns with gigantic male figures (8 m/26 ft high) between. Scattered around it are the remains of minor shrines and treasuries. In the Classical and Hellenistic periods the whole area was monumentalized with embellishments such as porticoes and piazzas. Still standing in the sanctuary precinct dedicated to the chthonic divinities, Demeter and Persephone (Kore) – whose cult was linked with the colony's agricultural activity – are four elegant columns of the so-called Temple of Castor and Pollux, datable to the 5th century BC but altered in Roman times. The Temple of Heracles (*c.* 510 BC) is a classic Doric structure, which may have had an open-air *cella*.

But the most splendid of Agrigento's gems is the celebrated Temple of Concord – in fact probably dedicated to the Dioscuri – still in a perfectly preserved state. Its meticulously calibrated and harmonious proportions are the result of a kind of standard for temple architecture, which seems to have been developed around 450 BC. It was doubtless influenced by Callicrates' stylistic experiments which reached their peak with the realization of the Parthenon and the almost contemporary Theseum, in the agora of Athens. Less well-preserved – but in chronological and stylistic respects very similar to the previous temple – is the Temple of Hera Lacinia, notable for its elegant peristyle.

270–271 (above)
The modern town of Agrigento forms the backdrop for the Temple of Concord. The deities of this subcolony of Gela had a magnificent and spectacular setting for their temples.

270 (right) This view of the so-called 'Temple of Hera Lacinia' from below brings out its spectacular position, anticipating the theatrical and spectacular architecture of the Hellenistic age.

272–273 (overleaf)
The blue Sicilian sky and the warm colour of stone: a perfect combination that enhances the beauty of the powerful and elegant Temple of Concord in Agrigento.

271 (right, above)
The surviving structures of the so-called 'Temple of Hera Lacinia' clearly reveal the search by the anonymous architect for marked effects of light and shade.

271 (right, below)
The columns of the 'Temple of Heracles' at Agrigento, a Doric building of Archaic date (late 6th century BC) have the heaviness characteristic of the age.

274 (left) Until recently the remains of the Greek theatre in Segesta were the city's most significant archaeological treasure. But excavations now in progress are throwing new light on the city's history and on details of its urban fabric and architecture.

274–275 (above) Standing alone on the hill, beautiful though perhaps unfinished, the Doric temple of Segesta is surrounded by an air undefinable mystery in its wonderful natural setting of green tranquil hills, dominated in the past by the ancient Italic population of the Elymians.

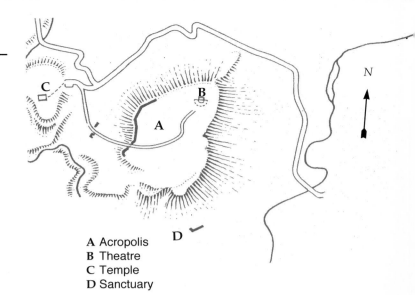

SEGESTA, THE GODS UNDER THE STARS

Capital of the Elymians, rival of Selinus and faithful ally of Rome, Segesta is one of the best known archaeological sites of ancient Sicily but also one of the least explored of the Greek world. Politically, Selinus did not in fact belong to this world but it assimilated its forms of civilization, most effectively illustrated by two buildings: the temple and the theatre. The temple, dedicated to an unknown deity, was built in classic Doric style in the last thirty years of the 5th century BC and its peristyle – of grand proportions, with 6 x 14 unfluted columns – and entablature are still perfectly preserved. The absence of a *cella* may not be due to the sudden interruption of building work in the troubled times of the last decade of the century, but rather may be a unique case in Greek architecture, perhaps arising from specific religious attitudes of the Elymians. In other words, the temple could have had an open-air cult *peribolos*, with sacred rites celebrated on movable altars, or ones made from perishable materials, under the 'concave vault of the heavens' – in Homer's words – rather than in smoky interior gloom. The proportions and dimensions of the temple's travertine forms derive from Attic models, and possibly also reflect the political links between the two cities at the end of century, when Segesta's growing ambitions were made manifest in this building. Although a monument with an evident political message, its design no longer follows the gigantism of the late Archaic and Severe style, but fits the architectural criteria of the second half of the 5th century BC.

Segesta's theatre, usually dated to the 3rd century BC, is very well preserved, at least in its lower part. An important feature, typical of Siceliot theatre architecture, is a scene-building with lateral projections or wings.

275 Two views of the famous Doric temple of Segesta, dedicated to an unknown deity. It was built according to classical models, with balanced proportions, though there are signs of decline in the artistic creativity of the architects and sculptors who worked on it during the last three decades of the 5th century BC.

SELINUS, A BRIGHT, SHORT-LIVED STORY

1	Site of the ancient city	7	Temple B
2	Theatre	8	Temple A
3	Sanctuary of	9	Temple O
	Demeter Malophoros	10	Temple G
4	Acropolis	11	Temple F
5	Temple D	12	Temple E
6	Temple C	13	Ancient harbour

Selinus (Selinunte) was an agricultural and trading town founded on the southwest coast of Sicily in 628 BC by subcolonists from Megara Hyblaea. Initially governed by an oligarchic regime, in the 5th century BC it was ruled by a tyranny, like many other Siceliot cities. The sack of the city by the Carthaginians in 409 BC marked the start of its decline; a period of modest recovery was followed by further destruction (250 BC) and its final end. The acropolis, with the most ancient temples and probably some residential blocks, is situated on a vast low-lying plateau jutting out into the sea. The town's residential quarters occupied gently sloping land to the north. The almost-perfect grid plan of roads and street blocks testifies to an urban scheme developed in the first quarter of the 6th century BC. Among its most interesting features are the rational arrangement of residential quarters, separate from the sacred area; the close relations between residential quarters, acropolis and harbour; and the orientation of the sanctuaries outside the walls, identical to that of the urban area.

The remains of the rich Archaic temple architecture of Selinus demonstrate a rational and aesthetic approach to configuring urban space and monuments within the landscape. Temples C and D and the vast southeast area of the acropolis, also reserved for worship, were spectacularly located within sight of the sea, at exactly the right distance from the main roads which imposed an orthogonal pattern on the plateau. Prominent on the acropolis was Temple C, built in 540–530 BC and dedicated to an unidentified deity.

276 (opposite, above left) Temple C at Selinus is the only sacred building of the acropolis of which a few columns of the peristyle still exist, in the Doric style. It had sculptured metopes in the high Archaic style.

276 (opposite, above right) A view of Temple E at Selinus, in the sacred area of the eastern hill outside the walls. Its peristyle and cella have been reconstructed.

276–277 (left) Temple C dominates the ruins of the acropolis of Selinus.

277 (above) The colossal Temple G at Selinus is now in ruins, with just one column still standing, the only witness to this huge building, begun around 510 BC and never completed.

278 Perseus brutally buries his sword in the throat of the Gorgon Medusa, whose blood gives life to the winged horse Pegasus. One of the famous metopes from the Doric frieze of Temple C, dating around 575–550 BC, and considered as one of the best examples of Sicily's Archaic style.

283 A damaged but still beautiful marble head of a goddess from one of the metopes of Temple E at Selinus (470 BC).

279–282 A reconstruction of Selinus in the mid-5th century BC, at the time of its greatest prosperity, before the dispute with Segesta and Carthage caused its decline. Note the location of the harbour at the mouth of the river.

Temple C was a classic Doric building with an elongated plan; its peristyle (6 x 17 columns), like the other structural elements, appears to be airy and filled with light. Many of its elements reveal a fruitful blend of Ionic influences with traditional Doric forms. Perhaps not always exceedingly elegant, the results are at least original. In the vicinity of Temple D are remains of Punic dwellings from the 4th and 3rd centuries BC, evidence of the reoccupation of the city by the Carthaginians.

The colossal Temple G, in a spectacular position on the east hill was probably dedicated to Apollo and dates to the last quarter of the 6th century BC. Its size (110 x 50 m or 360 x

164 ft) was perhaps one of the reasons why its construction took so long – at least half a century. The building is of the Doric order, with a large space between the *peribolos* and the walls of the *cella*. From the *pronaos*, three doorways gave access to the corresponding three naves of the *cella*, whose columns directed the gaze of the faithful to the small *adyton*, or inner shrine, where the oracle must once have been located. On the opposite side of the temple the *opisthodomos* conforms to the typical Doric blueprint. The voluminousness of the building is Ionic, reflecting a predilection for monumentalism typical of tyrants, who also came to power in Selinus.

Temple G is just one element in a crowded ensemble of sacred buildings sited on a small hill east of the city. But following a model common to other western colonies it is an expression – even more eloquent than Temple C – of the tyrants' desire to advertise the prosperity and prestige of the city under their power by excessive reverence to the city's deity and cult, a practice followed by contemporary tyrants in Athens and Asia Minor. In these monumental schemes propaganda, demogoguery and a touch of paternalism were mixed with traditional cultural and spiritual values of 'Greekness'.

Also of strong visual impact is Temple E, dating from the Severe style period, with unadulterated Doric forms, from which magnificent carved metopes have been recovered. Much of its peristyle and *cella* have been reconstructed.

Before reaching the 5th-century BC sanctuary of Demeter Malophoros (cultic prototype of the Christian Madonna of the Pomegranate Tree) and the cemetery, both outside the city walls, it is worth stopping to admire the substantial fortifications north of the acropolis. These include a long, covered gallery, a defensive ditch with towers and protected ramparts.

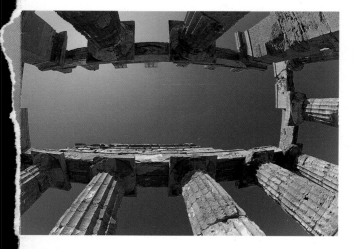

284 (top) An unusual view of the Doric columns of Temple E at Selinus against the sky. They stand almost as a tribute to the constant search of the Greeks to unite buildings and nature.

284 (above) The skill of the architect of Temple E is also apparent in the accurate layout of triglyphs and corner columns on the same axis.

284–285 and 285
(right) The peristyle
of Temple E, built
around 480 BC, has
fine, harmonious
proportions.

286–287 (overleaf)
It is generally agreed
that Hera, goddess of
marriage and fertility,
was the fortunate
deity to whom the
beautiful Temple E
was dedicated.

GLOSSARY

ABACUS a slab-shaped element, either square (Doric) or rectangular (Ionic), placed between the capital and the architrave.

ACROPOLIS the upper part of the city, often fortified with walls and embellished with temples.

ACROTERIUM decorative architectural element placed at the top or on both sides of the pediment.

AGORA marketplace, where public meetings were held.

BOULEUTERION building in which the council of the representatives of the *polis*, gathered.

CANON a body of established rules used as a model to determine the proportions of statues, according to a standardized ideal of beauty.

CELLA the principal chamber of a temple.

CHRYSELEPHANTINE made of gold and ivory, relating in particular to statues.

CREPIDOMA the base of a temple.

CYMA the upper part of a temple cornice or other monumental building, decorated with paintings or sculptural friezes, serving as eaves for the collection of rain water.

DIPTERAL a temple surrounded by a double order of columns.

DROMOS a corridor leading to the entrance of a monumental tomb.

ECHINUS the convex element of the Doric and Ionic capital, placed under the abacus.

ENTASIS the bulge of the column, used as an optical adjustment.

GYMNASIUM a place devoted to the moral and intellectual education of young people. where athletes trained.

HECATOMPEDON a temple with a length equal to a hundred Samian feet.

HEXASTYLE a temple with six columns on its short sides.

HOPLITE an infantry soldier equipped with heavy armour, consisting of a shield, spear, sword, helmet, cuirass and shin guards.

HYDRIA a ceramic or bronze vase used for water, having a bellied body, foot, a high and narrow neck and three handles.

HYPAETHRAL a roofless building or temple.

IN ANTIS of a temple with two central columns in the front and two pillars at the end of the side walls.

KOINE the commonly spoken Greek language, based on the Attic dialect which became widespread from the 4th century BC onwards in the central-eastern Mediterranean area.

KORE a votive statue in the form of a clothed young woman, typical of Archaic Greek sculpture.

KOUROS a votive statue of a young, naked, standing male typical of archaic Greek sculpture.

KRATER a large vase with a wide mouth, with a foot and two handles, in which water and wine were usually mixed.

MEGARON the largest and most sumptuous room in the palaces of the Mycenaean period, usually with a central hearth. A term later used to designate a large room.

METOPE in the trabeation of the Doric order, each of the square panels between triglyphs, carved with sculptures in bas-relief of marble or terracotta, or with floral patterns or with rounded shields.

NAOS in temples, the room in which the statue of the god was kept.

OINOCHOE a small jug, with a single handle, for drawing and pouring the wine.

OPISTHODOMOS the back part of a temple, opposite the pronaos, used for storing treasure.

PALAESTRA usually an outdoor space, used by young pupils for physical exercise, generally located next to the gymnasium.

PEDIMENT the triangular space in the gable of a temple or other monumental building.

PERIBOLOS an area surrounded by a wall around the temple, often adorned with statues, altars and votive monuments.

PERIPTERAL building or temple surrounded by an order of columns separated by the wall of the cella.

PERISTASIS a colonnade encircling the cella of a peripteral temple, or, more rarely, a building of another type.

PERISTYLE in Greek houses but also in sanctuaries, a court surrounded by a colonnade.

PRONAOS in the temple, the space between the cella and the colonnade of the front.

PROPYLAEUM gate building or buildings forming the entrance to the sacred enclosure of a temple or group of buildings, often monumental in scale.

RHYTON either a drinking vessel, of metal or pottery, in the shape of curved horn, often ending with the head of an animal; or a ritual vase with one hole for filling and another to allow liquids to flow out.

SKYPHOS a conical vase, with foot and two horizontal handles at the level of the rim.

STELE a tall upright slab of stone, used as a grave marker.

STYLOBATE the platform or base of a temple on whch the columns rested.

STOA a portico with colonnade, usually with a wall on the back, used as a gathering place.

TEMENOS a sacred enclosure, usually delimited by a wall or by boundary stones.

THALASSOCRACY a state founded on maritime supremacy.

THOLOS a temple, building or part of a building, with a circular plan, encircled by columns and usually with a dome- or a conical-shaped roof. Also a round, domed tomb, often monumental, particularly in the Mycenaean period.

TORUS a moulding of semicircular convex profile, forming a sort of ring at the base of a column.

TRABEATION in classical architectural orders, the frame resting on the columns, composed of the architrave, the frieze and the cornice.

TRIGLYPH in Doric trabeation, an ornament of the frieze alternating with the metope, consisting of a square or rectangular slab of stone or terracotta, with two vertical central channels and two half channels on the sides.

FURTHER READING

HISTORY AND CIVILIZATION

Boardman, J. et al (eds) *The Oxford History of Greece and the Hellenistic World* (Oxford, 1991)
Bury, J.B. and Meiggs, R. *History of Greece to the Death of Alexander the Great* (London, 4th ed. 1975)
Caratelli, G.P. *The Western Greeks. Classical Civilization in the Western Mediterranean* (London, 1996)
Chadwick, J. *The Mycenaean World* (Cambridge, 1976)
Coldstream J.N. *Geometric Greece* (London 1977)
Desborough, V.R. d'A. *The Greek Dark Ages* (London, 1972)
Dickinson, O. *The Aegean Bronze Age* (Cambridge, 1994)
Finley, M.I. *Ancient Sicily* (London, 1968)
Green, P. *A Concise History of Ancient Greece* (London and New York, 1979)
Green, P.A. *Alexander to Actium. The Hellenistic Age* (London and New York, 1994)
Harris, H. *Greek Athletes and Athletics* (London 1964)
Hood, S. *The Minoans* (London and New York, 1971)
Levi,P. *Atlas of the Greek World* (Oxford, 1980)
Marinatos, S.N. and Hirmer, M. *Crete and Mycenae* (London, 1960)
Meiggs, R. *The Athenian Empire* (Oxford, 1972)
Sandars, N.K. *The Sea Peoples* (London and New York, 1978)
Snodgrass, A.M. *Arms and Armour of the Greeks* (London, 1967)
Taylour, W. *The Mycenaeans*, 2nd ed. (London and New York, 1983)
Vermeule, E. *Greece in the Bronze Age* (Chicago, 1972)
Warren, P.M. *The Aegean Civilizations*, 2nd ed. (Oxford, 1989)

ART AND ARCHITECTURE

Boardman J. *Athenian Black Figure Vases* (London and New York, 1974)
Boardman J. *Athenian Red Figure Vases. The Archaic Period* (London and New York 1975)
Boardman J. *Athenian Red Figure Vases. The Classical Period* (London and New York 1989)
Boardman, J. *Greek Art* (London and New York, rev. ed. 1996)
Boardman J. *Greek Sculpture. The Archaic Period* (London and New York, 1978)
Boardman, J. *Greek Sculpture. The Classical Period* (London and New York, 1987)
Boardman, J. *Greek Sculpture. The Late Classical Period* (London and New York, 1995)
Cadogan, G. *Palaces of Minoan Crete* (London, 1980)
Coulton J.J. *Greek Architects at Work* (London, 1977)
Charbonneaux, J. et al. *Archaic Greek Art* (London and New York, 1971)
Cook, R.M. *Greek Painted Pottery* (London, 1960)
Demargne, P. *Aegean Art. The Origins of Greek Art* (London and New York, 1964)
Dinsmoor, W.B. *The Architecture of Ancient Greece* (London, 1950)
Doumas, C. *The Wall-Paintings of Thera* (Athens, 1992)
Fitton, L. *Cycladic Art* (London, 1989)
Graham, J.W. *The Palaces of Crete*, 2nd ed. (Princeton, 1987)
Higgins, R.A. *Minoan and Mycenaean Art* (London and New York, rev. ed. 1997)
Hood, S. *The Arts in Prehistoric Greece* (London and New Haven, 1995)
Immerwahr, S.A. *Aegean Painting in the Bronze Age* (Philadelphia, 1990)
Jenkins, I. *The Parthenon Frieze* (London 1994)

Lawrence, A.W. *Greek Architecture* (Harmondsworth and Baltimore, 3rd. ed. 1973).
Onians, J. *Art and Thought in the Hellenistic Age* (London, 1979)
Paton, J.M. (ed.) *The Erechtheum* (Harvard, 1927)
Pedley, J.G. *Greek Art and Archaeology* (London, 1993)
Pedley, J.G. *Greek Sculpture of the Archaic Period. The Island Workshops* (Mainz, 1976)
Pollit, J. *Art of Ancient Greece* (Cambridge, 1990)
Renfrew, C. *The Cycladic Spirit* (London and New York, 1991)
Richter, G.M.A. *A Handbook of Greek Art* (Oxford, 9th ed. 1987)
Robertson, M. *History of Greek Art* (Cambridge, 1976)
Smith, R.R.R. *Hellenistic Sculpture* (London and New York, 1991)
Spivey, N. *Understanding Greek Sculpture. Ancient Meanings, Modern Readings* (London and New York, 1996)
Williams, D. and Ogden, J. *Greek Gold. Jewellery of the Classical World* (London, 1994)
Woodford, S. *The Parthenon* (Cambridge, 1981)

ARCHAEOLOGICAL SITES AND GUIDES

Andronikos M., *Vergina. The Royal Tombs and the Ancient City* (Athens 1987)
Baedeker, *Greece* (Basingstoke, 1995)
Bruneau, P. and Ducat, J. *Guide de Délos* (Paris, 1965)
Camp, J.M. *The Athenian Agora. Excavations in the Heart of Classical Athens* (London, 1992)
Chrimes, K.M.T. *Ancient Sparta* (London, 1949)
De Miro E., *La Valle dei Templi* (Palermo 1994)
Doumas, C. *Thera. Pompeii of the Ancient Aegean* (London and New York, 1983)

Evans, A.J. *The Palace of Minos at Knossos*, vols I–IV (London, 1921–35).
Finley, M.I. *Atlas of Classical Archaeology* (London,1977)
Finley, M.I. and Pleket, H.W. *The Olympic Games: The First Thousand Years* (London and New York, 1976)
Forrest, W.G. *A History of Sparta, 950–192 BC* (London and New York, 1968)
Guido, M. *Sicily. An Archaeological Guide. The Prehistoric and the Roman Remains, and the Greek Cities* (London, 1977)
Hansen, E.V. *The Attalids of Pergamum* (Ithaca and London, 2nd ed., 1971)
Hill, I.T. *The Ancient City of Athens* (London and Cambridge, MA, 1953)
Lechman, K. *Samothrace. A Guide to the Excavations and the Museum* (Locust Valley, NY, 1970)
Loicq-Berger, M.P. *Syracuse. Histoire culturelle d'une cité grecque* (Brussels, 1967)
Macadam, A. *Sicily. Blue Guide* (London and New York, 1993)
Meyer, J.W. *The Aerial Atlas of Ancient Crete* (London 1992)
Parke, H.W. and Wormell, D.E.W. *The Delphic Oracle*, 2 vols (Oxford, 1956)
Pedley, J.G. *Paestum. Greeks and Romans in Southern Italy* (London, 1990)
Platon, N. *Zakros, the Discovery of a Lost Palace of Ancient Crete* (New York, 1971).
Poulsen, F. *Delphi* (London, 1920)
Schede, M. *Die Ruinen von Priene* (Berlin, 2nd ed., 1964)
Schliemann, H. *Mycenae* (London, 1878)
Travlos, J. *Pictorial Dictionary of Ancient Athens* (London and New York, 1971)
Wace, A,J.B. *Mycenae. An Archaeological History and Guide* (Princeton, 1949)

ILLUSTRATION CREDITS

Antonio Attini / Archivio White Star: pages 4–5, 160, 160–161, 161 top left, 162 top right, 184, 185, 192–193, 214, 215, 216, 217, 222, 224, 225, 228, 229, 237, 240 centre left, 240 top left, 240 right, 241, 242, 243, 245 top.

Marcello Bertinetti / Archivio White Star: pages 2–3, 158–159, 170–171, 170 bottom.

Giulio Veggi / Archivio White Star: pages 6–7, 162, 163, 164, 165 bottom right, 168 bottom right, 178 top, 179 top, 181, 182, 183, 204, 205, 206, 206–207, 207 bottom, 208, 209, 250, 250–251, 251, 252, 252–253, 253, 259 top, 260 bottom left, 260–261, 263, 264–265, 268, 269, 270, 271, 272–273, 274, 275, 276, 277, 284, 285, 286–287.

Felipe Alcoceba: pages 230–231, 231.

AKG Photo: pages 26 second from left, 117, 120 bottom, 123 bottom, 128 top left, 148 left, 148 right, 198, 207 top.

Ancient Art & Architecture Collection: pages 36 top, 80 top, 114 bottom.

P. Bernard / Photo R.M.N. Paris: page 147 left.

The British Museum: pages 8–9, 14–15, 35 third from left, 48, 66–67, 72 bottom right, 73 top and centre, 74 top, 75 bottom, 76 top, 76–77 bottom, 77, 88, 94 bottom, 96 centre, 104 third and fourth from left , 118 top, 118 bottom, 120 top, 122 right, 128 top right, 133 bottom, 142–143.

Hervé Champollion / Agence Top: pages 178–179.

Chuzeville / Photo R.M.N. Paris: pages 102, 121, 130.

Gerald Clyde / Barnaby's Pictures Library: pages 168–169, 176 bottom.

Giovanni Dagli Orti: pages 1, 10–11, 12–13, 16 right, 18–19, 21, 22 right, 23, 24 left, 25, 26 third and fifth from left, 36 bottom, 40 right, 41 right, 42 left, 43, 45, 46 left, 49, 51, 52 top, 53, 54 ,58, 60, 61, 64, 68, 69, 70, 74–75, 75 centre, 78 left, 80 centre and bottom, 81, 89, 92, 93, 99, 104 first, second from left, 105 first and third and fourth from left, 107, 108, 110 top, 111, 112 top, 113, 114 top, 115, 116, 118 centre, 119, 120 centre, 122 left, 124–125, 125 bottom, 127, 132, 134, 135, 140 left, 140 right, 154, 155 bottom, 155 top, 169 bottom, 176–177, 180, 188, 200, 201, 210, 211, 212, 213, 244 bottom left, 244–245, 254 bottom, 254 top, 255 top, 256 top, 257, 260 bottom right, 262, 263, 266 right, 278.

Araldo De Luca: pages 70 top and centre, 72 bottom left, 72–73, 76–77 top, 145, 248–249, 283.

Joel Ducange / Agence Top: page 168 bottom left.

E.T. Archive: pages 16 left, 46 right, 202–203.

Foschi / Focus Team: page 166 bottom left.

Robert Frerck / Odyssey / Agenzia Speranza: page 230 top.

Studio Koppermann / Staatlichen Antikensammlungen und Glyptothek München: pages 100–101, 144 left.

Johannes Laurentius / Staatliche Museen Zu Berlin / Prelißischer Kulturbesitz Antikensammlung: page 44.

Erich Lessing / Art Resource: pages 62, 103, 156, 157, 232.

H. Lewandowski / Photo R.M.N. Paris: pages 41 left, 123 top right, 147 right, 151.

Luciano Pedicini / Archivio dell'Arte: pages 35 first from left, 94 top, 95 left, 95 right, 255 bottom, 265 top.

Photo Nimatallah / Agenzia Luisa Ricciarini: pages 16 centre, 17, 22 left, 24 right, 26 fifth from left, 38–39, 39 top, 65, 96 top and bottom, 105 second from left, 106 right, 109, 112 bottom, 125 top, 126 centre, 128–129, 133 top, 137, 149, 153, 165 top right, 171.

Photo R.M.N. Paris: page 37 left.

Guido Alberto Rossi / The Image Bank: pages 184–185, 190–191, 191, 194 left, 195, 196, 218, 219, 223, 258–259, 266 left, 267.

Archivio Scala: pages 14, 15, 20, 26 first from left, 35 second from left, 42 right, 47, 83, 126 bottom, 136, 138, 139 left, 139 right, 142–143, 144 right, 150, 152, 174, 175, 189, 190, 265 centre.

Emilio F. Simion / Agenzia Luisa Ricciarini: pages 37, 110–111.

Henri Stierlin: pages 8, 38, 76 bottom, 78 right, 79, 106 top, 106 bottom left, 177 bottom, 179 bottom, 194 right, 226, 240 bottom.

Agenzia Luisa Ricciarini: pages 39 bottom, 50, 52 bottom, 55, 63, 71 bottom, 75 bottom, 90, 94 centre, 123 top left, 126 top, 131, 146, 199, 244 top left, 256 centre, 256 bottom, 258, 265 bottom.

E&C Valentin AG HOA-QUI / Agenzia Speranza: page 227.

MUSEUMS AND ART COLLECTIONS

Acropolis Museum, Athens: pages 26 fifth from left, 49, 61 bottom, 99 top, 124 top, 125 bottom, 126 top, 127, 134, 169 bottom, 174, 175.

Antiquarium of Metaponto: page 254 top.

Archaeological Museum, Delphi: pages 18–19, 26 fourth from left, 105 second from left, 123 bottom, 124–125, 132 top, 209 top, 210, 211 right, 211 left, 212 left, 213.

Archaeological Museum, Florence: page 124 bottom.

Archaeological Museum, Iraklion, Crete: pages 22, 23, 24, 104 first from left, 110 top, 110–111.

Archaeological Museum, Istanbul: pages 61 top, 63.

Archaeological Museum, Nauplion: pages 104 second from left, 114 top.

Archaeological Museum, Olympia: pages 131, 146, 198, 199.

Archaeological Museum, Palermo: pages 266 top, 278.

Archaeological Museum, Piraeus: pages 53, 56, 80 centre.

Archaeological Museum, Salonika: page 46 right.

Archaeological Museum, Syracuse: page 42.

Archaeological Museum, Thessalonike: pages 45, 58, 78 left, 79.

The British Museum, London: pages 8–9, 35 third from left, 66–67, 72 right, 73 top, 73 centre, 74 top, 75 bottom, 76 top, 76 bottom, 76–77 bottom, 77, 88, 94 bottom, 96 centre, 104 third and fourth from left, 118 top, 118 bottom, 120 top, 122 top, 128 top right, 132 bottom, 142–143.

Capitoline Museums, Rome: page 144 right.

Collezioni Ceccanti, Florence: page 94 centre.

Corinth Museum: pages 41 right, 48 centre, 120 centre.

Document Jean Vinchon, Paris: page 46 left.

Dresden Staatliche Kunstsammlungen: page 148.

Kanellopulos Museum, Athens: page 69.

Karlsruhe Badisches Landesmuseum: page 120 bottom.

Louvre Museum, Paris: pages 1, 35 fifth from left, 40 right, 41 left, 102, 103, 121 top and bottom, 123 top, 130, 147, 151, 155 bottom, 156, 157.

National Museum, Mycenae: page 189 top.

National Museum, Naples: pages 35 second from left, 47, 152.

National Museum, Paestum: pages 105 right, 258, 262, 263, 265.

National Archaeological Museum, Athens: pages 10–11, 20, 21, 25, 26 first and third from left, 26 second from left, 36 bottom, 38 top, 38–39, 39 bottom, 40 left, 43, 51, 52, 57, 64, 65, 83, 89, 92 top, 92–93, 93 top, 96 bottom, 105 first from left, 105 third from left, 106, 107 top, 107 bottom left, 107 bottom right, 108, 109, 111 right, 112, 113, 114 bottom, 114–115, 116, 117, 119, 122 bottom, 123 centre, 128–129, 133, 140 right, 149, 153, 165 top, 171 top, 189 bottom, 190 top.

National Archaeological Museum, Naples: pages 35 first from left, 35 fourth from left, 60, 71, 72, 72–73 bottom, 74 bottom, 90 bottom, 94 top, 95, 96 top, 140 left, 248–249, 250–251.

National Museum, Reggio Calabria: pages 50, 68, 81, 136, 137, 138, 139, 250 bottom, 251 bottom.

National Archaeological Museum, Taranto: pages 75 centre, 76–77, 92 centre and bottom, 236, 257.

Pella Museum: pages 202–203.

Pio Clementino Museum, Vatican, Rome: pages 145, 150.

Rhodes Museum: pages 154, 155 top.

Staatliche Antikensammunlung und Glyptothek, Monaco: pages 80 bottom, 100–101, 128 top left, 135, 144 left.

Staatliche Museen zu Berlin, Prenßischer Kulturbesitz Antikensammlungen: page 44.

Staatliche Museum Pergamonmuseum, Berlin: pages 62, 232, 233.

Thermae Museum, Rome: pages 140–141.

Thermos Museum: page 124 centre.

Volos Museum: pages 70, 74–75.

Text credit:
Page 27: from Pausanias. *Guide to Greece, vol. I Central Greece*, translated by Peter Levi, Harmondsworth 1971, p. 194 (Book II, 27, 3).